# The Law of Child Custody: Development of the Substantive Law

# The Law of Child Custody: Development of the Substantive Law

**Shirley Wohl Kram**
Judge of the Family Court of the
State of New York

**Neil A. Frank**
Member of the Bar of the
State of New York

**LexingtonBooks**
D.C. Heath and Company
Lexington, Massachusetts
Toronto

**Library of Congress Cataloging in Publication Data**

Kram, Shirley Wohl.
  The law of child custody.

  Includes index.
    1.  Custody of children—New York (State).  2.  Custody of children—
United States.  I.  Frank, Neil A.  II.  Title.
KFN5130.K725                          346.74701'7                          79-7717
ISBN 0-669-03183-6                    347.470617                           AACR2

Published simultaneously in Canada

Printed in the United States of America

International Standard Book Number: 0-669-03183-6

Library of Congress Catalog Card Number: 79-7717

*This book is dedicated, with love and reverence, to the late Bernard Kram and the late Aaron Frank.*

# Contents

Contents

# Acknowledgments

We thank Mindy Hass for her assistance in the preparation of this book. Leora Binstok, whose dedication to scholarship and love of the subject matter greatly aided our work, is especially acknowledged.

We express our appreciation for the encouragement and patience shown by Margaret Zusky, Mike McCarroll, and many other people at Lexington Books.

Last, we take note of the help, faith, unwavering support, and inexhaustible spirit of the inimitable Iris B. Frank.

# Introduction

In the New York metropolitan area, the practice of domestic relations law is dominated by, if not restricted to, a fraternity of specialists (usually individuals or small firms) who have founded reputations of expertise among both members of the bar and consumers of legal services. Those who enjoy standing at the apex of professional renown naturally accept only affluent clientele. But the inclination among lawyers toward specialization in matrimonial matters is not confined to the privileged. At every social and economic level and in every geographic, demographic, and ethnic classification, there is always a certain number of attorneys reputed to specialize in matrimonial matters who become familiar to domestic-relations tribunals. A maxim among attorneys (even those who describe themselves as general practitioners) reluctant to take on domestic-relations cases is that they "won't handle a matrimonial matter" but "refer it out."

We do not suggest that the rejection of a domestic-relations matter is the inevitable knee-jerk reflex of any lawyer not in the specialty. Nonetheless, many practitioners will affirm the description given here concerning the specialization of legal labor in the matrimonial field.

The widespread hesitation of qualified professionals to accept retention in the domestic-relations arena is not a reflection of the particular difficulty or complexity of the subject matter, the obscurity of the decisional or statutory law, or a lack of potential lucrativeness. Rather, the aversion appears to be predicated on the seemingly inevitable inability to satisfy *any* matrimonial client and the resultant frustration for all but those practitioners bearing the thickest of hides and the most formidable abdominal composure. Often, no matter how favorable the result, no matter how impressive the lawyer's display of adversary skills, and no matter how diligent the lawyer's preparation, the client expresses or conveys the sentiment that the adversary somehow has escaped retribution. A matrimonial client, it seems, like a nymphomaniac, always wants more than anyone has to give.

To set forth a strenuous professional effort in pursuit of a client's cause and to lose is a bitter experience for any advocate. To set forth such an effort and to achieve all or most of one's realistic goals, by any objective professional standard, only to receive the most tenuous gratitude and vague disaffection often is yet a more bitter conclusion. Yet reflecting on this not-uncommon occurrence, even the practitioner who chooses not to overcome his distaste for domestic-relations cases should recognize how predictable this lawyer-client scenario is.

Nothing in our culture is more intimately connected with emotional, subjective responses than those affairs involving love, sex, domesticity, childbearing, and child-rearing. People may maintain a certain level of objectivity when issues of money, property, power, or even possible commitment to prison are at stake. But sexual and romantic affairs are altogether different. Every issue directly or indirectly connected with a domestic-relations matter that may be either litigated or negotiated has the same potential for emotional excess and resultant sensational behavior. The emotional bonds forged at the inception of a marriage, a liaison, or shared parenthood commonly are not eradicated when the formal ties of a relationship are dissolved or when the positive emotions are transformed to negative ones. The intensity often remains and, indeed, expands to encompass satellite parties, such as parents, siblings, and successor spouses and paramours, not to mention the lawyers involved.

Thus it should be no surprise that contention among adults for the company and control of infants in whom they have an emotional interest, by reason of blood or affinity, may well be the most sensational of all the varieties of disputed domestic-relations proceedings. Contested child-custody themes generate notable audience interest in some of the more current cinema and television screenplays. (For example, *Kramer v. Kramer; Hide in Plain Sight.*) Although child-custody is only tangentially sexual, in dispute it attains the sensationalism associated with erotic drama.

Treatment of child-custody contests in all its various permutations (*parent* v. *parent, parent* v. *grandparent, natural* v. *adoptive parent,* and so forth) from the psychosociological horizon is current, fashionable, and abundant. Numerous treatises designed to explain the psychosociological material in relation to legal principles, decisional law, and statutory law are also readily available.

The aim of this book is somewhat less sensational and, to some degree, more modest. Our objective is to present a comprehensive analysis of the conceptual evolution of judicial and legislative policy toward the resolution of disputed child-custody proceedings. We selected, analyzed, and commented on decisional and statutory language in an effort to perceive trends of policy and theory to date. Ultimately, we wish to enable the practitioner or any serious student to discern and distinguish continuing prospective trends of policy and theory and anticipate modifications that will bear on the disposition of a disputed child-custody matter. We approached the material in as dispassionate, objective, and unsensational a manner as the subject matter allowed.

In selecting research material for analysis, we placed emphasis on decisional and statutory authority in the state of New York. One reason for this choice is our familiarity with that particular jurisdiction, but there were other factors. New York has a longer history of reported case law than most other jurisdictions and thus presents a particularly abundant resource for developmental analysis of judicial thinking. Further, New York's character, encompassing both metropolitan and rural life-styles as well as broad ethnic and economic contrasts, allows us diversity and volume from which to select more recent cases for analysis. The result, we hope, is a more coherent and integrated presentation of the material.

Other jurisdictions have been selected for in-depth analysis with the intent of providing contrast and comparison to New York law, both current and historic. Our objective is to provide a means by which valid conclusions may be drawn on a broad national scope with regard to judicial and legislative policy on the issue of child custody. Although other jurisdictions have been selected mostly at random, we have made an attempt to include those with representative divergent aspects in the sociopoliticoeconomic composition of various states. The object is to make comparative legal study more productive and more challenging.

Our work in this area has been conceived in terms of two volumes. This volume is directed to the substantive law in terms of the relief that a court of law may award. The substantive relief devolves into three basic categories: (1) custody, or choosing which contestant will have the ultimate control and/or physical possession of a minor child; (2) visitation, or the extent to which an adversary party will obtain the company and limited control of a minor child for a specified time; and (3) counsel fees, which concerns the liability of the parties to the potentially crippling expense of litigating the first two enumerated issues.

The area of counsel fees falls within the substantive definition inasmuch as the exposure to considerable expense or the favorable prospect of fee recovery significantly influences potential adversaries in the decision to begin or to continue custody litigation that might otherwise never have been disputed. When faced with the prospect of protracted litigation, the party who risks the greatest exposure for legal fees is immediately placed in an inferior bargaining position compared to his adversary.

Practical experience tells us that a negotiating position is an integral component of any legal system that encourages settlements of disputes prior to litigation. This is even truer in family-law litigation, which is emotionally as well as financially draining. Thus to place one party in an inferior negotiating position at the outset—not by reason of the merits of the case but because of potential financial exposure—significantly affects the substantive result. The effect must be deemed of such importance that the award of counsel fee and the theoretical development of the policy behind such awards must be considered more than the procedural nicety or incidental relief that it is sometimes deemed.

Chapter 1, Jurisdiction, provides integral background for the discussion contained in this first volume. Failure to understand the acquisition of the subject-matter jurisdiction forces the reader to examine the substantive law in a partial vacuum.

The concept of the projected second volume encompasses those topics that may generally be classified as procedural or ancillary to the three basic forms of substantive relief examined in the first volume. Our present outline includes the analysis of such topics as evidence, enforcement, appeals, and the alternative remedies offered by the statutory schemes of the Adoption and the Child Abuse Codes.

This is not a handbook for the practitioner. For example, this book does not give the reader advice on dealing with a hysterical client who telephones in the middle of the night to report that her ex-husband has not yet returned the children from weekend visitation. We do not tell you where to file your papers or which term or department of the court is designated for particular hearings. Our purpose is to provide the practitioner, the serious student, or anyone with an intellectual interest in the subject of child custody with a solid intellectual framework on which specific cases and practical examples can be fastened and clearly organized to allow deeper comprehension and more thorough, productive problem-solving.

# 1 Jurisdiction

## Powers of the Supreme Court of the State of New York

### General Original Jurisdiction

The Supreme Court of the State of New York possesses "general original jurisdiction in law and equity" under the New York Constitution.[1] This general jurisdiction in law and equity makes the supreme court heir to all powers possessed by the Court of Chancery in England on July 4, 1776.[2]

As heir to the general powers of the Chancery Court of England, the New York Supreme Court possesses the inherent power of a court of equity to decide custody disputes brought before it by petition and order to show cause.[3] The theoretical background of this authority has been described by Justice Cardozo in the following terms:

> The chancellor in exercising his jurisdiction upon petition does not proceed upon the theory that the petitioner, whether father or mother, has cause of action against the other or indeed against anyone. He acts as *parens patriae* to do what is best for the interest of the child. He is to put himself in the position of a "wise, affectionate and careful parent" [citation omitted], and make provision for the child accordingly. He may act at the intervention or on the motion of a kinsman, if so the petition comes before him, but equally he may act at the instance of anyone else. He is not adjudicating a controversy between adversary parties to compose their private differences. He is not determining right "as between a parent and a child" or as between one parent and another [citation omitted]. He interferes for the protection of infants *qua* infants, by virtue of the prerogative which belongs to the crown as *parens patriae*.[4]

### Authority under Habeas Corpus Proceedings

The supreme court, as inheritor of the chancellor's general equity power, derives its *habeas corpus* authority over custody disputes from two sources. Under Section 7002 of the CPLR, "a person illegally imprisoned or otherwise restrained in his liberty within the state, or one acting on his behalf," may petition any justice of the supreme court or, under certain circumstances, a county-court judge.[5] "The writ of *habeas corpus* was limited in its origin to cases of restraint under color or claim of law."[6] This is to say, it was limited to cases of false imprisonment by authorized law-enforcement agencies and others with a colorable claim to such authority. "In time, however, it was extended to controversies touching the custody of children, which were governed not so much by consideration of strictly legal rights, as by those of expediency and equity, and above all, the interests of the child."[7]

There is a second source of supreme court jurisdiction by means of *habeas corpus* provided in Section 70 of the Domestic Relations Law. Under Section 70, "where a minor is residing within this state, either parent may apply to the supreme court for a writ of habeas corpus" and have such child brought before the court for a determination of custody and related issues.[8] This particular statute limits the remedy to application by either parent and to situations in which the subject child is found within the state. The remedy provided by Section 7002 of the CPLR, the general *habeas corpus* jurisdiction of a court of equity, is not so limited. The plain language of Section 7002 provides that any person acting in behalf of the detainee may apply for relief.[9] The scope of Section 7002 has been extended, moreover, in child-custody cases to circumstances in which the court may have a claim to jurisdiction over the respondent, even though the subject child, himself, is *not* residing within the state.[10]

The ancestor statute of Section 70 of the Domestic Relations Law was enacted to provide the mother with a specific remedy for gaining custody of her child when living in a state of "separation from the father."[11] This remedy was necessitated by the father's preferred right, under common law, to the custody of his children.[12] This preferential treatment of the husband's right to child custody was also recognized under Roman law and the Civil Code of France.[13] It is of great interest to compare this ancient approach with its subsequent reversal and the preferential treatment given to the mother's claims to custody under the Tender Years Doctrine.[14]

The statute was ultimately amended to grant the remedy of *habeas corpus* relief in child-custody disputes to *both* the father and mother, as it stands in its present form.[15]

*Habeas corpus* relief has also been specifically extended by statute to enable grandparents to claim visitation rights.[16] But to obtain custody, as distinct from visitation, grandparents, like any other third party, must proceed under the *general habeas corpus* statute (CPLR) or the general equity powers of the authorized courts by petition or order to show cause.

## Authority under the Domestic Relations Law

The jurisdictional basis on which most custody cases arise is that granted by statute in the Domestic Relations Law to the supreme court in all such disputes connected with an action for annulment, divorce, or separation.[17] Dispositions of custody questions can be made "in the final judgment in such action or proceeding, or by one or more orders from time to time before or subsequent to final judgment, or by both such order or orders and the final judgment"[18] A disposition as to custody may be made incidental to such a divorce, annulment, or separation action, even though the primary relief sought, the separation or marital dissolution, is *not* granted.[19] For good measure, the general equity powers of the court over custody by petition, and by means of *habeas corpus*, are codified within the same Domestic Relations Law section.[20]

## Powers of the Surrogate's Court

Under the Surrogate's Court Procedure Act, the Surrogate's Court has concurrent jurisdiction to appoint a "guardian of the person or of the property or of both of an infant, whether or not the parent or parents of the infant are living."[21] The surrogate's powers, however, are limited to those cases in which the infant is domiciled in the county or has resided there for over 1 year immediately preceding the application.[22] The petition may be brought by anyone, on the infant's behalf, or by the infant himself, if over the age of 14 years.[23]

The origin of the surrogate's court's powers are also found in the equity powers of the Chancellor of England as *parens patriae*.[24] While the surrogate's court has concurrent jurisdiction with the supreme court over custody,[25] the surrogate is discouraged from exercising such jurisdiction where the supreme court or family court are more appropriate forums due to related matrimonial issues.[26]

Hence, the surrogate's court chiefly exercises its jurisdiction over custody in those cases relating to its authority over abandoned or neglected children, or those voluntarily surrendered under the Social Services Law, or when a question arises relating to adoption of a child.[27] Occasionally, the surrogate will exercise custody jurisdiction under the guise of its guardianship authority when the matter is initiated in surrogate's court, and there is no outstanding conflict with the jurisdiction of another forum.[28]

## Jurisdiction of the Family Court

Under section 651(a) of the Family Court Act, the Family Court of the State of New York may deal with custody issues referred to it by the supreme court and county courts with "the same powers possessed by the supreme court in addition to its own powers."[29] This grant refers to *habeas corpus* proceedings and proceedings brought by petition and order to show cause.[30] Under Section 651(b), the family court has original jurisdiction to determine issues of custody with "the same powers possessed by the supreme court in addition to its own powers," where such an action is initiated by petition, order to show cause, or writ of *habeas corpus*.[31]

Authority for the delegation of the powers enumerated in Section 651 of the Family Court Act is derived from the New York Constitution.[32] The family court's mandate is limited by the constitution, and, hence, it is a court of limited jurisdiction.[33] As such, there is a pronounced tendency on the part of the courts to read all statutes implementing the family court's jurisdiction with a strict constructionist's view.

Thus, it has been held that, when Section 651 grants to the family court "the same powers possessed by the supreme court . . . [in] proceedings brought . . . for the determination of the custody of minors, . . . [i]t follows, therefore, that if the Family Court has the same powers as the Supreme Court in regard to custody of minors, it has *all* of the same powers held by the Supreme Court under the New York State Constitution."[34]

By specific statutory grant in Section 651, under authority of the New York Constitution, and by virtue of the plain meaning of the statutory language, the family court is now deemed to possess *all* of those powers of the supreme court in all such custody cases in which it has jurisdiction, either by referral or by initial commencement. By analogy, the family court now wears the same mantle of the chancellor as *parens patriae* as attribtued to the supreme court.[35]

There are, of course, two sides to the strict construction trend. Prior to the 1978 amendment, Section 651(b) referred to initiating a family court proceeding by order to show cause or petition but was silent as to *habeas corpus*. Thus it had been held that a writ of *habeas corpus* to determine custody, when initiated in family court, was beyond the statutory mandate, whereas initiation by petition and order to show cause is within the court's authority.[36] This, of course, is a distinction more of form than of substance. The same relief might have been had in family court under the same circumstances on redrafting the same set of papers and changing the title and caption.

Section 651(a), regarding referral of custody matters commenced in supreme court, has been interpreted literally to prohibit any family court modification "in the absence of a specific provision in the Supreme Court decree giving the family court authority to do so."[37] The court noted that "a contrary decision could be interpreted as a precedent countenancing an effort by an unsuccessful litigant in a contested matrimonial action to relitigate the issue before a different judge."[38]

Where a proceeding is brought under Article 4 of the Family Court Act for support, the court may, in conjunction with such a proceeding, make an order of custody or visitation in the absence of a prior order by the supreme court.[39] Such an order may be terminiated or adopted on a super-seding order of the supreme court.[40] A similar provision provides for a custody or visitation award pursuant to a paternity proceeding under the Family Court Act.[41]

The family court may also exercise jurisdiction over custody and vis-itation under Sections 467 and 652 of the Family Court Act.[42] Sections 467 and 652 provide for referral of custody matters brought on in supreme court incident to proceedings for divorce, separation, or annulment.[43] The refer-ral provisions under Section 651(a) are addressed to the more general powers of the supreme court or county courts to hear custody issues brought on by petition, order to show cause, or writ of *habeas corpus.* The referral provisions under the Family Court Act Sections 467 and 652 are directed toward those custody issues connected with marital dissolution under the appropriate sections of the Domestic Relations Law.[44]

When an application to modify the custody order of the supreme court is referred to the family court under any one of the aforementioned means, the family court is statutorily prohibited from making any such modifica-tion except on a clear showing of subsequent changed circumstances and a resulting necessity.[45] The object of this limitation is to discourage relitiga-tion in another forum under the guise of "modification."

Any proceeding commenced in family court over which it has no juris-diction or which has not been transferred to it by another court must be transferred out of family court to the appropriate forum.[46]

The family court *may* make dispositions as to child custody and even modify a prior supreme court order *without* specific referral when such dis-position is made pursuant to an order of protection issued in a family offense proceeding under Family Court Act Articles 4, 5, and 8.[47] Finally, the family court may now exercise jurisdiction over visitation under a Uniform Support of Dependents Law (U.S.D.L.) proceeding but only wherein the petitioner resides with the child within another county in New York State.[48]

**Development under Louisiana Law**

Although the law of Louisiana is heavily influenced by the French origins of its society and by the Code Napoleon in particular, the concept of the remedy of *habeas corpus* as a means to litigate the custody of children has long been recognized.[49] The use of the writ of *habeas corpus* under such circumstances dates back to 1812, the year in which Louisiana was first admitted to the Union.[50] It is noteworthy that the long and elaborate deci-sion on the use of *habeas corpus,* contained in *Prieto* v. *St. Alphonsus Convent of Mercy,* decided in 1900,[51] makes numerous references to New York decisions in explaining the origins of a writ of *habeas corpus* in child-custody litigation.[52] Thus the evolution of the remedy in Louisiana and in New York discloses common decisional ancestors.

There seems to be no question that the remedy of *habeas corpus* was always available in Louisiana, at least to parents seeking to regain custody from a nonparent. In New York, specific *habeas corpus* relief in custody matters is given to parents of a child against any party, including the other parent.[53] In Louisiana, *habeas corpus* relief for child custody in cases involving *both* parents has evolved by decisional law with some reluctance.


## Habeas Corpus *Relief as between Parents*

In a 1901 case, the Supreme Court of Louisiana considered the arguments against allowing a writ of *habeas corpus* brought by a husband against a wife who had deserted him along with their small daughter.[54] The dissenting opinion took the view that, under existing statutory law, a husband and wife could not avail themselves of a writ of *habeas corpus* against each other.[55] They were required to litigate their custody dispute in connection with an action for separation or divorce and were prohibited from any other remedy under the codes then in effect.[56] The court took the view that resort to a writ was justified inasmuch as the custody of a child was not simply an issue between husband and wife, but one of interest to the state, and hence to the courts, for the benefit of the child.[57] This reasoning is redolent of the same *parens partriae* position expressed by the New York courts, although the phrase itself is not employed.[58] The majority concluded that a married couple should not be forced into an action for separation or divorce in order to have the custody of their child determined.[59]

In a 1910 case, the Louisiana Supreme Court upheld a lower-court decision granting custody to a maternal uncle against a natural father.[60] Citing *Lassere* v. *Michel,* the court held: " These proceedings by *habeas corpus* can scarcely be regarded as a suit between the relator and the defendant. It is a matter . . . in which that state has an interest which goes beyond the mere right and authority of the father. The welfare and happiness of the child have to be considered by the court."[61] The tone of much of the Louisiana decisional law is apologetic in affirming the use of *habeas corpus.* There is a tendency to look on its use by parents, particularly against each other, not as a matter of right to them, but as an exception that the courts make in the interest of the child.

There is less equivocation on the part of the courts in recognizing the use of *habeas corpus* as a remedy in the litigation of custody disputes between natural parents of a child born out of wedlock.[62] The reservations seem to be directed chiefly toward those parents still legally married to each other, no matter what the state of their actual relationship.

*More Recent Cases*

Under more recent case law, the use of a writ of *habeas corpus* between parents in a custody dispute is more clearly recognized as a "proper procedural device" for obtaining custody of a child, "even in domestic matters where other procedures, summary or ordinary, are available."[63] However, the issues that gave rise to *State ex rel. Lassere* v. *Michel, supra* (that is, whether the Louisiana prohibition against interspousal suits precludes resort to *habeas corpus* by married parents) were not finally resolved until 1977.

Louisiana statutory law still prohibits suits between spouses with certain enumerated exceptions.[64] *Habeas corpus* was not among the enumerated exceptions.[65] In a 1977 decision, the Supreme Court of Louisiana, citing *State ex rel. Lassere* v. *Michel, supra,* with approval, held that the statutory exceptions to the prohibition against interspousal suits were *illustrative,* not *exclusive.*[66] The court held further, adopting the dissenting view of the lower appellate court

> There is no sound or cogent reason which should dictate that in matters of custody, where children of tender years are involved, the rules governing the award of custody should differ, depending upon the legal status of the contesting parents. Such determination is clearly contrary to the sage reasoning announced in [Lasserre v. Michel], that neither husband or wife, should be driven to the necessity of instituting an action of separation from bed and board or divorce in order to have the matter of legal custody of the children judicially inquired into.[67]

*Remedies under Louisiana's Divorce and Separation Statute*

Under Louisiana statutory law, permanent custody may be granted to either parent based on the best interests of the child, in accordance with the court's discretion. An in-camera hearing to determine custody is mandated.[68] The present statute, providing for a custody award based on the best interests of the child, was amended in 1970. The previous form provided for an award to the party that prevailed in the underlying action for divorce or separation.[69] In other words, the winner went home with all the spoils, including the infant children. This earlier view is generally discredited in most jurisdictions.[70]

During the pendency of a divorce or separation proceeding, however, the mother is mandated to receive custody of the children unless there is a compelling reason to the contrary, in the court's discretion.[71]

Under the statute, the decision of the court as to custody *pendente lite* has *no effect whatever* on the final determination of custody.[72]

Grandparents are authorized by statute to claim reasonable visitation with grandchildren after the divorce or separation of the infant's parents, if the parent who was *their* child is deceased.[73] This mandate is distinct from New York's in that it is included in Louisiana's general divorce or separation codes, rather than under a specific *habeas corpus* remedy.[74] Additionally, the New York statute is broader in allowing grandparental visitation, in the court's discretion, even when the divorced or separated parent is *not* deceased.[75] Nor is divorce or separation of the parents a specific prerequisite for grandparental visitation under the New York statute.[76]

### Habeas Corpus *Relief Codified*

Louisiana's *habeas corpus* relief is codified.[77] Venue is determined by statute according to the parish in which the defendant is domiciled or the parish in which the person detained is in custody.[78]

### *Other Forms of Statutory Relief*

Louisiana provides in its codes for a juvenile court having jurisdiction over neglected or abused children.[79] In accordance with proceedings thereunder, courts may award custody to third parties consistent with the child's best interests.[80] The courts have clearly held, however, that a finding of neglect and assignment of custody to a third party against either parent may not be made by a court during pendency of a custody proceeding under the divorce and separation statutes.[81] Such an action is beyond the jurisdiction of the court, unless the state initiates a neglect or abuse proceeding under the appropriate statute.[82] "[F]orfeiture of parental right . . . is not authority for awarding custody to a third person over a parent solely on the *best interest* premise."[83]

### Development under California Law

### *General Statutory Remedies*

California is a particularly good example of a jurisdiction in which the emphasis is laid on statutory means for the resolution of custody disputes. The superior court has authority to determine custody of minors in relation to the dissolution of marriage,[84] although a "husband or wife" may file a petition for exclusive custody without commencing a dissolution action.[85]

Courts of competent jurisdiction are mandated, by statute, to determine custody in accordance with various specific guidelines, in descending order of preference,[86] and with certain weight given to the preference of the child.[87] This governing statute, Section 4600 of the California Civil Code,[88] is held to govern as to *standards* of determination, no matter what form the custody proceeding takes.[89] Thus, in applying Section 4600, the Supreme Court of California held that

> Although the present appeal concerns a custody order under the Juvenile Court Law, this procedural setting is fortuitous; the issue of custody could as readily have been raised by an application for letters of guardianship, a writ of habeas corpus, or . . . an action for dissolution of marriage. In fact California has at least eight separate proceedings in which custody questions can be litigated.[90]

Among these statutory remedies noted herein and in addition to those connected with the dissolution of marriage, or petition for exclusive custody without dissolution,[91] are those under the Juvenile Dependency Law. This is a body of law similar to the New York's Child Neglect Statutes, which are contained in Article 10 of the New York Family Court Act.[92]

The definition of a child who comes under the jurisdiction is expressed in terms similar to the definition of a neglected child under the New York statute.[93] The order of disposition may provide for custody to be taken from the parent and awarded to an appropriate person or institution.[94] The authority to act under this particular statutory framework is granted to the superior court "and while sitting in the exercise of such jurisdiction shall be known and referred to as the juvenile court."[95] Once jurisdiction has been established in accordance with the definitions contained within the statute, "that jurisdiction continues as long as the best interests of the minor so require.[96]

The power to appoint a custodian of a child may also be exercised by the superior court under various provisions of the California Probate Code.[97] This grant of jurisdiction is analogous to that under New York's Surrogate's Court Procedure Act.[98] As in New York, it has been held that the court will not exercise jurisdiction under probate proceedings so as to interfere with the jurisdiction of another court previously established under divorce preceedings.[99]

In addition, custody can be determined under the body of statutory law dealing with termination of parental rights and adoption.[100]

*Development under Case Law*

The power of the superior and other courts of California to grant writs of *habeas corpus* is granted by the California Constitution. There is considerable case law to the effect that the *habeas corpus* jurisdiction may be used to litigate child-custody matters.[101] *Habeas corpus* is recognized as "an additional remedy" in child-custody proceedings and "will lie when a person entitled to custody of a minor child is denied possession thereof."[102] It has been held that *habeas corpus* is "well established" as a proper proceeding as relates to the fitness of parties in a custody proceeding and the determination of the "temporal, moral and spiritual welfare of the child."[103]

> But in addition to such general power of the court in such matters, it is clear in principle that, although possibly from abstract reasoning the relief in a *habeas corpus* proceeding should be limited to an inquiry into the question of the validity and regularity of the authority upon which the respondent may base his right to the detention of the petitioner, in a *habeas corpus* proceeding involving the custody of an infant, where the issue of the fitness of each of the opposing litigants is made and evidence of such issue is introduced and received at the hearing, the judgment by the court thereon is a valid adjudication of the rights of the parties and binding upon them.[104]

The use of *habeas corpus* as a remedy in custody litigation goes well back into the nineteenth century in California cases. In addition, there is a line of decisions that holds that the courts have inherent power to dispose of a custody issue when brought before it on petition, without any statutory authority, so long as the child is a resident within the state and within the county wherein the court exercises such jurisdiction.[105] This concept is reminiscent of the *parens patriae* principle that marks the development of the law in New York. (See Powers of the Supreme Court of the State of New York, *supra.*)

## Federal Jurisdiction

The federal courts generally will not take jurisdiction of custody matters unless jurisdiction can be based on some special circumstance.[106] In an 1890 decision, the U.S. Supreme Court ordered the release from prison of a grandfather, incarcerated by the order of a federal district court judge for contempt. The contempt commitment arose out of a custody dispute between the grandfather and the natural father of his grandchild.[107] In deciding that the U.S. District Court had no jurisdiction to make such an order in the first place, the Supreme Court held

> The whole subject of the domestic relations of husband and wife, parent and child, belongs to the laws of the States and not to the laws of the United States. As to the right to control and possession of this child, as it is contested by its father and its grandfather, it is one in regard to which

neither the Congress of the United States nor any authority of the United States has any special jurisdiction. Whether the one or the other is entitled to the possession does not depend upon any act of Congress or any treaty of the United States or its Constitution.[108]

*In re Burrus, supra,* from which the above quotation derives, was more recently cited, with approval, in support of the continuing policy of the U.S. courts, "to avoid handling domestic relations cases . . . in absence of important concerns of a constitutional dimension."[109]

The same principle was adopted in a decision denying relief to a mother who sought to bring her custody dispute within the purview of a federal civil-rights statute.[110] In finding that there was no factual basis to the mother's claim of a conspiracy to violate her civil rights, the court found there was no cause of action under the U.S. statute invoked.[111] Having found no violation of the petitioner's civil rights, the court, citing *In re Burrus, supra,* affirmed the judgment of the district court in granting summary judgment to the defendant.[112]

Pragmatic reasons, in addition to the lack of specific jurisdiction, have also figured in the general posture of the federal judiciary in avoiding custody litigation.

Although neither the Constitution nor the statutes governing federal jurisdiction mandate this refusal to entertain domestic relations cases, the reasoning underlying these decisions is clear and well-founded. Because state courts traditionally have adjudicated domestic relations cases, they have developed a proficiency and expertise in the area that is almost completely absent in the federal courts [citation omitted]. In addition, this rule respects the special interests of the states in domestic relations matters. Furthermore, the Court is unwilling to increase the workload of this already overburdened Court by ignoring the rule that has existed for over 100 years without any intimation of Congressional disapproval [citation omitted].[113]

## Federal Statutory Jurisdiction

Under the U.S. Constitution, "The Judicial Power shall extend to all cases in Law and Equity, arising under this Constitution, the Laws of the United States, and Treaties made, or which shall be made under their authority."[114]

Thus, the federal courts exercise jurisdiction over those custody cases that, for one reason or another, fall under the jurisdiction of the U.S. government. For example, the U.S. Virgin Islands, ruled under U.S. law as a territory, has its judicial power vested in a district court of the Virgin Islands by U.S. statute.[115]

The district court has general original jurisdiction over all causes in the Virgin Islands arising under local laws.[116] The local laws are codified in a

Virgin Islands Code, also pursuant to U.S. statute.[117] Under such local self-governing authority, U.S. courts can be called on to decide issues of custody.[118]

Then there are such exotic instances of federal intervention in child-custody cases as those arising under the following statute:

> The privilege of the writ of habeas corpus shall be available to any person, in a court of the United States, to test the legality of his detention by order of an Indian tribe.[119]

Based on this statute, a U.S. Court of Appeals upheld a writ granted by a district court in a child-custody case against the Tribal Court of the Blackfoot Indian Tribe.[120]

### Constitutional Jurisdiction

When a custody issue rises to constitutional proportion (that is, where an argument can be made that a party is being deprived of the equal protection of the laws, as guaranteed by the Fourteenth Amendment) then, of course, the federal courts will assume jurisdiction. Probably the best example in more recent years is the U.S. Supreme Court decision in *Stanley* v. *Illinois*. In *Stanley,* the court overturned an Illinois statute denying the same rights of custody to unwed fathers of children as were granted to fathers of those children born *in* wedlock.[121]

Another significant example finds the U.S. Supreme Court striking down as unconstitutional a New York statute that denied to unwed fathers the same rights to withhold consent to adoption as were granted to the mothers of children born out of wedlock.[122] In both instances, denial of equal protection of the laws, in violation of the Constitution's mandate, formed the basis for intervention by the court.

### Full Faith and Credit

The U.S. Constitution requires each of the states to give full faith and credit to the "public Acts, Records and Judicial Proceedings of every other State."[123] Custody decisions are the most notable exception to this rule. In holding that the Full Faith and Credit Clause did not bind an Ohio court to recognize a Wisconsin custody decree, Justice Frankfurter, in a concurring opinion, held as follows:

> Property, personal claims, and even the marriage status [citation omitted], generally give rise to interests different from those relevant to the discharge

of a State's continuing responsibility to children within her borders. Children have a very special place in life which law should reflect. Legal theories and their phrasing in other cases readily lead to fallacious reasoning if uncritically transferred to determination of a State's duty towards children. . . . Interests of a State other than its duty towards children may . . . prevail over the interest of national unity that underlies the Full Faith and Credit Clause. But the child's welfare in a custody case has such a claim upon the State that its responsibility is obviously not to be foreclosed by a prior adjudication reflecting another State's discharge of its responsibility at another time.[124]

This doctrine has been fully recognized and implemented by the New York courts.[125]

The logic of the position expressed in *May* v. *Anderson* becomes somewhat more apparent when one considers that most custody and/or visitation orders are subject to modification in the courts that originally rendered them on a showing of change of circumstances. In view of this, "the State of the forum has at least as much leeway to disregard it, or to depart from it as does the State where it was rendered."[126]

The whole question of the applicability of the Full Faith and Credit Clause is now largely preempted by the Uniform Child Custody Statute.[127] The Uniform Child Custody Statute depends on voluntary adoption by individual jurisdictions as an interstate compact, and thus does not affect the current federal law. As a practical matter, however, it provides an alternative to the worst abuses of the child-custody exception to the full faith and credit doctrine.

### Notes

1. N.Y. Const. arts. VI, § 7(a).
2. N.Y. Jud. Law. § 140b (Mc Kinney).
3. *Finlay* v. *Finlay,* 240 N.Y. 429, 433, 148 N.E. 624 (1925); *Matter of Mack,* 81 Misc. 2d, 802, 805, 367 N.Y.S.2d 644 (Fam. Ct. 1975).
4. *Finlay* v. *Finlay,* 240 N.Y. at 433–434.
5. N.Y. Civ. Prac. Law §§ 7002(a), 7002(b) (McKinney).
6. *Reisner* v. *New York Nursery & Child's Hosp.,* 230 N.Y. 119, 124, 129 N.E.2d 341 (1920).
7. *Id.*
8. N.Y. Dom. Rel. Law § 70 (McKinney). *See* chapter 6, Visitation.
9. N.Y. Civ. Prac. Law § 7002 (McKinney).
10. *Spreckles* v. *DeRuyter,* 150 Misc. 323, 269 N.Y.S. 100, (Sup. Ct. 1934); *Portnoy* v. *Strasser,* 303 N.Y. 537, 104 N.E.2d 859 (1952).
11. *Sternberger* v. *Sternberger,* 12 A.D. 398, 400, 42 N.Y.S. 423 (1st Dept. 1896).

12. *Id.,* at 399.

13. *Brooks* v. *Brooks,* 35 Barb. 85 (1861).

14. See chapter 2, Custody Disputes between Natural Parents, *infra.*

15. N.Y. Dom. Rel. Law § 70 (McKinney). *See also Sternberger* v. *Sternberger, supra,* 12 A.D., at 398.

16. N.Y. Dom. Rel. Law § 72 (McKinney). See chapter 6, Visitation, *infra.*

17. N.Y. Dom. Rel. Law § 240 (McKinney).

18. *Id.*

19. *Id.*

20. *Id.*

21. N.Y. Surr. Ct. Proc. Act § 1701 (McKinney 58A).

22. *Id.,* at § 1702(1).

23. *Id.,* at § 1703.

24. *In re Camp,* 126 N.Y. 377, 389, 27 N.E. 799 (1891); *In re Thorne's Estate,* 126 Misc. 96, 213 N.Y.S. 419, 421 (Sur. Ct. 1925); *In re Lamb's Estate,* 139 N.Y.S. 685 (1912); *Matter of Stuart,* 280 N.Y. 245, 20 N.E.2d 741 (1939); *Matter of Bock,* 280 N.Y. 349, 21 N.E.2d. 186 (1939).

25. *In re Yardum,* 228 A.D. 854 (2d Dept. 1930).

26. *Id. See In re Stillman,* 117 Misc. 61, 190 N.Y.S. 495 (Sur. Ct. 1921), and chapter 6, Visitation, note 45, *infra.*

27. *Matter of Raana Beth N.,* 78 Misc. 2d 105, 355 N.Y.S.2d 956 (Sur. Ct. 1974). *See N.Y. Dom. Rel. Law* § 110 (McKinney); N.Y. Const. art. VI, § 12 (e); N.Y. Surr. Ct. Proc. Act § 201 (McKinney 58A).

28. *Matter of Leslie L.,* 75 Misc. 2d 305, 348 N.Y.S.2d 46 (Sur. Ct. 1973); *Matter of Raana Beth N.,* 78 Misc. 2d, at 105. *See also* N.Y. Surr. Ct. Proc. Act § 2001(a) (McKinney 58A), which provides that the surrogate court shall have all powers that the supreme court would have in like actions, where the surrogate's jurisdiction applies.

29. N.Y. Fam. Ct. Act § 651(a) (McKinney 29A). See also note 9, *supra.*

30. *Id.*

31. *Id.*

32. N.Y. Const. art. VI, § 13(b), 13(c).

33. *Harrington* v. *Harrington,* 60 A.D.2d 982, 983, 401 N.Y.S.2d 342 (4th Dept. 1978); *Borkowski* v. *Borkowski,* 38 A.D. 752, 330 N.Y.S.2d 106 (2d Dept. 1972).

34. *Matter of Mack,* 81 Misc. 2d 802, 805, 367 N.Y.S.2d 644 (Fam. Ct. 1975).

35. *Finlay* v. *Finlay,* 240 N.Y., at 429; *Matter of Mack,* 81 Misc. 2d, at 802. *See generally and compare Sturm* v. *Sturm,* 71 Misc. 2d 577, 336 N.Y.S.2d 660 (Fam. Ct. 1972), *and Donne* v. *Pace,* 74 Misc. 2d 127, 344 N.Y.S.2d 398 (Fam. Ct. 1973), for background on the extent to which fam-

ily court jurisdiction was limited prior to the enactment of N.Y. Fam. Ct. Act § 651 (McKinney 29A).

36. *King* v. *King,* 83 Misc. 2d 1019, 373 N.Y.S.2d 944 (Fam. Ct. 1975).

37. *Harrington* v. *Harrington,* 60 A.D.2d, at 983.

38. *Id.,* at 984.

39. N.Y. Fam. Ct. Act § 447(a) (McKinney 29A).

40. *Id.,* at § 447(b).

41. *Id.,* at § 549.

42. *Id.,* at §§ 467, 652.

43. *Compare* N.Y. Fam. Ct. Act § 651(b) with §§ 467, 652 (McKinney 29A).

44. N.Y. Fam. Ct. Act §§ 652, 467 (McKinney 29A); and chapter 3, Current Standards for Determination of Custody Disputes between Parents, *infra.*

45. *Id.*

46. N.Y. Const. art. VI § 19(e), cited in *King* v. *King,* 83 Misc. 2d, at 1021.

47. N.Y. Fam. Ct. Act § 842(e), (McKinney 29A); N.Y. Fam. Ct. Act § 446(e); N.Y. Fam. Ct. Act § 551(e).

48. N.Y. Dom. Rel. Law § 34a (McKinney).

49. *Prieto* v. *St. Alphonsus Convent of Mercy,* 52 La. Ann. 631, 27 So. 153, 171 (1900); *Billington* v. *Sacred Heart Orphan Asylum,* 134 La. 883, 98 So. 406 (1923).

50. *Bermudez* v. *Bermudez,* 2 Mart. (O.S.); 181 *see Prieto* v. *St. Alphonsus Convent of Mercy,* 27 So., at 171; *Billington* v. *Sacred Heart Orphan Asylum,* 98 So., at 407.

51. *Prieto* v. *St. Alphonsus Convent of Mercy,* 27 So., at 153.

52. *People* v. *Porter,* 1 Duer 709 (1853); *People* v. *Wilcox,* 22 Barb. 179, 187 (1854); *People* v. *Cooper,* 8 How. Pr. 288, 294 (1853); *Mercein* v. *People,* 25 Wend. 163, 80 (1840).

53. N.Y. Dom. Rel. Law § 70 (McKinney).

54. *Lassere* v. *Michel,* 105 La. 741, 30 So. 122 (1901).

55. *Id.,* at 125–126.

56. *Id.*

57. *Id.,* at 125.

58. See Powers of the Supreme Court of the State of New York, *supra.*

59. *Lassere* v. *Michel,* 105 La. at 741.

60. *Ex parte Ryan,* 126 La. 449, 52 So. 573 (1910).

61. *Id.,* at 575.

62. *Neal* v. *White,* 362 So. 2d 1148 (La. Ct. App. 1978); *Creppel* v. *Thornton,* 230 So. 2d 644 (La. Ct. App. 1970); *Stein* v. *Wade,* 207 La. 177,

20 So. 2d 747 (1944); *Jagneaux* v. *Jagneaux,* 206 La. 107, 18 So. 2d 913 (1944).

    63. *Benoit* v. *Blassingame,* 249 So. 2d 302 (La. Ct. App. 1971). *See also Smith* v. *Martin,* 269 So. 2d 558, 560 (La. Ct. App. 1972).

    64. La. Rev. Stat. Ann. § 9:291 (West).

    65. *Id. See also Stelly* v. *Montgomery,* 347 So. 2d 1145, 1148 (La. 1978).

    66. *Stelly* v. *Montgomery,* 347 So. 2d, at 1148.

    67. *Id.*

    68. La. Civ. Code Ann. art. 157(A). (West).

    69. *Id.*

    70. See chapter 3, Current Standards for Determination of Custody Disputes between Parents, *infra.*

    71. La. Civ. Code Ann. art. 146 (West).

    72. *Id.,* at art. 157(A).

    73. *Id.,* at art. 157(B).

    74. See note 16, *supra;* see chapter 6, Visitation, *infra.*

    75. *Id.*

    76. *Id.*

    77. La Code Civ. Pro. Ann. art. 3821 (West).

    78. *Id.,* at art. 3822.

    79. La. Rev. Stat. Ann. § 13:1570 (West).

    80. *Id.,* at § 13:1580.

    81. *Lulich* v. *Lulich,* 361 So. 2d 451 (La. Ct. App. 1978). *Compare* La Civ. Code Ann. arts. 146, 157 (West) *with* La. Rev. Stat. Ann. § 13:1570 (West).

    82. *Lulich* v. *Lulich,* 361 So. 2d, at 452. *Compare with Wood* v. *Beard,* 290 So. 2d 675 (La. 1974), particularly concurring opinion of Braham, J.

    83. *Hall* v. *Hall,* 367 So. 2d 162 (La. Ct. App. 1979).

    84. Cal. Civ. Code § 4350 (West).

    85. *Id.,* at § 4603.

    86. *Id.,* at § 4600.

    87. *Id.*

    88. *Id.*

    89. *In re B.G.,* 523 P.2d 255, 144 Cal Rptr. 444 (1974); *In re Reyna,* 55 Cal. App. 3d 288, 126 Cal. Rptr. 138, 143 (1976).

    90. *In re B.G.,* 523 P.2d, at 255.

    91. See notes 84 and 85, *supra.*

    92. N.Y. Fam. Ct. Act art. 10 (McKinney 29A).

    93. Cal. Welf. & Inst. Code § 300 (West).

    94. *Id.,* at § 727.

    95. *Id.,* at § 245.

96. *In re B.G.,* 523 P.2d, at 252.

97. Cal. Prob. Code §§ 1400, 1405 (West).

98. See Powers of the Surrogate's Court, *supra.*

99. *Green* v. *Superior Court,* 37 Cal. 2d 307, 231 P.2d 821 (1951).

100. Cal. Civ. Code §§ 221-230, 232-238 (West).

101. *In re B.G.,* 523 P.2d, at 255; *In re Reyna,* 126 Cal. Rptr., at 143.

102. *Ex parte Barr,* 243 P.2d 787, 788, 39 C.2d 25 (Cal 1952), *In re Matthews,* 176 Cal. 156, 158, 167 P. 873 (1917).

103. *Ex parte McDaniel,* 265 P. 884, 885 (Cal. 1928).

104. *Id.*

105. *See In re Chambers,* 22 P. 138 (1889); *In re Matthews,* 176 Cal., at 156 (1917); *In re Gates,* 95 Cal. 461, 30 P. 396 (1892).

106. *In re Burrus,* 136 U.S. 586, 593 (1890); *Hernstadt* v. *Hernstadt,* 373 F.2d 316 (2d Cir. 1967).

107. *In re Burrus,* 136 U.S., at 586.

108. *Id.,* at 593-594.

109. *Overman* v. *United States,* 563 F.2d 1287, 1292 (8th Cir. 1977).

110. *Harris* v. *Turner,* 329 F.2d 918 (6th Cir. 1964), *cert. denied,* 379 U.S. 907, *rehearing denied,* 379 U.S. 98.

111. *Id.,* referring to 42 U.S.C. §§ 1983, 1985.

112. *Id.*

113. *Cherry* v. *Cherry,* 438 F. Supp. 88 (D. Md. 1977).

114. U.S. Const. art. III, § 2, cl. 1.

115. 48 U.S.C.A. § 1611 (West).

116. *Id.,* at § 1612.

117. *Id.,* at § 1574(c).

118. *See Bergen* v. *Bergen,* 439 F.2d 1008 (3d Cir. 1971); *Brown* v. *Stevens,* 331 F.2d 803 (D.C. Cir. 1964).

119. 25 U.S.C. § 1303.

120. *Cobell* v. *Cobell,* 503 F.2d 790 (9th Cir. 1974), *cert. denied, Sharp* v. *Cobell,* 421 U.S. 999.

121. *Stanley* v. *Illinois,* 405 U.S. 645 (1972). See chapter 4, Effect of Illegitimacy, *infra.*

122. *Caban* v. *Mohammed,* 441 U.S. 380 (1979). See chapter 4, Effect of Illegitimacy, *Infra.*

123. U.S. Const. art. IV §1.

124. *May* v. *Anderson,* 345 U.S. 528 (1953). *See also Hernstadt* v. *Hernstadt,* 373 F.2d 316, 318 (2d Cir. 1967).

125. *Bachman* v. *Mejias,* 1 N.Y.2d 575, 580, 154 N.Y.S.2d 903 (1956).

126. *Hernstadt* v. *Hernstadt,* 373 F.2d 316 (2d Cir. 1967). *See Halvey* v. *Halvey,* 330 U.S. 510, 615 (1947), cited in chapter 6, Visitation, *infra,* note 98.

127. N.Y. Dom. Rel. Law §§ 75 a-z (McKinney).

# 2 Custody Disputes between Natural Parents

## Superiority of Maternal Rights in Custody Disputes

*Historical Background and Development*
*of the Tender Years Doctrine*

**Common-Law Preference for Father.** The Tender Years Doctrine, the rule of law that enshrined the mother as the preferred parent in most custody disputes, is presently considered a relic of the past and a casualty of the sexual revolution. The impression of the Tender Years Doctrine is of an ancient rule that only recently has come under scrutiny and subsequent disapproval. Tender Years, however, is a relatively recent tenet dating from the early part of the twentieth century.[1] Prior to that time, the general rule, going back into ancient English law, gave the father the preferred status in a custody dispute.

In an 1837 decision, the New York Supreme Court found a *prima facie* right in the father to the custody of a child, citing an impressive list of old English decisions as authority.[2] "The father is the natural guardian of his infant children, and in the absence of good and sufficient reasons shown to the court, such as ill usage, grossly immoral principles or habits, want of ability & c. is entitled to their custody, care and education."[3]

This particular decision was remarkably favorable to the primacy of the paternal right to custody, so much so that it cited one English decision wherein the father was confirmed as the custodian of the child "even though he was living in a state of adultery," so long as he did not bring the child into contact with his paramour.[4] This was rather a noteworthy position to maintain, considering the morality of the times. Even more remarkable to contemporary ears is the following passage by which the court rationalized the doctrine according to the prevailing socioeconomic values of the time.

> The interference of the court with the relation of father and child, by withdrawing the latter from the natural affection, kindness and obligations of the former, is a delicate and strong measure; and the power should never be exerted except for the most sound and solid reasons. In this country, the hopes of the child in respect to its education and future advancement, is mainly dependent upon the father; for this he struggles and toils through

life; the desire of its accomplishment operating as one of the most powerful incentives to industry and thrift. The violent abruption of this relation would not only tend to wither these motives to action, but necessarily in time, alienate the father's natural affections; and if property should be accumulated, the child under such circumstances could hardly expect to inherit it.[5]

The father's *prima facie* right to custody was so solidly established that a statute prevailing at the time allowed the father to effectively dispose of the custody of the child to other persons by "deed or will duly executed."[6] The only relief afforded to the mother was the right to bring a *habeas corpus* proceeding when living in a state of separation from the father.[7] But such relief could only be had on some showing by the mother that the father was somehow at fault for the separation *and* unfit to have custody of the child.

> It may be well doubted, I think, whether this statute was intended to apply where the wife withdraws from the protection of the husband and lives separate from him without any reasonable excuse. . . . The legislature could not have intended that the court should ever award to the mother the care and education of her minor children, when she had willfully and without pretense of excuse, abandoned her family and the protection of her husband if he was in a situation to take care of them and no well founded objection existed in the case.[8]

In 1860, the New York Legislature "constituted and declared" every married woman "to be the joint guardian of her children with her husband, with equal power, rights and duties in regard to them with her husband."[9] On the surface, this revision would appear to afford the mother equal footing with the husband, and, coupled with the *habeas corpus* relief grant in prior legislation, improve the mother's prospects in disputed custody proceedings. Additionally, the courts continued to recognize their own inherent powers of *parens patriae,*[10] to decide a custody dispute in the child's interest when sufficient reason was shown to overcome the father's *prima facie* common-law preference.[11]

Nevertheless, the court continued adamantly to support the *prima facie* custody preference for the father. In the *Brooks* case,[12] the court held that the recently enacted statute making the mother joint guardian of her children was only applicable to those circumstances wherein the mother and father resided together.

> So far as this guardianship includes the custody and care of the person, it must be exercised with her husband, and not away from or exclusive of him. It is only in connection with her husband that she takes any right of guardianship, under the statute. The common law right of the husband remains, except as modified by joining the wife with him. . . . There is no

evidence of intent in the statute to confer any rights upon the wife as rights to be exercised in severalty, or separate from her husband. . . . The law can only be carried into effect while the parents are living together. When they are separate from . . . each other . . . *the husband is remitted to his common law rights* [emphasis added].[13]

The court's conclusion was the the father's "paramount right" must prevail, despite the statute, if he "is in all respects fit and proper to have the care of the child and to superintend its education and other things are equal between the two."[14] What rights were granted to the mother under the statute were forfeited if she was living separately from her husband "without just cause or provocation."[15]

In an 1857 decision, the court clearly recognized the powers of an equity bench to overrule the father's common-law right in cases in which the mother would be entitled to divorce or when "the father had abused or forfeited the right by cruelty or misconduct towards the children, or is of such character, or has been guilty of such conduct that their welfare, either physical or moral, requires that they shall be removed from him."[16]

The court decided in the father's favor, finding that the mother's refusal to return with the child to live with her husband was the result of invidious interference by the maternal grandmother. As such, her separation was considered voluntary and not justified under the law.[17]

The whole frame of government and law has been said to exist only to protect and support the *family* [emphasis in original]. . . . Such an institution is to be cherished and guarded. . . . The hand that has been raised against its sanctity must be stricken down. . . . But if a relative may stir up strife between them and separate them, as has been done in the case now before me, public policy requires that the party sinned against shall not bear all the punishment; that the offenders shall not escape animadversion.[18]

**Exceptions to the General Rule—The Watershed of Tender Years.** In those cases in which the mother emerged the victor in a custody litigation, the victory was usually rationalized as an exception to the general rule recognizing the father's superior rights. In an 1881 Supreme Court case, the decision seems to actually overrule the doctrine of the father's *prima facie* right.

The referee is of the opinion that under the facts both parents are irreproachable. If that be so, it might well be urged that as far as the welfare of the children is concerned, and which is the matter considering their *tender years* [emphasis added), which is to be now chiefly considered, it would be best to leave them with their mother.[19]

In that particular decision, however, the judge was influenced by the failure of the record to sufficiently disclose whether or not the husband had ever struck his wife. Anxiety was expressed by the court that until that issue was resolved, the father might not be considered fit: "For I must conclude that as a man is to his wife in this regard, so he would be towards his children."[20] Hence, the case may be seen as distinguishable on its facts, rather than the advent of new law.

In *People ex rel. Sternberger* v. *Sternberger,*[21] an 1896 decision, the appellate division continued to recognize the potency of prior authorities that placed a burden on the mother to show either unfitness on the father's part or justification for her decision to leave him or both.[22] *Sternberger* mitigated, to some degree, the burden of justification placed on the mother, holding that, "the remedy sought in proceedings of this character [that is, *habeas corpus]* may be furnished to a wife under the statute when it appears to the court that she is living separate and apart from her husband for some good and substantial reason, which justified her morally in the course she has pursued, although that reason may not be sufficient basis for a decree of divorce. . . ."[23]

The court's analysis of the facts in this case led it to the conclusion that the verbal abuse and harrassment suffered by the wife at her husband's instigation was "beyond endurance," . . . although it "did not go to the extent of actual brutality or physical injury."[24]

The Tender Years Doctrine strictly speaking, had not made its debut in the Sternberger case. The decision of the court was in the mother's favor, it is true, but it did not specifically throw out the prior common-law *prima facie* rights of the father. Further, the mother was still held to some degree of justification for her desertion. The case can be distinguished on its facts from the rule expressed in *People ex rel. Nickerson, supra,*[25] because of the circumstances of the mother's voluntary separation. Still, even if through dicta, all those signal words and phrases that will appear in later cases marking the reign of Tender Years Doctrine are included in this court's opinion.

> We consider it to be satisfactorily established that it is much better for [the children] to remain at the present time with their mother than with their father, and that consideration arises from the proven fitness of the mother to take charge and control of them; their *tender years,* the *delicate condition,* of the boy, the *necessity* that exists for the girl having *maternal care and guidance* [emphasis added].[26]

The Tender Years Doctrine gained ground in *Osterhoudt* v. *Osterhoudt,* an 1899 decision.[27] The court held for the mother in spite of her living in a state of *de jure* adultery, the result of the failure of the New York court to recognize a North Dakota divorce. The mother's superior wealth, ability to provide for her children, and the father's infrequent contacts with the children during the separation compounded a set of conditions that influenced the court in the mother's favor.[28]

Once again, the decision is couched in language that recognizes the old rule favoring the father and finds special circumstances in the case to distinguish it from the [new] rule: "Were no other considerations . . . involved the plaintiff . . . would also have control and custody of the two minor children."[29]

The decision in the appellate division affirming *Osterhoudt*[30] distinguished the case further in finding that the mother believed herself legally divorced from the father when she contracted her invalid marriage with and commenced cohabitation with her paramour.[31] Further, the court recognized that the mother had given her daughter "the care and attention which daughters require from a mother."[32] These words are key ingredients in the *Tender Years Formula* that was becoming dominant.

(The dissenting opinion in the appellate division decision is worth some attention, if only for entertainment value, as an outrageously stereotypical, puritanical sermon on morality that even then was fast becoming a relic of the prior half-century.)[33]

In a 1904 decision, *People ex rel. Sinclair* v. *Sinclair,*[34] the court does little more than pay lip service to the "undoubted rule that the husband is regarded in the law as the head of the household and the law awards him the care and the custody of the children. . . ."[35] For having confirmed that rule, the Court holds that it may interfere with the rule on sufficient reason presented. In its opinion, the court finds that the tender years of the children is reason enough.

In all cases, however, where the custody of tender infants is involved, the prime consideration is the welfare of the child. The right of the husband must always yield to such considerations. Nature has devolved upon the mother the nurture and care of infants during their tender years, and in that period such care, for practical purposes, in the absence of exceptional circumstances, is almost exclusively committed to her. At such periods of life courts do not hesitate to award the care and custody of young infants to the wife against the paramount right of the husband where the wife has shown herself to be a proper person and is able to fully discharge her duty toward the child.[36]

Custody was awarded to the mother, though no finding of unfitness was made against the father, and no attempt was made to justify the mother's willful abandonment of the father.[37] The paramount right of the father turns up to be something less than paramount as a result of this decision. The old common-law rule is effectively dead at this point, though a few more years would pass until it was properly buried.

Eight years after *Sinclair,* the common-law rule favoring paternal primacy was effectively, if not specifically, overruled in *Ullman* v. *Ullman.*[38]

I consider that the rule in its entirety is not stated .. . if it be intended to say that only the misconduct or incapacity of the father or a cause of action for divorce in the mother authorizes the court to give the mother custody of the child. The mother may have been in fault and the father blameless, and yet the age or condition of the child may require a mother's care. . . . The child at tender age is entitled to have such care, love and discipline as only a good and devoted mother can usually give.[39]

## The Reign of Tender Years

The Tender Years Rule, having come to full maturity in the *Ullman* decision, completely reversed the previous state of the law. The father, under the old common law, had the *prima facie* right to custody unless the mother could carry a heavy burden to persuade the court otherwise. Subsequent to *Ullman,* the burden was reversed. The preference for maternal custody was never specifically elevated to the dignity of a *prima facie* right. There was, at the time of *Ullman,* a statutory standard that remains the law today; that is, making both parents equally entitled to custody and denying a preference to either.[40] Nevertheless, the percentage of cases in which mothers were awarded custody was deemed by one authority to be as high as 90 percent in 1973.[41] For a period of approximately 60 years following *Ullman,* there was a "pattern of at least cursory invocation of the courts in New York and elsewhere, of the presumption that children of tender years, all other things being equal, should be given into the custody of their mother."[42]

This undeclared but ever-present presumption became sufficiently well-established so that in many cases, courts felt secure in applying the rule without the need of citing authority. In reversing a lower-court decision awarding custody to the father because the mother had failed to honor her prenuptial agreement to instruct the children as Roman Catholics, the appellate division held, in a 1961 decision that "the welfare of such very young children will be better served by allowing them to remain with their mother." No authority was cited.[43]

In direct contrast to the old common-law rule,[44] the mother's position post-*Ullman,* was so well-favored that "one act of adultery" was "not a justifiable basis upon which the mother may be denied custody," considering that the welfare of the child was the court's primary concern and that "the age or condition of the child may require a mother's care."[45] In spite of statutory authority to the contrary, the court makes the blanket statement that, "Generally, children of tender years should be awarded to the mother."[46]

The rule in *Ullman* continued to retain its vitality into the early 1970s.[47] Those instances in which the father was awarded custody were usually announced as exceptions to the general rule of maternal preference, in that some special circumstances were deemed to exist in holding the mother unfit. The old common-law rule had been turned around 180 degrees.

*Exceptions to Tender Years during Its Reign*

There was no shortage of exceptions to the Tender Years Doctrine during its unofficial sovereignty. The burden was, of course, reversed, in that now the father needed to show good cause as to why the "natural" advantages of maternal love and affection were insufficient reason to confirm the mother as custodian.

In *People ex rel. Fields* v. *Kaufman,*[48] the parties were divorced after the mother was stricken with polio and confined to a wheelchair. Thus the mother was physically unable to care for the children for a period of approximately 6 years.[49] The father assumed the care of the children with the aid of his second wife. The mother, displaying iron determination, acquired some degree of physical rehabilitation and resumed her career as a nursing supervisor at a comfortable salary.[50] On achieving this measure of recovery and independence, the mother brought a writ of *habeas corpus* to regain custody of her children. Her efforts failed.[51]

The extent to which the mother was physically disabled was never mentioned as an influence on the court's decision, but it is difficult to believe this factor was totally ignored. The court appeared to be more plainly influenced by the phsychiatric report, which evaluated the mother as a "driven woman with a high degree of impulsive behavior."[52] Her impulsiveness, and perhaps her capriciousness, was underlined to the court's mind by her failure to keep in touch with the children during the period in which she fought to recover her physical mobility and career stability.[53]

If there had bccn no better reason, the court could not bring itself to uproot the children from the secure, happy, and stable environment that had surrounded them for 6 years in order to comply with the Tender Years Doctrine, even though the children had expressed a preference for their mother as custodian.[54]

Other scenarios that resulted in an award to the father included a mother with a clear history of mental instability and an uncertain future[55] and a case in which the mother had a serious problem with alcoholism.[56]

*Mother's Adultery as an Exception to Tender Years*

The extent to which adultery on the part of the mother will overcome the Tender Years presumption was a close question, even in a period of more puritanical mores. No one could have been more flagrant in her adulterous flings than Mrs. Ethel Bunim,[57] who, at her divorce trial, admitted "numerous deliberate adulteries"[58] with a man who was married and had children of his own.[59] Not content with her admission of behavior, which she knew to be considered disgraceful by her community, Mrs. Bunim justified her recreational activities as the natural result of her dissatisfaction with her husband; she demonstrated no repentence whatsoever and perjured herself during part of the proceedings as well.[60] Mrs. Bunim certainly did not leave much leeway for even the most promother court to grant her custody, considering the prevailing mores of the time. The outcome, in the father's favor, was no surprise.[61]

In another example, in reviewing a family court award of custody to the mother, the appellate division found her circumstances grossly unfavorable compared to those of the father. The Court reached this conclusion due to her "conduct over a prolonged period in which she openly lived with a married man known to her to be an ex-convict and a suspected drug addict and mothered his child."[62] That particular scenario left few major sins out of the script. Open adultery was compounded by drugs, an out-of-wedlock pregnancy, and a criminal conviction. How could the court apply Tender Years against the alternative afforded by the father of a "home atmosphere," a steady job, and a stable remarriage?[63]

Custody was also denied to a mother in a case in which she had carried on an adulterous affair for 3 years, including one occasion at her marital home while her children were present.[64]

In those instances in which a mother had been less flagrant in deviation from moral rectitude, the courts were inclined to forgive the lapse and apply the Tender Years Doctrine. In a case in which a father had won a divorce against his wife on grounds of adultery, the court found that, "aside from a single moral lapse," which could "be attributed in large measure" to the husband's "ill treatment of her," the mother had been devoted in her care of the child, and her custody of him was confirmed.[65]

It has been specifically held that "[a]dultery alone is not a bar" to the mother's retention of custody.[66] This general rule was applied, in one case, where there were only two admitted acts on the part of the mother and there was "no evidence that the indiscretions were notorious or that they occurred in the presence of the children.[67]

### The Decline of the Tender Years Rule

The Tender Years Rule, originally announced in *Ullman* v. *Ullman,*[68] came under increasing criticism toward the end of the late 1960s.

In a 1969 third-department decision, *Ullman* and the Tender Years Doctrine was unequivocally criticized, and the long-ignored statutory mandate that "there is no *prima facie* right to custody in either parent" was specifically cited.[69] The degree to which the Tender Years Doctrine had achieved recognition, despite its inconsistency with prevailing statutory law, was illustrated by the court's summary of the mother's argument. "Petitioner contends that the record does not support the (lower court) determination because there are no overriding considerations present to deny the general principle of the propriety of committing a child of tender years to its mother. . . ."[70]

Custody was awarded to the father. The court was influenced largely by the fact that, at the time of the decision, he had already maintained the child in a comfortable, wholesome atmosphere for 3 years. To have granted custody to the mother would have meant uprooting the child; that is, a change in a satisfactory status quo, which the court could not countenance.[71] The Tender Years Rule was overcome, in this case, by an insufficient change of circumstances to justify removal of the custodian.[72]

The same criticism of *Ullman* and the Tender Years Rule was voiced in another third-department decision, *Matter of F.F.* v. *F.F.*[73] The appellate court affirmed the family court's decision, confirming custody to the father.[74] The trial-court record showed the mother absent for long periods in the evening, while leaving the children with the father or neighbors during the time that she was the custodian.[75] Such behavior on the part of the mother was characterized by the appellate court as reflecting "a certain degree of immaturity on petitioner's part and either an unwillingness or inability to accept and fulfill fully and completely her maternal responsibilities."[76]

The rationale in this decision is significant in that the courts did not hold the father to a heavy burden of proving outrageous immoral behavior or serious mental or physical disability on the mother's part in order to overcome the sway of the the Tender Years Rule. Fear of uprooting the children was not as significant in this particular case as the period in which they had been in the father's care at the time of the hearing was short.[77] This is the beginning of the wane of the Tender Years Doctrine, as the courts attempt to make a custody decision based simply on which parent would do a better job, without presuming the mother to be the natural choice.

*People ex rel. Watts* v. *Watts,*[78] a 1973 family court decision, directly and vigorously attacked the Tender Years Doctrine.

> Until recently . . . there has been a pattern of at least cursory invocation by the court in New York and elsewhere, of the presumption that children of tender years, all other things being equal, should be given into the custody of their mother. In fact, this approach to deciding custody cases, since the Domestic Relations Law was amended to forbid such preferences, constitutes judicial error, error, moreover which does not promote the best interest of the children involved.[79]

Further, the court squarely analyzed the whole 60-odd-year history of Tender Years as a substantive presumption, no less powerful because of its inconsistency with statutory law and its failure to be openly enunciated as such a presumption.[80] The court labeled it as a plainly arbitrary sexist rule, which might even be subject to constitutional attack as violative of the "equal protection" clause under the Fourteenth Amendment to the U.S. Constitution.[81]

By the time the decision in *Salk* v. *Salk* came down,[82] the Tender Years Doctrine had been effectively buried. The *Salk* decision postulated that, "Under well-settled statutory and case law neither parent has a *prima facie* right to custody of a child [citing authority]. The issue is one of *comparative fitness* [sic] with the paramount and controlling consideration being the best interest and welfare of the child [citing authority]."[83]

Now the courts have gotten to the point where a judge can hold for an evenhanded approach in determining custody, citing as "well-settled," a rule that was honored more in the breach than in its application. The court does not even mention Tender Years by way of eulogy or reminiscence, thus acting as though it had never existed. It would seem, if this decision was read in a vacuum, that an award to the father without a finding of unfitness, simply because he was the *better parent,* was in conformity with the way things had always been. The opinion makes it very plain that the case was decided exactly on that basis.

> The court is convinced that both parties exhibit genuine love and affection for the children. Neither parent has been neglectful of their parental duties, nor in any way can be characterized as being an unfit custodian of the children.
>
> However, from all the evidence before the court it has been clearly established that the best interests of the children would be served if permanent custody is awarded to the one parent that appears to more adequately satisfy the emotional and cultural needs of the children. . . . [I]t is the opinion of this court that [the father] can best nurture the complex needs and social development of these chilren.[84]

The court, in reaching its decision, relied heavily on the expert testimony of three psychiatrists and one psychologist.[85] The children expressed preferences for their father, but the court hastened to point out that it was influenced but not controlled by that factor.[86] The anecdotal evidence was also significant to the court in finding that the father was the more sensitive, motivated parent.[87]

The emphasis in the future, it appears, will be placed on determining which parent is the better or the "exclusive" psychological parent for the child.[88]

Having defined a rule of awarding custody according to the best "psychological" qualifications, it remains to be determined how this standard will be refined and effectively applied. The behavioral sciences are highly speculative, subjective disciplines at best. An opinion from an expert, no matter how distinguished, as to what is psychologically best for a child in terms of emotional support, nurturing, or other such now-familiar phrases, is certainly more speculative than weighing, for example, the worth of the disability caused by a fractured leg.

Will custody suits evolve into detailed evaluations by the judge of interminable psychological reports, sometimes barely distinguishable in their findings? The comforting thing about the old rules was their relative predictability in application. First, the father was by "natural law," or some other such metaphysical criterion, the head of the household and entitled to custody unless proven unfit. Then "nature" and the courts decreed a child of tender years to be sorely in need of the care that only a mother could provide unless she was unfit.

The sheer unpredictability occasioned by the current standard tempts one to say that lawyers should push for out-of-court settlements in all but the most exceptional circumstances. But child custody is an emotionally supercharged issue, and life is not so bloodless. The actual physical day-to-day custody of a child can only be in one place or another. Joint custody is rarely a realistic alternative. How does one divide a child? The dilemma illustrated by the biblical parable of King Solomon and the two women comes to mind with new and unexpected relevance. A child's custody cannot be compromised like the monetary worth of an injury or partitioned like real property, or sold for equitable division of the proceeds.

## The Tender Years Doctrine in Other Jurisdictions

The courts in New York evolved at first into and then away from the Tender Years Doctrine, often with painstaking deliberation. New York decisions have recognized the Tender Years Rule tentatively, always open to finding some justifiable factual exception to the rule. When the New York courts abandoned the doctrine, they did not do so unequivocally but pretended, in many decisions, that it had never been the rule at all.[89]

### Iowa

The Iowa courts, by contrast, are far less equivocal generally in their judicial pronouncements on child custody.[90] Iowa never gave more than the most minimal recognition to the Tender Years Doctrine. "[W]e generally infer that the mother is the better choice in the care of small children, but the inference yields to evidence tending to show otherwise [citing case]. No hard and fast rule governs which parent should have custody [citing case]."[91]

Never having held much support in Iowa, the rule was scrapped altogether in 1974, just as the decline of the Tender Years Doctrine was accelerating in many other jurisdictions.

> We do not think either parent should have a greater burden than the other in attempting to obtain custody in the dissolution proceeding. It is neither necessary nor useful to infer in advance that the best interests of young children will be better served if their custody is awarded to their mothers instead of their fathers. We previously emphasized the weakness of the inference; we now abandon it.[92]

The court noted the social changes in our evolving society that gave rise to the total abandonment of the rule. This inference is partly based on the assumption a mother keeps the home, performs household duties, and will have more time to devote to the children and their welfare. . . . Modern redefinition and adjustment to traditional parental roles has greatly diluted the strength of the inference. . . .[citations omitted]."[93]

The court even goes so far as to question the constitutionality of the doctrine as violative of the Equal Protection Clause of the Fourteenth Amendment and cites the New York decision in *Watts* v. *Watts* in connection with this dicta.[94] The court found it, however, "unnecessary to decide the constitutional issue because we hold the inference is no longer wise. It is simply not justified as an a priori principle. . . . The real issue is not the sex of the parent but which parent will do better in raising the children."[95]

The rejection of the Tender Years Doctrine remains the unequivocal policy of the Iowa courts. In a 1978 decision, an intermediate appellate decision reversing the trial court's award of custody to the mother was affirmed by the Iowa Supreme Court. The opinion held that the trial court erroneously "indulged the inference that the best interests of younger children are served by placing them in their mother's custody. We abandon such inference in *In re Marriage of Bowen* . . ."[96]

*Pennsylvania*

Although little credit was given by the Iowa courts to the Tender Years Rule, the presumption was until recently treated reverentially in Pennsylvania decisions. Not a little sanctimonious state chauvinism was intermingled with this esteem for the Tender Years Doctrine, as evidenced by the language in this 1973 decision.

> In Pennsylvania, supported by the wisdom of the ages, it has long been the rule that in the absence of compelling reasons to the contrary, a mother has the right to the custody of her children over any other person, particularly

so, where the children are of tender years [citing cases]. In fact, that the best interests of children of tender years will be best served under a mother's guidance and control is one of the strongest presumptions in the law [citing case].[97]

The court cited a long list of authorities in support of this position, including one decision dating from 1813.[98] This view was adopted in its entirety in an intermediate appellate decision in 1974, *Commonwealth ex rel Spriggs* v. *Carson.*[99] But in 1977 *Spriggs* v. *Carson* was reversed on appeal to the Pennsylvania Supreme Court, and the trial court's award of custody to the father was reinstated.[100] The leading case up to that time, *Commonwealth ex rel. Lucas* v. *Kreischer,* was especially criticized.[101] This represented a major shift away from Pennsylvania's devotion to the Tender Years Doctrine, although it was not just yet totally abandoned.

We . . . question the legitimacy of a doctrine that is predicated upon traditional or stereotypic roles of men and women in a marital union. Whether the tender years doctrine is employed to create a presumption which requires the male parent to overcome its effect by presenting compelling contrary evidence of a particular nature; [citing cases], or merely as a makeshift where the scales are relatively balanced; [citing cases], such a view is offensive to the concept of the equality of the sexes which we have embraced as a constitutional principle within this jurisdiction [citing authority]: Courts should be wary of deciding matters as sensitive as questions of custody by the invocation of "presumptions."[102]

In a decision 6 months after *Spriggs,* an intermediate appellate court was describing the opinion as one that changed the law and precluded reliance on the Tender Years Rule.[103] In a 1979 Pennsylvania Supreme Court opinion, the bench ruled flatly that the Tender Years Presumption . . . has now been abandoned.[104] Thus, the evolution of Pennsylvania's decisional law in abandoning the Tender Years Rule was rather abrupt.

## *Illinois*

The development of Illinois decisional law on the Tender Years Doctrine was considerably less abrupt, compared to the trend in Pennsylvania and Iowa. In that sense, it bears more similarity to the development in New York cases. The result, as in New York, has been more equivocal than in Pennsylvania or Iowa. The leading case, decided in 1952,[105] rings with the classic language of the Tender Years Doctrine and has never been overruled.

It is usual in [custody] cases, due to the tender years of the child and in consideration of its best interests, to entrust its care and custody to the mother, she being a fit and proper person to rear the child [citing cases].

The maternal affection is more active and better adapted to the care of the child. Especially is this true in the case of a minor daughter, where the care and guidance of a mother's hand is doubly important.[106]

The court indicates that, such being the rule, it has enjoyed recognition in Illinois for a considerable period: "This principle has become so well fixed and followed in this State that this court has not in recent years been called to rule upon it."[107] The court held that, "compelling evidence" of unfitness on the part of the mother would have to be proven before the mother would be divested of custody.[108] The decision, however, did express the dicta that "[u]nder our divorce statute the court is clothed with a larger discretion in determining to which parent a child will be given."[109] It is this last phrase that will prove a basis for reconciling the leading case with later, seemingly inconsistent decisions.

The vitality of the leading case, the *Nye* decision, was demonstrated by its citation with approval in a 1978 decision by an intermediate appellate court.[110] The court did not apply the rule in that particular case, because it found the Tender Years Doctrine inapplicable to a contest between a parent and a grandparent. But it did not disapprove or comment adversely on either the *Nye* decision or the Tender Years Doctrine.[111]

In a 1967 case that distinguished *Nye* v. *Nye,* the court affirmed the trial court's award of custody to the father with whom the children had resided during the mother's 18-month commitment to a mental hospital.[112] The court rejected the application of the tender-years presumption under the facts of the case and emphasized the language in *Nye,* that "clothed [the court] with large discretion" in determining to which parent the children should be given.[113]

In a 1974 decision, also affirming a custody award to the father, the court downgraded the Tender Years Doctrine from a tentative presumption to just one factor of consideration.

A court when making a determination as to the children's best interests must weigh a variety of factors. Undoubtedly, as plaintiff argues, an infant of tender years may benefit more by being placed in the custody of its mother rather than with its father [citing case]. . . . Whether their age and maturity were such as would bring this preference into operation was for the trial court to decide. Yet, even if invoked, this is just one factor among many which a court must look at when viewing the totality of the evidence presented.[114]

Another 1974 decision, while not mentioning the *Nye* case, implicitly overrules it and unequivocally criticizes the Tender Years Doctrine.

. . . [I]t should be noted that there is today no inflexible rule which requires that custody of children, especically of tender age, be vested in the mother.

Equality of the sexes has entered this field. The fact that a mother is fit in only one facet of the situation and, standing by itself, it does not authorize a denial of custody to the father, when this appears necessary because of other considerations [citing cases].[115]

A 1975 decision further disapproved of the presumption. "The wife contends that she should have been awarded custody of the child because the child is one of tender years and the wife is the child's mother. However, as a result of the recent social and legal trends, this court cannot recognize a presumption in favor of the mother in the contest for a child of tender years [citing case]."[116] These decisions, seemingly inconsistent with the *Nye* case, the leading decision of a higher tribunal,[117] were reconciled to some extent in another 1975 decision. "[T]here is no inflexible rule that the custody of children, even of tender age, be vested in the mother [citing cases], but the fact that an infant of tender years may benefit by being placed in the custody of its mother is a fact to be considered [citing cases]."[118]

A more adept attempt to reconcile *Nye* v. *Nye* with those decisions critical of the Tender Years Doctrine was made in a 1976 decision, *Drake* v. *Hohimer.*[119] In that case, the court, recognizing that *Nye* v. *Nye* was still the law, refused to reach the issue raised by the father that a presumption in the mother's favor was unconstitutional sexist discrimination.[120] The court held that, "The constitutional question need not be reached in this case because we do not read *Nye* as requiring the award of custody to the mother if she is found to be fit."[121] The court held further that the presumption in favor of the mother could no longer be recognized and that this was consistent with *Nye,* which had held that, "The guiding star is and must be, at all times, the best interest of the child."[122] In the most recent decision on the question, the presumption of Tender Years was held "no longer recognized" by the court.[123]

The trend in Illinois decisions in the intermediate appellate courts is certainly against the Tender Years Rule. Some of the decisions are emphatically disapproving; other justices are inclined to read the *Nye* decision so as not to be constrained to recognize the presumption in the first place. But in *Nye* there is an outstanding decision by the state's highest court that has never been reversed. Hence, one cannot say with complete assurance that the Tender Years Doctrine is dead in Illinois, although it might be considered a safe bet.

## Alabama

Alabama presents a situation different from other jurisdictions already discussed, in that it has codified the Tender Years Doctrine as applied to children under 7 years of age.[124] Appellate decisions have been consistent in interpreting the presumption as a rebuttable one and upholding that the facts of each case must be considered in applying the doctrine.[125] But the Tender Years Doctrine still has considerable force in Alabama where an appellate court held, as late as 1975, that, "The courts follow a compelling presumption that a female child of tender years will be best cared for by its mother unless she is shown to be unfit."[126] This is classic Tender Years Doctrine language, now dated in other jurisdictions such as New York, Illinois, and Pennsylvania, and has been held to be equally applicable to male children of tender years.[127]

The Alabama courts could not entirely ignore the gathering criticism of the Tender Years Doctrine in the 1970s. But prevailing judicial opinion met the challenge head-on with a strong defense of its position. The courts rejected the argument that the statute was unconstitutional or violative of a father's right to equal protection of the laws.[128] The statutory presumption was held not to be arbitrary because it was rebuttable and not absolute.[129] The court held that the basis of the presumption was rational as applied in Alabama.

> It has evolved over many decades and has been refined by actual experience of many able judges and attorneys. It is aimed at the legitimate good of providing the most favorable environment for young children. The presumption was fashioned in the context of observed reality, not abstract contemplation.[130]

There is a hint in a 1976 decision that the courts are beginning to recognize some inconsistency between a statutorily established tender-years presumption and the male parent's right to equal protection of the laws. ". . .[T]he unfitness of the mother need not be established to rebut the presumption of the tender years doctrine. Rather, the father can obtain custody upon showing that he is relatively more fit [citing case]. Such a result is a necessary consequence of the natural father's rights to due process and equal protection [citing cases]."[131]

The court, however, recognized that the Tender Years Doctrine continued to be the prevailing law in Alabama and gave no hint of rejecting or disapproving it.[132] The case can probably be distinguished by the fact that the mother was applying for a modification of a prior custody order that had placed the child with the father, and the court was loath to upset a satisfactory status quo in the absence of sufficient change of circumstances.[133] On balance, one must conclude that the Tender Years Doctrine is still very much alive in Alabama.

## California

California is an example of another jurisdiction that has dealt with the tender-years presumption on a statutory, rather than a decisional basis. The current form of the applicable statute,[134] effective as of 1972, provides that in any proceeding to determine custody of a child, an award should be made in the "following order of preference: (a) To either parent according to the best interests of the child. . . ."[135]

The 1970 form of the statute include the words, "To either parent according to the best interest of the child, *but other things being equal, custody should be given to the mother if the child is of tender years.* " [emphasis added].[136] Thus, by the 1972 amendment, California made it clear that it was unequivocally *rejecting* the Tender Years Doctrine as a presumption of law.

The form of the statute that preceded the 1970 act (known prior to 1970 as Section 138), was even more specific and more sexist in its assignment of presumptions for the disposition of custody disputes.[137] The old Section 138 provided that in determining custody, "the court is to be guided by the following considerations . . .:

> (2) As between parents adversely claiming the custody, neither parent is entitled to it as of right; but other things being equal, if the child is of tender years, custody should be given to the mother; if the child is of an age to require education and preparation for labor or business, then custody should be given to the father.[138]

There is, however, considerable authority demonstrating that California was in the forefront of rejecting the Tender Years presumption as long ago as 1946, even while Section 138 was still in effect.[139]

In a 1953 decision, the Supreme Court of California was already setting a standard that would not be considered by other jurisdictions until some 20 years later, holding that even under the statute then in effect either parent was "entitled to custody and no showing or finding of unfitness is necessary to enable the court to award custody to one or the other in accordance with what, in its sound discretion, is deemed the best interests of the child."[140]

It is inescapable to conclude that the trend in U.S. law is away from the tender-years presumption, although the pace of evolution from jurisdiction to jurisdiction varies. Some jurisdictions, while tending to water down the Tender Years Doctrine, have been more reluctant than others to pronounce against it. The social and political trends in this country in favor of eschewing sexual stereotypes do not enhance the prospects of the Tender Years Doctrine.

**Notes**

1. *Ullman* v. *Ullman,* 151 A.D. 419, 135 N.Y.S. 1080 (2d Dept. 1912).
2. *People ex rel. Nickerson,* 19 Wend. 16 (1837).
3. *Id.*
4. *Id.,* at 17.
5. *Id.,* at 19.
6. *People ex rel. Nickerson,* 19 Wend., at 18 *See* 2 R.S. 150 § 1.
7. *Id. See* 2 R.S. 148, 149 (§ 1, 2). See, chapter 1, Jurisdiction, *supra.*
8. *People ex rel. Nickerson,* 19 Wend., at 18.
9. 1860 N.Y. Laws 157, cited in *Brooks* v. *Brooks,* 35 Barb. 85 (1861).
10. See chapter 1, Jurisdiction, *supra* and chapter 6, Visitation, *infra.*
11. *Brooks* v. *Brooks,* 35 Barb., at 87.
12. *Id.*
13. *Id.,* at 91–92.
14. *Id.*
15. *Id.*
16. *Olmstead* v. *Olmstead,* 27 Bar. 9, 15 (1857).
17. *Id.,* at 33.
18. *Id.,* at 33–34.
19. *In re Pray,* 60 How. Pr. 194, 195 (1881).
20. *Id.*
21. *Sternberger* v. *Sternberger,* 12 A.D. 398, 42 N.Y.S. 423 (1st Dept. 1896), *appeal dismissed,* 153 N.Y. 684.
22. *Id.,* 12 A.D., at 401.
23. *Id.,* at 403.
24. *Id.,* at 406.
25. *People ex rel. Nickerson,* 19 Wend., at 16.
26. *Sternberger* v. *Sternberger,* 12 A.D., at 405.
27. *Osterhoudt* v. *Osterhoudt,* 28 Misc. 285, 59 N.Y.S. 797 (Sup. Ct.), *aff'd,* 48 A.D. 74 (1st Dept. 1900), *appeal dismissed,* 168 N.Y. 358.
28. *Id.,* 28 Misc., at 285.
29. *Id.,* at 287.
30. *Id.,* 48 A.D., at 74.
31. *Id.,* at 78.
32. *Id.,* at 76.
33. *Id.,* at 83. "Are these children then, to be taught to hate their blameless father and to love his successor? Are they to learn as they grow up, that there is no inherent sanctity in the marriage bond, that the duty is an old fashioned notion, that the desire of the heart or the craving of the senses is the essential thing, and that all acts are righteous which lead to

their gratification? It would be better for these children—better for their future here, and better for that wider future which lies beyond—that they should share the modest and humble environment of their innocent father than enjoy the material advantages, or even a mother's love, at the expense of principle and morality.''

34. *Sinclair* v. *Sinclair,* 91 A.D. 322, 86 N.Y.S. 539 (1st Dept. 1904).

35. *Id.,* at 325.

36. *Id.*

37. *Id.*

38. *Ullman* v. *Ullman,* 151 A.D. 419, 135 N.Y.S. 1080 (2d Dept. 1912).

39. *Id.,* at 424–425. Compare this language with the concurring opinion of Senator Paige, sitting on what was then called the court for the Correction of Errors, in *Mercein* v. *Barry,* 25 Wend. 64, 105 (1840). The language therein seems to have overturned the common-law rule some seventy years prior to *Ullman, supra,* but somehow it never made an authoritative impression on subsequent opinions.

40. Now codified in N.Y. Dom. Rel. Law §§ 70, 240 (McKinney).

41. *Watts* v. *Watts,* 77 Misc. 2d 178, 350 N.Y.S.2d 285 (Fam. Ct. 1973).

42. *Id.,* at 179.

43. *Begley* v. *Begley,* 13 A.D. 2d 961, 216 N.Y.S.2d 417 (2d Dept. 1961).

44. *People ex rel. Nickerson,* 19 Wend. at 17.

45. *Sheil* v. *Sheil,* 29 A.D. 2d 950 (2d Dept. 1968).

46. *Id.,* citing *Fischel* v. *Fischel,* 286 A.D. 842, 142 N.Y.S.2d 236 (1st Dept. 1955); *Walker* v. *Walker,* 282 A.D. 671, 122 N.Y.S.2d 385 (1st Dept 1953); *Thiele* v. *Thiele,* 277 A.D. 1025, 100 N.Y.S.2d 634 (1st Dept. 1950).

47. *Pritchett* v. *Pritchett,* 1 A.D.2d 1009, 151 N.Y.S.2d 481 (2d Dept.), *aff'd,* 2 A.D.2d 692, 153 N.Y.S.2d 591 (2d Dept. 1956); *Matter of Desiree T.,* 64 Misc. 2d 28, 35, 314 N.Y.S.2d 480 (Fam. Ct. 1970).

48. *Fields* v. *Kaufmann,* 27 Misc. 2d 625, 207 N.Y.S.2d 870 (Sup. Ct. 1960).

49. *Id.,* at 627, 628.

50. *Id.*

51. *Id.,* at 631.

52. *Id.,* at 629.

53. *Id.,* at 630.

54. *Id.,* at 631.

55. *Reinhart* v. *Reinhart,* 33 Misc. 2d 80, 227 N.Y.S.2d 39 (Sup. Ct. 1961).

56. *Goodson* v. *Goodson,* 301 N.Y.S.2d 406 (1st Dept.); Bloustein,

*Goodson* v. *Goodson,* N.Y.L.J., Jan. 7, 1969, at 2, col. 5. With reference to the unfitness of an alcoholic parent, generally see chapter 3, Current Standards for Determination of Custody Disputes between Parents *infra;* *Application of Cleaves,* 6 A.D.2d 138, 175 N.Y.S.2d 736 (3d Dept. 1958); *Matter of Gustow.* 14 A.D.2d 756, 220 N.Y.S.2d 373, 377 (3d Dept. 1976).

57. *Bunim* v. *Bunim,* 298 N.Y. 391 (1949).

58. *Id.,* at 393. When is adultery not deliberate, except in the case of rape?

50. *Id.,* at 393, 394.

60. *Id.*

61. *Id.*

62. *Bishop* v. *Bishop,* 34 A.D.2d 834, 835, 308 N.Y.S.2d 998 (2d Dept. 1970).

63. *Id.*

64. *Johnson* v. *Johnson,* 47 Misc. 2d 805, 263 N.Y.S.2d 404 (Sup. Ct. 1965), *aff'd,* 25 A.D.2d 672 (2d Dept. 1966). This case was specifically distinguished from *Kruczek* v. *Kruczek,* 29 N.Y.S.2d 385 (Sup. Ct. 1941), *See also Ragona* v. *De Saint Cyr,* 207 Misc. 194, 137 N.Y.S.2d 275 (Sup. Ct. 1954).

65. *Kruczek* v. *Kruczek,* 29 N.Y.S.2d 385 (Sup. Ct. 1941), *mod.,* 264 A.D. 242, 35 N.Y.S.2d 289 (1st Dept. 1942), *aff'd,* 289 N.Y. 826.

66. *Geismar* v. *Geismar,* 184 Misc. 897, 907, 54 N.Y.S.2d 747 (Sup. Ct. 1945), citing *Lefkon* v. *Lefkon,* 267 A.D. 83 (2d Dept. 1944); *Rizzo* v. *Rizzo,* 246 A.D. 838 (2d Dept. 1936); *Teinan* v. *Teinan,* 267 A.D. 173, 45 N.Y.S.2d 226 (1st Dept. 1943).

67. *Geismar* v. *Geismar,* 184 Misc., at 907.

68. *Ullman* v. *Ullman,* 151 A.D. 419, 135 N.Y.S. 1080 (2d Dept. 1912).

69. *Wout* v. *Wout,* 32 A.D.2d 709, 710 (3d Dept. 1969). *See* N.Y. Dom. Rel. Law § 70 (McKinney).

70. *Wout* v. *Wout,* 32 A.D., at 710.

71. *Id.*

72. See chapter 3, Current Standards for Determination of Custody Disputes between Parents, *infra,·* on change of circumstances as equally important a basis for custody determination as "tender years" once was.

73. *F.F.* v. *F.F.,* 37 A.D.2d 893 (3d Dept. 1971).

74. *Id.,* at 894.

75. *Id.*

76. *Id.*

77. *Id. Compare with Wout* v. *Wout,* 32 A.D.2d, at 709.

78. *Watts* v. *Watts,* 77 Misc. 2d 178, 350 N.Y.S.2d 285 (Fam. Ct. 1973).

79. *Id.,* at 179–180.

80. *Id.,* at 180.

81. *Id.,* at 182–183.

82. *Salk* v. *Salk,* 89 Misc. 2d 883, 393 N.Y.S.2d 841 (Sup. Ct. 1975), *aff'd,* 53 A.D.2d 558, 385 N.Y.S.2d 1015 (1st Dept. 1976).

83. *Id.,* 89 Misc. 2d, at 886.

84. *Id.,* at 887.

85. *Id.,* at 890–892.

86. *Id.,* at 889.

87. *Id.,* at 888.

88. *Golden* v. *Golden,* 95 Misc. 2d 447, 449, 408 N.Y.S.2d 202 (Fam. Ct. 1978).

89. See *Historical Background and Development of the Tender Years Doctrine, supra; Salk* v. *Salk,* 89 Misc. 2d 883, 393 N.Y.S.2d 841 (Sup. Ct. 1975); *Golden* v. *Golden,* 95 Misc. 2d 447, 449, 408 N.Y.S.2d 202 (Fam. Ct. 1978).

90. See chapter 5, Custody Disputes between Natural Parents, *infra. See generally Painter* v. *Bannister,* 260 Iowa 1082, 140 N.W.2d 152 (1967); *Garvin* v. *Garvin,* 258 Iowa 1390, 152 N.W.2d 206 (1966).

91. *In re Marriage of Callahan,* 214 N.W.2d 133, 136 (Iowa 1974).

92. *In re Marriage of Bowen,* 219 N.W.2d 683, 688 (Iowa 1974).

93. *Id.*

94. *Id. See also Watts* v. *Watts,* 77 Misc. 2d 178, 350 N.Y.S.2d 285 (Fam. Ct. 1973).

95. *In re Marriage of Bowen,* 219 N.W.2d at 688.

96. *In re Marriage of Meir,* 267 N.W.2d 46 (Iowa 1978), citing *In re Bowen,* 219 N.W.2d 683, 688 (Iowa 1974). *See also In re Marrige of Teepe,* 271 N.W.2d 740 (Iowa 1978).

97. *Lucas* v. *Kreischer,* 450 Pa. 352, 299 A.2d 243, 245 (1973).

98. *Id.*

99. *Spriggs* v. *Carson,* 229 Pa. Super. Ct. 9, 323 A.2d 273 1974).

100. *Spriggs* v. *Carson,* 470 Pa. 290, 368 A.2d 635, 639 (1975).

101. *Id.,* citing *Lucas* v. *Kreischer,* 450 Pa. 352, 299 A.2d 243 (1973).

102. *Spriggs* v. *Carson,* 368 A.2d, at 639–640.

103. *Gulas* v. *Gulas,* 254 Pa. Super. Ct. 516, 386 A.2d 70 (1978).

104. *Rummel* v. *Rummel,* 39 Pa. 570, 397 A.2d 15, 14 (1979).; *McGowan* v. *McGowan,* 247 Pa. Super Ct. 41, 374 A.2d 1306 (1977).

105. *Nye* v. *Nye,* 411, Ill. 408, 105 N.E.2d 300 (1952).

106. *Id.,* at 303.

107. *Id.*

108. *Id.*

109. *Id.*

110. *Barclay* v. *Barclay,* 66 Ill. App. 3d 1028, 384 N.E.2d 564, 567 (1978).

111. *Id.*

112. *Carlson* v. *Carlson,* 80 Ill. App. 2d 251, 225 N.E.2d 130 (1967).

113. *Id.*

114. *Mulvihill* v. *Mulvihill,* 20 Ill. App. 3d 440, 314 N.E.2d 342, 345 (1974).

115. *Marcus* v. *Marcus,* 24 Ill. App. 3d 401, 320 N.E.2d 581, 585 (1974).

116. *Pratt* v. *Pratt,* 29 Ill. App. 3d 214, 330 N.E.2d 244, 246 (1975), citing *Marcus* v. *Marcus,* 24 Ill. App. 3d 401, 320 N.E.2d 581 (1974).

117. *Nye* v. *Nye,* 411 Ill. 408, 105 N.E.2d 300 (1952).

118. *Christensen* v. *Christensen,* 31 Ill. App. 3d 1041, 335 N.E.2d 581, 583 (1975), citing *Marcus* v. *Marcus,* 24 Ill. App. 3d 401, 320 N.E.2d 581 (1974); *Pratt* v. *Pratt,* 29 Ill. App. 3d 214, 330 N.E.2d 244 (1974); *Nye* v. *Nye,* 411 Ill. 408, 105 N.E.2d 300 (1952); *Mulvihill* v. *Mulvihill,* 20 Ill. App. 3d 440, 314 N.E.2d 342 (1974).

119. *Drake* v. *Hoheimer,* 35 Ill. App. 3d 529, 341 N.E.2d 399 (1976).

120. *Id.,* at 400, citing Ill. Const. of 1970, art. I, § 18.

121. *Id.,* at 400, citing *Nye* v. *Nye,* 411 Ill., at 415.

122. *Id.*

123. *In re Marriage of Farris,* 69 Ill. App. 3d 1042, 388 N.E.2d 232, 234 (1979), citing *Drake* v. *Hoheimer,* 35 Ill. App. 3d 529, 341 N.E.2d 399 (1976); *Pratt* v. *Pratt,* 29 Ill. App. 3d 214, 330 N.E.2d 244 (1975).

124. Ala. Code of 1940, tit. 34, § 35 (1958). *Compare with N. Y. Dom. Rel.* §§ 70, 240 (McKinney), which specifically prohibited such a presumption although the prohibition was substantially ignored for many years. See Superiority of Maternal Rights in Custody Disputes, *supra.*

125. *Statham* v. *Statham,* 276 Ala. 675, 166 So. 2d 403, 407 (1964); *Free* v. *Free,* 52 Ala. App. 651, 296 So. 2d 735, 738 (Civ. App. 1974).

126. *Hubbard* v. *Hubbard,* 55 Ala. App. 521, 317 So. 2d 489, 492 (Civ. App.), *cert. denied,* 294 Ala. 759, 317 So. 2d 492 (1975).

127. *Thompson* v. *Thompson,* 57 Ala. App. 57, 326 So. 2d 124, 127 (Civ. App.), *cert. denied,* 57 Ala. App. 62, 326 So. 2d 129 (1975).

128. *Id.,* 326 So. 2d, at 126.

129. *Id.*

130. *Id.,* at 127.

131. *Wambles* v. *Coppage,* 333 So. 2d 829, 835 (Ala. Civ. App. 1975).

132. *Id.*

133. *Id.,* at 836.

134. Cal. Civ. Code § 4600 (West).

135. *Id.*

136. *Id.*

137. *Id.* See historical note at 319.

138. *Id.,* at 320.

139. *Munson* v. Munson, 27 Cal. 2d 659, 166 P.2d 268, 272 (1946).

140. *Davis* v. *Davis,* 41 Cal. 2d 563, 565, 261 P.2d 729, 730 (1953). *See also Holsinger* v. *Holsinger,* 44 Cal. 2d 132, 279 P.2d 961 (1955).

# 3

# Current Standards for Determination of Custody Disputes between Parents

## Mores and Life-Styles of Parents Relative to Custody Award

### Sexual Practices

During the reign of the Tender Years Doctrine, which presumed that a young child was best off in the custody of the mother,[1] one principal exception to the application of the rule was flagrant adulterous behavior on the part of the mother.[2] Adultery by one parent, in and of itself however, has never been considered the sole basis for a custody award to the other.[3] This remains the general rule in New York.

In a 1977 decision, the appellate division reversed the family court that had awarded custody of two children, 6 and 2 years of age respectively, to the father.[4] The parents were separated but not divorced. The mother had left the father and taken the two children to live with her. At the time of the separation, she had the father's tacit approval.[5] The father's petition for custody was inspired by the mother's commencement of cohabitation with a male companion some weeks after her leaving the marital residence. The appellate court's reading of the record on appeal brought it to the conclusion that, "the Family Court, to the exclusion of all other factors, denied the mother custody solely because of her participation in the adulterous relationship."[6]

This presents the issue of "whether or not a mother who loves and properly cares for her children automatically forfeits her right to custody solely because of her participation in that relationship."[7] The court held emphatically that the mother's adultery could not be a basis for such forfeiture and laid down the following guidelines for factors that must be considered in determining a custody award:

> Determining that which is in the child's best interest requires that consideration be given to many factors, namely, the care and affection shown; the stability of the respective parents; that atmosphere of the homes; the ability and availability of the parents; the morality of the parents, the prospective educational probabilities, the possible effect of custodial change on the children; the financial standing of the parents and parents' past performance are but a few of the areas requiring exploration.[8]

The appellate division disapproved of the trial court's failure to weigh all of the "competing considerations" and of its allowance of the mother's adultery to "abuse or confuse the issue."[9] The case was reversed and remanded for a new trial.[10]

A 1975 miscellaneous decision presented a set of facts in which the parents had been separated and subsequently divorced with custody granted to the mother by separation agreement.[11] The child had thereafter resided with the mother and her paramour for approximately 3½ years when the father petitioned the court for modification in his favor.[12] The father did not rely totally on moral or religious arguments but sought to prove, with evidence of specific symptoms and the aid of expert witnesses, that the child was psychologically damaged by "continued residence . . . in the prevailing 'adulterous' atmosphere."[13]

The court found, in weighing the objective evidence, and based on an in-camera interview with the child that the father's contentions were not supported.[14] It further held that the "criterion to be applied to determinations of custody is not whether the court condones the mother's mode of living or considers it to be contrary to good morals, but whether the child is best located with the mother and there well behaved and cared for [citing case]."[15] The judge further distinguished the case from those in which the mother's adultery *might* have led to a different result. One basis of distinction was the absence of any "behavioral patterns of conduct" that involved such "gross moral turpitude as would render [the mother] unfit for custody [citing case]."[16] The other basis of distinction, interestingly, was that the mother was divorced and hence not actually guilty of adultery in the literal sense.[17] "Residence together of an unmarried male and female without the benefit of a sermonized marriage is not per se evil nor one of immorality."[18] Custody was retained by the mother.

In *Feldman* v. *Feldman,* a 1974 appellate division decision, the court reversed the trial court's transfer of custody from the mother, with whom the children had resided from birth.[19] The trial-court's order, in the father's favor, was based on the mother's freewheeling sexual activities and evidence of her interest in, and possession of, pornographic literature in her home.[20] The appellate division found no evidence of the mother's unfitness or of any effect whatsoever between the children and the mother's private sexual activities.[21] The appellate division disapproved of the trial court's unwarranted reliance on its "subjective evaluation" of the mother's life-style in reaching its decision in the father's favor.[22] The court ruled that

[T]he right of a divorced woman to engage in private sexual activities, which in no way involve or affect her minor children, is within the penumbra of that yet ill-defined area of privacy mandated by the specific guarantees of the Bill of Rights [citing cases]. . . . The courts have on occasion recognized the right of an unmarried male to engage in extramarital sexual relations without being branded a "social leper," and there appears to be no rational basis to impose a more stringent standard upon a divorced woman.[23]

There is every indication that a father seeking custody will be at no disadvantage under the law solely because of his own extramarital sexual activities. In *People ex rel. Repetti* v. *Repetti,* the trial court had awarded custody of all five children to the mother, despite the wishes of the three oldest, all teenagers, to continue residence with their father and his paramour.[24] The two youngest children had always lived with the mother.[25] The appellate division modified the trial-court's order and allowed the three elder children to remain with the father. The appellate court took note of the fact that the father's household consisted of himself, the three teenagers, his paramour, a child born to himself and his paramour out of wedlock, and the paramour's mother. The court concluded that, "[a]side from the irregularity of the relationships" between the father and his lady, "the household appears to present a propitious atmosphere for the children."[26] The court mentioned, with approval, that the father had often stated his desire to marry his paramour, if only his wife would consent to a divorce [the father admittedly having no grounds].[27] The court concluded that "[t]he moral effect this unfortunate situation may have on the children will not be abated by forcing [them] to live in sullen resentment with the other parent. . . ."[28]

Of course, where evidence of the mother's moral character is sufficient to indicate a lack of fitness on her part, custody will be taken from her. But in such cases, her sexual activities will be factor *bearing* on her fitness, not a reason sufficient, in itself, to find her unfit.[29]

Homosexuality is another matter. It has been plainly held, in at least one published miscellaneous decision, that a situation in which a mother was living with a female lover in a lesbian relationship *was* emotionally disturbing to the welfare of the child, and custody was transferred to the father.[30] There was nothing in that particular case that would have amounted to unfitness on the part of the mother other than her sexual orientation. Inasmuch as, at the time of this writing, gay consciousness is a relatively new phenomenon, it may be that the courts will come to liberalize their attitude toward the adversity of homosexual orientation on the welfare of a minor child. This is an area in custody law that has only begun to develop.

*Religious Practices*

Other indications of lax morality, such as failure to adhere to religious precepts, are generally given little weight by the courts if the parent is, in all other respects, fit to continue as the custodian.

In a 1967 miscellaneous decision involving a strictly Orthodox Jewish family, the wife brought an action for separation against the husband and was granted *pendente lite* custody of the couple's two children.[31] In moving for reargument, the husband contended that his wife's failure to adhere rigorously to the tenets and precepts of Hebrew Orthodoxy constituted a defense to her action for separation and was inimical to the welfare of the children.[32] The court held at the outset that secular, rather than religious, law was determinative of the issue,[33] and that even if the wife's lack of religious observance would constitute a defense to her action in chief, the only basis for the determination of the custody question was the best interests of the child.[34]

In adhering to its original decision, the court held that it was "not persuaded that the [mother] should be denied . . . custody because of her alleged backsliding unless it is demonstrated that this has and will have . . . such profound adverse effect upon the infant's welfare as to justify [it]. . . . "[35]

In another miscellaneous decision, the parents and all three of their children had been baptized and raised as Roman Catholics. The mother converted to the Jehovah's Witnesses, and the dissension occasioned by her conversion ultimately led to a family court order of protection directing the father to leave the home.[36] The mother made no attempt to convert the children and continued to allow them to be reared and taught as Roman Catholics. The father sought custody on the contention that the children were being adversely affected by continued residence with the mother.[37] The court ruled that there was no adverse effect on the children nor was the mother otherwise unfit in any way so as to justify a change of custody.[38]

## Effect of Fault of Parent in Causing Dissolution of Marriage

The general rule on parental fault in marital dissolution as a factor in custody awards was announced in a court of appeals decision in 1943.

> Apportionment between the parents of the blame for the broken marriage may not be the decisive factor in the determination [citing case]. Nonetheless, the past conduct of the parents, the unwillingness of one or both to carry out their marital obligations are factors which may not be disregarded in determining which parent will provide the better home.[39]

The significance of the rule, though often quoted, is inconclusive as to its specific application. For instance, in *Sheil* v. *Sheil,* the father was granted a separation after a nonjury trial against the mother on grounds of adultery.[40] The court held that the one act of adultery did not make her unfit to have custody, and that ordinarily children of tender years should be awarded to the mother.[41] Nevertheless, the court cited *Harrington* to the effect that the mother's prior conduct in the marital breakup was a factor worthy of consideration.[42] The court affirmed the trial-court's decision in awarding custody to the father on the basis of his apparent ability to provide a better home.[43] Thus all of the court's statements, both on the Tender Years Doctrine and on the predissolution fault, are essentially dicta, and although the rule as stated in *Harrington* is cited, it is difficult to see how it applied.

In the *Repetti* case, the court made two blanket statements.[44] First, it held that the father was plainly at fault for the events leading to the separation of the parties.[45] Second, it held that the custody award did not depend in the least on those circumstances.[46]

In *Salk* v. *Salk,* the court cited the *Sheil* case and the rule in favor of taking past conduct into consideration as part of a long summary of principles involved in reaching a custody determination.[47] However, no specific application of the rule was made to the facts of *Salk.* In the action in chief, both the parties were granted divorces on their individual complaints on grounds of cruel and inhuman treatment.[48] Possibly the equality of fault on the part of both parties was such as to make the factor irrelevant on the issue of custody.

Even the *Harrington* case itself, in which the rule was announced, is conclusive only on the point that parental fault in the marital break-up must be given some weight. But the case is inconclusive as to actually how much weight it is to be given.[49] Again, in a 1965 appellate division decision, in which the background of the marital dissolution was described in terms of "disintegration" and "termination," there was no guidance given as to specific application of the rule, although it was invoked.[50]

The best guidance available for specific application of the rule appears to be in those cases where the predissolution behavior of the parent is particularly flagrant and of such nature as to put the question of actual fitness into issue. There is strong indication that when there is a pattern of physical assault by one party on the other and when such physical cruelty forms a basis for a complaint in a separation or divorce action, that factor will weigh strongly against the parent found to be guilty of such assaultive conduct.[51]

Although as has been demonstrated, adultery is rarely in and of itself a factor to be considered, it has been held that the past conduct of a parent with regard to his or her private sexual affairs is a factor warranting scrutiny in that such matters "could affect the availability of a parent when such parent's presence is vitally necessary."[52]

When dealing with such factors as physical cruelty and sexual affairs leading to neglect, it would seem to be more of a case of dealing with unfitness on the part of the guilty parent, as such, rather than with predissolution fault. Inasmuch as the current bases for divorces are, in so many cases, either on a no-fault basis, or on grounds of mental cruelty, neither of which bear much relation to parental fitness, it is likely that the rule as expressed in *Harrington* will have little actual significance in determinations of child custody. That which is sufficient fault, on the part of a guilty parent in bringing about a marital dissolution, such as would justify a deprivation of custody, would likely be sufficient to amount to plain unfitness in the first place.

## Preference of Child

The general rule concerning the weight to be given the preference of children in custody determinations is clearly stated and easily applied.

> [A]lthough the expressed desires of children are not controlling in custody matters, such desires are, however, an important factor in the over-all determination as to what is in their best interests. This is especially so where the children are advanced in age and have indicated a strong preference for one of their parents.[53]

The quotation is taken from a decision in which the two children involved were 16 and 17 years of age respectively. The same rule was applied in weighing the preference of a 15-year-old girl for her father's custody in a 1975 decision.[54] In the latter case, the child's preference was held "not determinative" as a factor, "but it obviously should be considered when, as here, the child is not of tender years."[55] The latter case was distinguished from another decision in which the childrens' preference was given less weight because they were only 13 and 8 years of age respectively.[56] It has been held specifically that, "[p]references for custody enunciated by infants below 13 years of age are not determinative of their best interests."[57]

There is also authority to the effect that, even under the age of 13, the child's wishes will be given weight, although correspondingly less weight than if the child were older.[58] In the *Salk* case, the court held that the "expressed wishes of a child of sufficient age and discretion are a factor to be considered by the court," even though the younger child was 11 years old.[59] In *Repetti,* the preferences of the three older children (ranging from 13 to 16 years in age) for their father was held to be of sufficient importance to override the adverse impact of splitting their custody from that of their two younger siblings.[60] A similar conclusion was reached in the case of two girls, 12 and 9 years of age respectively, in which the older daughter expressed a strong preference to reside with her father and his current wife.[61]

The court, placing great reliance on expert psychiatric and psychological testimony, concluded that the relationship between the girls was not close enough to overrride the strong preferences of the older daughter for a change of custody. Hence, the general rule that siblings are best reared together could not justifiably be applied.[62]

Generally, the more advanced a child is in age, the more weight will be attached to that child's stated preference in custody matters. As a rule of thumb, although by no means an absolute presumption, it may be said that great weight attaches to the preference of a child over the age of 14 years and less weight to the wishes of a child under that age in descending degrees as the age of the child decreases.[63] Even those decisions, however, that give heavy weight to the preference of a child of mature age mandate the need for evaluating such preference against a more objective criteria. In cases in which a strong preference is shown, it has been held that expert psychological opinion must be sought to evaluate the choice as objectively as possible.[64] Moreover, the court should be cautious of the influences brought to bear on a child, even of mature age, that will induce the child to express such preferences.[65] Such influences cover the whole range of potential parental manipulation: bribery, brainwashing, comparatively lax discipline, inducing feelings of guilt in the child, and so forth.[66] An in-camera interview to determine preference is not sufficient to resolve the issue even when the court is inclined to accord consideration to preference.[67]

## Separation of Siblings

It is now generally held that when the circumstances of the case warrant it, and the best interests of the children require it, courts will not hesitate to award custody of one or more children to one parent, and the custody of a sibling or siblings to the other.

In a case in which a 14-year-old girl had become seriously estranged from her mother and chose to reside with her father, the appellate division held that "[r]egardless of fault, the alienation between mother and daughter requires that they reside apart. . . ."[68] The court held that, at 14 years of age, the daughter was entitled to have her preference seriously considered, and, further, that the need for sibling association could be met through sufficient visitation as ordered by the court.[69]

In sustaining an award dividing the custody of two daughters in the *Porges* case, the appellate division found that the record demonstrated a breakdown in the relationship between one child and the mother.[70] Further, the mother's behavior toward the one child had "been characterized by intermittent harrassment" whereas she had demonstrated a "close and caring relationship" with the other daughter.[71] Based on a thorough and

thoughtful evaluation of expert opinion, the court reached a similar decision in the *Pact* case, noting that, "[i]f at all possible, it is assumed that
children should be reared together rather than partitioned off."[72]

In the *Repetti* case, the court awarded the three eldest children to the
father and the two youngest to the mother but attempted to maintain the
sibling relationship by ordering visitation between all five children, "at least
one day each week, alternatively at the two homes."[73]

There is no shortage of cases, however, emphasizing the importance of
maintaining siblings in the custody of one parent when the circumstances
warrant it. Many of such reported cases involve factual situations in which
one parent has refused to return one or more of the siblings after visitation
and proceeds to seek permanent custody, while another child remains with
the other parent. This was the case in *Ebert* v. *Ebert,* wherein the father
sought to retain the two older children after their summer visitation with
him.[74] The Court of Appeals reversed the appellate division and reinstated
so much of the family court order that had maintained custody of all three
children in the mother.[75] The holding expressed the view that, "the separation of siblings, where, as here, the custodial parent in whose care all three
had been entrusted is fit and willing and able to function as such, is to be
frowned upon."[76] The court's rationale for this view was expressed as follows:

> Close familial relationships are much to be encouraged. By building iden-
> tity, countering feelings of isolation, and encouraging healthy adjustments
> to and with others, they provide an important additional dimension to
> long-term stability [citing cases]. . . . A family unit is struck a vital blow
> when parents divorce; it is struck an additional one when children are sep-
> arated from each other.[77]

A similar state of facts characterized the decision in *Obey* v. *Degling,* in
which the father refused to return the son in violation of the custody provisions of the divorce judgment, while the girl remained with the mother.[78]

> Courts should be reluctant to permit separate custody of siblings [citing
> cases]. Young brothers and sisters need each other's strengths and associa-
> tion in their everyday and often common experiences, and to separate
> them, unnecessarily, is likely to be traumatic and harmful. The importance
> of rearing brothers and sisters together, and thereby nourishing their famil-
> ial bonds, is also strengthened by the likelihood that the parents will pass
> away before their children.[79]

In a 1977 appellate division decision, the court warned against the
temptation in the emotional aftermath of a marital dissolution, to look on
children as items to be partitioned like real estate or furniture. "It is an
elemental principle . . . that custody of the children of a marriage should

not be split between the parents in the absence of unusual circumstances, and by no means as a compromise of the respective claims and feelings of the parents [citing cases]."[80]

The standards in this particular aspect of custody determination are not as illusive as in some others. The general rule is well established that siblings should remain together. However, it is not hard to distinguish, on their facts, those cases which, for some compelling reason, are exceptional.

## Weighing the Best Interests of the Child and Judging Standards of Parental Fitness

Fitness to maintain custody of a child is a concept that eludes specific determination. Reasonable people can generally agree as to what behavior amounts to *unfitness* such as to deny custody to one parent or the other. But how does one measure *relative fitness,* in the positive sense, between two competing parents?

Although, as demonstrated previously,[81] adultery in and of itself will not be sufficient to deny custody, when uninhibited sexual mores are of such nature as to create an unpropitious atmosphere for minor children, or indicate irresponsibility on the part of the parent concerned, custody *will* be transferred.

In *Zavasnik* v. *Zavasnik,* the appellate court upheld the trial court's award of custody to the father, finding that the record amply supported its decision.[82] Prior to the parents' separation, as indicated by the record, the mother was in the habit of leaving the home on four or five evenings per week and not returning until the early morning hours.[83] During these periods, the father assumed full responsibility for the care of the children.[84] There was further evidence that a great deal of the mother's time was spent in the pursuit of an extramarital love affair with a parolee who had been convicted of murder.[85] The appellate division held that these factors were a sufficient basis for the trial court's decision and its "close assessment of the character and temperament of the parents and their ability to fulfill responsibility."[86]

In *People ex rel. Bishop* v. *Bishop,* the appellate division held that

[the mother's] conduct over a prolonged period in which she openly lived with a married man, known to her to be an ex-convict and a suspected drug addict, and mothered his child, conclusively established her unfitness to care for the infant whose custody is here at issue.[87]

In *McAteer* v. *McAteer,* the parties' separation was brought about by the mother's plea of guilty to sexual abuse of several minors.[88] Although the mother's record was clear since the guilty plea and the court was favorably impressed by the psychiatric testimony elicited in her favor, her history did not demonstrate the degree of stability that would induce the court to change the status quo and award her custody.[89]

In *Harrison* v. *Harrison,* the court found that the mother prior to separation, was away from the home during most of the night hours and that she "frequently neglected to properly clothe, clean and feed the child, necessitating that "[the father] do those tasks.""[90] It is no surprise that the court held that custody entrusted to the father would be in the child's best interests.[91]

Gross neglect and/or abuse of a child will, of course, disqualify the custodial parent from continuing in that role, and the other parent can expect to prevail under such circumstances.[92]

The types of "unfitness" illustrated by those cases cited in this section do not present issues of subtle distinction. A parent who carouses at all hours, as a regular pattern of behavior, who associates intentionally with people of criminal inclination, and who has no redeeming aspects to his or her behavior, will be considered as unfit by the generally accepted standards of almost any community. A parent who neglects to properly care for a child or who is unavailable, as indicated by gross deviations from accepted norms of behavior, will likewise be considered "unfit" by a broad consensus of opinion.

The tougher questions, the more subtle issues, have to do with "psychological fitness, which does not reach the level of incompetence or institutionalization. In *Mouscardy* v. *Mouscardy,* in awarding custody of the two oldest of the couple's three children to the father, the appellate division observed that, "The weight of the credible evidence establishes that the [mother] may well be less fit to be a custodial parent, owing to certain psychological problems."[93] What those problems were was not specified, although the court is specific as to the weight and reliability of the expert opinions on which the conclusion was based.[94]

In *Krok* v. *Montagna,* the appellate division concluded, from the trial court's record, that the mother was "warm, kindly and flexible, while the father was . . . a methodical and disciplined person who leads a regimented life."[95] It further appeared that the child displayed symptoms of depression, instability, and uneven temperament when returned to his father's custody after weekend visitation with his mother.[96] The appellate court held that "ample evidence" supported the trial court's transfer of custody to the mother.[97]

In a 1976 miscellaneous decision, the court transferred custody of three children (15, 12, and 10 years of age respectively) to the father, basing its decision on the mother's general incompetence as a parent.[98] The record was characterized by hostility between the children and their mother and among the children individually, involving at least one family court petition by the mother against the oldest child as a person in need of supervision.[99] The mother admitted to being unable to "cope" with the children.[100] The court concluded that she was indeed "unable to function adequately as a custodial parent to the point where she is now currently unfit to care for these three children."[101] The family court judge hastened to recognize the mother's sincerity of love and concern for her children and added that, "this court does not intend to imply that she is an incompetent person. [B]ut it is very evident to this court that respondent, at this time, cannot properly meet the emotional demands and needs of [the three children]."[102] A fourth child, 14 years of age, was left with the mother, as she "has been adequately able to meet [his] emotional needs."[103]

The court, in transferring custody to the father, found that "turmoil, anxiety, anger and bitterness" demonstrated by the children, had significantly subsided in the short period of time during which they had resided with their father.[104]

The influence of expert psychological opinion in weighing best interests has led to custody awards based on factors even more abstract and vaguely defined than the comparative inability of the mother to cope in *Coleman,* [105] or the inflexibility and regimented personality of the father in *Montagna* v. *Krok.* [106]

In *Salk* v. *Salk,* the court declined to discuss the choice between parents in terms of "fitness" but chose rather "as the criterion . . . the use of an affirmative standard, which parent was 'better fit'."[107] On this criterion, the court concluded that the father was best able to "nurture the complex needs and social development of these children."[108]

The closest that the court came to citing specific behavior of the father, in support of its conclusion, was noting that it was he who "more often than [the mother] met the children after school, and clearly had more contact with school officials with respect to the childrens' educational development."[109]

Aside from that, the reasons in support of the award to the father were delivered in the following terms: "The father's successful relationship with his children is based, in part, on his ability to provide positive input into the children's development, specifically consistent affection, approval, acceptance, guidance, protection and control."[110]

Similar criteria for custody determinations have been expressed in other recent decisions, often in terms of who will be the "exclusive psychological parent."[111]

These are the standards of determination that raise as many questions as they answer. How can a court accurately evaluate the extent of "positive input into the children's development?" How fairly can a court determine that one parent is "warmer" than another and one more "regimented" in his or her thinking. All other things being equal, of course, a court can always make a choice when it has an opportunity to compare results. For example, in the *Coleman* case, *supra,* the court had an opportunity to compare the attitudes of the children before and after de facto transfer to their father's custody. The court found conditions much improved and so ratified the change.[112] They had an admission from the mother that she was unable to "cope."[113] Whether or not the court could make an accurate determination as to who was "psychologically" the best parent, it could content itself with results that were plainly favorable and the wish to leave well enough alone.

One may say the same of *Montagna* v. *Krok,*[114] wherein the child was just plain happier with his mother, although, at 9 years of age, too young to have his own choice weighed heavily in the decision. If the decision were, in fact, based on the relative warmth and flexibility of one parent versus the regimentation of another, what could be used for an objective measure? Who is to say what personality traits create an overall better environment for a child? Who is to measure the consistency of "affection, approval, acceptance, and so forth?" At what points do the courts abdicate their own function of decision-making and simply ratify the conclusions of the psychiatrist or psychologist who performs most convincingly on the stand? The introduction of the "better fit" theory, based on psychological factors, throws the determination of many custody disputes into a state of complete unpredictability. One can only guess how a trial judge will analyze and react to the wide range of potential expert psychological testimony that can be introduced. The disappointed party cannot look to the appellate courts for relief since, without some tangible evidence of "unfitness" as opposed to "better" fitness, there is usually enough on the record to support the trial court's decision one way or the other.

### Tangible Factors: Material Advantages
### and Quality of the Home Provided

The material aspects and the quality of the home provided are sometimes spoken of in terms of "fitness" and sometimes specifically distinguished from that aspect. In *People ex rel. Bishop* v. *Bishop,* the court found the mother unfit by reason of her flagrantly unacceptable morality and her inappropriate associates. After enumerating its reasons for the finding of unfitness, the court held that "[a]part from her unfitness, the record shows she has no facilities whatever to care for the child," as if to distinguish personal unfitness from inadequate facilities.[115]

In a 1974 appellate division decision, the trial court's award of custody of three children to the father was reversed.[116] The appellate court held that the award was made on an "inadequate record" due to "the complete absence of facts as to how defendant, a flight engineer [presumably required to spend long and frequent periods away from home] would be able to care for the children."[117] The inadequacy of facilities for care, either by reason of a parent's unavailability or by reason of the inadequacy of the physical conditions, is a significant factor, although not necessarily equated with personal unfitness.

In *Rowe* v. *Rowe,* the custody award to the father was reversed, again for the inadequacy of "proof to show that the father, who was living alone, could properly care for and supervise the children without assistance."[118]

In another fourth department decision, the family court order awarding custody to the father was reversed, and the mother was deemed to be the better custodian by reason of her remarriage and ability to "better provide for the daily needs of [the children]."[119] The father was deemed to be comparatively inadequate because he [kept] house alone and [was] at work all day."[120]

It is well established that the relative financial positions of parents competing for custody cannot be determinative in making an award, although they are factors to be taken into consideration.[121] If the financial position of a parent is so stressed as to call into question his or her ability to provide a suitable home for the child, then the financial aspects take on more weight in reaching a decision.[122]

## Effect Wherein a Custody Award to a Parent Is Tantamount to an Award to a Third Party

"The courts have generally taken the position that it is not in the best interests of the child to award custody to a parent, whether mother or father, if such action is tantamount to awarding custody to a grandparent or a third party."[123]

When, however, the substantial day-to-day care of minor children is left with a third party, such as a governess or grandparent who resides with the custodial parent, so that the custodial parent may engage in employment, then, all other factors being in the child's best interests, such an arrangement will not be disturbed by the courts.[124]

When both parents would be compelled to leave the child in the care of others during business hours, it has been held that the father's home (with his parents) was preferable to the mother's proposed plan, which would have provided hired, unrelated babysitters.[125] When, however, a parent is absent from the home for long periods of time due to travel, no matter how loving the attention of the grandparent left in charge, an award to the parent who lives with the child on a regular basis is considered preferable.[126]

### Effect of Contempt of Court Order
### or Violation of Prior Custody Agreement

The prevailing general rule in New York is stated as follows: "Priority, not as an absolute, but as a weighty factor, should, in the absence of extraordinary circumstances, be accorded to the first custody awarded in litigation, or by voluntary agreement,"[127] The rationale behind the rule is, "that if the best interests of all children are to be served, the abduction of children to avoid the effect of custody decisions must be deterred."[128] The court cited the passage of the Uniform Child Custody Jurisdiction Act by the legislature as manifesting this principle.[129]

In the leading case, *Nehra* v. *Uhlar,* the father had been awarded custody by a Michigan court after trial because of the "mother's misconduct and unfitness in the case of the children."[130] Both parents remarried, and, 5 days after her remarriage in 1973, the mother absconded with the children from Michigan to New York.[131]

It was nine months after the abduction before the father was able to locate the children and nearly 4 years of extended litigation, during which time the children remained in the custody of the mother, before the court of appeals made its determintion.[132]

Although the court recognized that the mother had provided a good home for the children over the 4 years she had retained them, there was sufficient evidence to indicate that the father would be equally as good a custodian.[133] Hence, the court was left to grapple only with the issue of the effect on the children wrought by a change in the status quo. The court adhered to the following principles.

> The mother's custody of the children for the last four and a half years, without more, is not a change in circumstances sufficiently extraordinary to justify upsetting the determination of the Michigan court. If it were, a parent, having lost a custody dispute in another state, might believe that by abducting the children, secreting them in New York, and waiting for time to pass, the prior custody decree could be effectively nullified. Of course, were there no tolerable alternatives to awarding custody to the abducting parent, as for example, if the other parent were not fit to raise the children, or could not provide a suitable home, or just too many years had passed, even the unlawful act might have to be ignored [citing cases]. In this case, the alternative, awarding custody to a father who is able and eager to provide a good home for his children, is the least difficult to accept.

> Applying these principles and considering the best interest of the children, the father is entitled to custody because the Michigan court so decreed, because he is a fit parent, because the mother obtained the possession of the children by lawless self-help, because the transitory harm caused by disruption past and future was caused by the mother, and because there is insufficient showing that the harm to the children if they be returned to the father is any more irreparable than that caused by the mother in creating the situation in the first instance.[134]

It should be borne in mind, however, that the necessity of discouraging child snatching can never be made totally subordinate to the children's best interests. "[T]he apparent imperative to discourage abduction must, when necessary, be submerged to the paramount concern in all custody matters: the best interest of the child. Otherwise, '[t]he dignity of the several courts would be preserved, but the welfare of the children would be destroyed.'"[135]

Thus, *Nehra* v. *Uhlar* was distinguished in a miscellaneous decision where the court found that, "while the [father] is to be strongly condemned for wrongfully taking the child and the court has considered this conduct as a factor in its decision, the court finds that it is in the best interests of the child that custody be granted to the petitioner at this time."[136]

This distinction was based on what the court considered to be a superior home environment provided by the father. The specific reasons for this conclusion are obscure in the decision, although the court expressed the opinion that the father had become the "exclusive psychological parent of the child."[137]

In further applying the principle that the welfare of the children must take final precedence over the vindication of the courts, the appellate division reversed a family court order transferring custody from the mother to the father as a sanction against the mother for contempt.[138] "For reasons which may or may not have been proper [the mother] failed to appear at a number of scheduled hearings in Family Court."[139] Her failure to appear resulted in a contempt citation, a warrant for her arrest, a counsel fee award to the father, and a transfer of custody.[140] The appellate division reversed, holding that the best interests of the child could not be served by "altering custody arrangements of 10 years" duration without a showing of severely changed circumstances or parental unfitness [citing cases].[141]

On this particular aspect of custody determination, attention is drawn to that part of *Nehra* v. *Uhlar* that holds that the priority of a previous award or agreement is entitled to be considered as a "weighty" but not an absolute factor.[142]

## Modification and Change of Circumstances

### General Principles

The general rule in New York is that custody of infants should not be modified so as to shift a child from parent to parent unless the custodial parent has been shown to be unfit or "perhaps 'less fit'" than the parent seeking modification.[143] Thus generally, the custody of children is to be established, whenever possible, on a long-term basis. Custody is not to be shuttled back and forth between divorced parents merely because of changes in their matrimonial status, economic circumstances, or improvements in their moral or psychological adjustment."[144]

When the family court specifically found the custodial mother to be fit, the appellate court reversed the transfer of custody to the father.[145] "We have reviewed the record and found that the mother is neither unfit nor less fit than the father. Under these circumstances, it was error for the Family Court to change custody to the father."[146]

The expressed preference of a child for a change of custody is not sufficient in and of itself to justify such change.[147] "We believe that custody should be established on a long-term basis and should not be changed merely because a child at some time states that he desires it."[148] The psychological aspects and the transitory nature of such choices were recognized by the court in the following language:

> There are periodic reorientations toward one or another parent, and this is especially true when young parents are involved and one or both remarries. The subjective changes in the children or the objective changes in the family relationship should not be followed automatically by changes in custody. The rearing of a child requires greater stability than a rollercoaster treatment of custody.[149]

In determining sufficient lack of fitness or relative unfitness in the custodial parent such as to justify a change of custody, the trial court must "delve into all the circumstances, educational, religious and health, which might effect the infant upon change of . . . custody."[150]

It is plainly held that the burden of "establishing a change in circumstances which would demonstrate a need to effect a change" rests on the noncustodial parent seeking relief.[151] Unless a record demonstrates compelling reason for such a change, the status quo will be affirmed.[152]

It has been held that contempt of a court order as to appearance in court and failure to allow the father his visitation rights, may not be sufficient in itself to justify a change in the mother's established custody without a showing of some specific detriment to the child.[153]

In cases in which custody has been established by agreement between the parties, either by stipulation or separation agreement, the law requires the same compelling demonstration of changed circumstances to effect a modification of custody.

### Specific Examples

The courts generally set a high standard of compelling reason to justify a change in the status quo. In *Lisa* v. *Lisa,* the mother sought to modify the existing arrangement whereby her infant sons were placed in the custody of the father.[155] The mother claimed that she was capable of providing a home as good as that which the father and the paternal grandparents with whom he resided could provide. In addition, she would provide a "mother's love."[156] The court ruled that, "[s]ince the children's custodial circumstances are entirely satisfactory, petitioner is not entitled to a change in the status quo [citing case]."[157]

In *Goho* v. *Goho,* the mother had retained custody of a 6-year-old girl since a 1973 divorce decision.[158] The court conceded on appeal of the father's application for modification that the mother had, at one time, "failed properly to safeguard her daughter's welfare."[159] Yet inasmuch as "the circumstances and conduct of the [mother] which supported this finding had ceased to exist about six months before the hearing," the status quo would not be changed in the absence of some presently compelling reason.[160].

Earlier in this text, it has been noted that the (1) sex of a parent alone is not sufficient, in and of itself to effect a change of custody,[161] and (2) the private life-style, mores, and sexual and religious practices of a parent are not sufficient in themselves to justify modification, except possibly in the case of homosexuality.[162] It has already been noted that the preference of the child and the parent's contempt of a court order are not sufficient in and of themselves to result in a modification, so strong is the law's concern with the harm implicit in "shifting" children. Yet there are exceptions to all of these general statements when the courts have found the particular circumstances of a case to be particularly compelling, and the distinctions can be very fine and difficult to comprehend.

The same set of circumstances that will motivate a court to modify custody or deny modification might have resulted in a different decision wherein the question of custody is to be initially determined. In any event, such determinations tend to be made on a case-by-case basis, depending on particular facts, as discussed in the foregoing sections of this chapter.

An interesting, if exceptional, example of circumstances deemed sufficient for modification is the decision in *Arcarese* v. *Monachino.*[163] Although the mother had custody pursuant to a divorce decree incorporated in a separation agreement, she had voluntarily allowed the child to reside with the father for a considerable period of time, during which she had maintained only minimal contacts.[164] Moreover, the mother's second husband was a participant in a Federal Witness Relocation Program, under which he and the mother would be concealed and relocated, their identities changed, and their contacts with friends and family limited.[165] For a time, they had lived in protective custody in a prison apartment. The change of circumstances was considered sufficient to sustain a change in custody to the father.[166] The circumstances under which the child would be reared by the mother were not considered in her best interests.[167]

In *Lee* v. *Lee,* a miscellaneous decision, the court posed the following question:

> May changes solely in the child and his interaction with the parents con-
> stitute sufficiently "material changes in circumstances" to warrant a
> change in custody, assuming that the objective characteristics of the
> parents have remained relatively constant since custody was awarded?[168]

The court concluded that, although neither parent was unfit, the best interest of the child required a change of custody to the father, in spite of the general policy considerations against changing the status quo.[169] The child was 15 years old, and, although minimally brain-damaged, was considered to have achieved a maturation level equivalent to a 13-year-old.[170] He suffered from severe emotional problems and attended a special school.[171]

Anecdotal testimony indicated that his emotional stability and other tangible factors, such as personal cleanliness and school work, improved when "he went to school directly after overnight visitation with his father."[172] The child expressed a strong desire to be in his father's custody during an in-camera interview, in which he impressed the court as remarkably free of parental influence or brainwashing in understanding and appreciating the choices available to him.[173]

The mother was characterized, both by anecdotal testimony and expert opinion, as unstable, hostile, uncooperative, inconsistent, "highly emotional, argumentative, tangential [and] provocative. . . ."[174] These characteristics were personally observed by the court, at least to some extent, during her appearances. The psychiatric opinion evidence was unanimously and unequivocally in favor of transferring custody to the father.[175] The overwhelming conclusion from all of the evidence, viewed as a totality, was that the child's best interests mandated a change of custody. In the face of such compelling reason, the general rule—discouraging change—could not stand. Unlike so many other "general rules" honored more in the breach than in the application, the rule, as expressed in *Nehra* v. *Uhlar, supra,* is a dependable one. It will usually take notably exceptional circumstances, such as exemplified in *Lee* v. *Lee, supra,* and *Aracarese* v. *Monachino, supra,* to effect a change in the status quo.

## Other Jurisdictions

Some aspects of custody-determination criteria, as analyzed in the foregoing sections of this chapter, are more or less uniformly accepted in other jurisdictions. Other aspects encompass a wider range of opinion. A comprehensive review on the law in each jurisdiction herein would be onerous and repetitive. Selected random examples from various jurisdictions will be considered with the object of conveying some general conclusions as to the state of the law nationwide and to furnish a basis for more detailed research for the reader with a specific question.

*Mores and Life-Styles of Parents*
*Relative to Custody Award*

The general rule in New York, with regard to the effect of adultery on custody disputes, is generally accepted in most other jurisdictions; that is, adultery or irregular sexual relations will *not* be sufficient in and of itself to deny custody to or transfer custody from a parent participating in such activities.

In *Moore* v. *Moore,* a Kentucky decision, the Supreme Court of Kentucky affirmed an intermediate appellate decision, which in turn, reversed a trial court award of custody to the father.[176] The trial court considered evidence of the mother's admitted extramarital affairs during the course of an out-of-town trip lasting several days.[177] It appeared to the supreme court that this was not the primary factor influencing the trial court's award to the father.[178] As such, the finding was improper in that, "both parties were equally fit to have custody of the daughter if the evidence of this instance of illicit sexual behavior is excluded."[179] The criteria for determining custody of a child is codified in Kentucky, and provides in part that, "The court shall not consider conduct of a proposed custodian that does not affect his relationship to the child."[180] In applying this subsection, the Kentucky Supreme Court held

> [T]here must be proof that the sexual misconduct affects the relationship of the parent to the child; otherwise, the evidence of such misconduct is irrelevant and should not be admitted into evidence. Here there is no showing, or even a suggestion that the child was aware of respondent's misconduct or that the relationship of the child and the respondent was in any way affected by this incident.[181]

In a Missouri decision, the appellate court overruled the trial court award of custody to the mother, based in part on her unsavory moral character.[182] There was more involved, however, than adultery, and the court found that the mother had been guilty of various acts of fraud with regard to funds jointly held by the parties and funds properly belonging to the paternal grandmother.[183] In addition, the mother had already given birth to two out-of-wedlock children at the time that she had married her husband.[184] The custody dispute involved two younger children of her marriage.

Altogether, the moral character of the mother was found to be habitually unpalatable. Her ongoing, remorseless affair with a married man, although conducted outside of the presence of the children, could only have enhanced the unfavorable picture.[185] The trial court had been reluctant to award custody to the mother and did so primarily on a "lesser of two evils" theory. The trial court's apprehensions as to the father's fitness as a parent concerned his severely handicapped state as a result of multiple sclerosis. This condition confined him to a wheelchair.[186] The appellate court, recognizing the delicacy of balancing the pertinent factors, agreed with most of the trial court's findings but tipped the balance in the opposite direction; that is, the appellate court considered the mother's generally adverse moral character as more potentially detrimental to the children than the father's physical handicap.[187] It is doubtful that the mother's adultery in and of itself would have been sufficient to deny her custody without other corresponding evidence of inadequacy. The court postulated that, "[i]n determining the best interests of the children, the morals and character of the parent to whom custody is to be awarded are proper objects of inquiry [citing cases]." [188] In applying that general rule, the court found that the award to the mother was against the weight of the evidence.[189] But there is nothing in the tone of this case to indicate that irregular sexual relations was the critical factor.

In a 1976 decision by the Supreme Court of Pennsylvania, a clear distinction is drawn between those cases in which nonmarital sexual relations have an adverse effect on the children and those where no harm is discernible.[190]

> It is now beyond dispute that the mere fact of a parent's nonmarital relationship is insufficient to deny him or her custody of the children [citing cases]. Nevertheless, a parent's non-marital relationships must be given close scrutiny in determining custody matters. The prevailing issue must remain the best interests of the child, and a non-marital relationship is merely one of the circumstances which the court must consider before reaching its decision. . . . it is the effect of the non-marital relationship on the child and not the fact of the relationship itself which is crucial to a custody decision.[191]

In an Illinois decision, *De Franco* v. *De Franco,* the transfer of custody from the mother to the father was affirmed, based, primarily and unabashedly, on the mother's continuing adulterous relationship.[192] The court held that the adulterous relationship, in which the paramour and the mother resided together with the children, was "flagrant" and *did* adversely affect the relationship between mother and children, so as to endanger their moral health, within the meaning of statutorily mandated criteria for determining custody disputes.[193] The court specifically rejected the mother's argument that, inasmuch as she and her paramour intended to marry as soon as he was able to obtain a divorce, the court should place, "minimal importance upon the adulterous aspects of her relationship."[194] To do so, the court held, would "severely undermine any attempt at reconciliation between [the paramour] and his wife in contravention of" existing statutory authority and public policy.[195]

The court distinguished the *De Franco* case from *Jarrett* v. *Jarrett,* where the appellate court reversed the trial court's transfer of custody from the mother to the father on similar grounds.[196] The court in the *De Franco* case found that the relationship between the mother and the paramour therein amounted to adultery, whereas in *Jarrett,* it involved fornication.[197] "[A]dultery is viewed as the more opprobrious offense since it is a class A misdemeanor while fornication is class B. . . . 'Adultery involves an affront to a specific marriage relationship, in addition to an affront to the institution of marriage in general. It was felt this more seriously offended the public peace.'"[198]

The *De Franco* case appears to be something of an anomaly in its unashamed moralistic approach to a parent's sexual mores. It may, in fact, not even be representative of the state of the law in Illinois, considering how strained the distinction is between *De Franco* and *Jarrett* and the long line of case law cited by Jarrett in support of a contrary ruling.[199]

### Preference of Child in Other Jurisdictions

Generally in other jurisdictions, as in New York, the courts will give weight to the preference of children in determining custody, although such preference alone will not be the deciding factor. Generally, as well, the courts will be found giving more weight to the preferences of a child over the age of 14, which is also consistent with the rule in New York.

In Louisiana, it has been held that the preferences of three children (16, 12, and 9 years of age respectively) was an appropriate factor to be taken into consideration by the court in determining custody.[200] The general rule is to the same effect in Illinois, particularly with regard to a modification of custody.[201]

In Vermont, the courts are mandated to give weight to the preference of a child over the age of 14 years of age.[202] "Until that time . . . the wishes or preferences of the child are not controlling factors in the court's decision upon the issue of custody and the court is not bound by the child's preference."[203] It has been held in Vermont, that, where a child under 14 years of age is involved, there was no error in the trial judge exercising his discretion by *not* examining the child to determine preference.[204]

Washington has a statutory requirement that the courts consider the preference of the child, with no set minimum age. This requirement, however, is just one of many factors enumerated in the statute in rather general language, compelling the court to consider all "relevant factors."[205]

In Georgia, children over the age of 14 years have a statutory right to choose the parent with whom they live, and such choice "is controlling in the absence of a finding that such parent is unfit."[206] The rule in Georgia is altogether uncommonly strong in favor of child preference.

> It is not a new or novel concept that a minor child may well be capable of making a wise selection. . . . Under [the statute], no parental right of custody by judgment or decree can defeat the right of a child reaching 14 years of age "to select the parent with whom such child desires to live."[207]

The preference is accorded such weight that it cannot be defeated by a history of past unfitness on the part of the chosen parent but only by a showing of present unfitness.[208]

Other jurisdictions are not inclined to give such credit to a 14-year-old. In an Illinois case, the court ruled that there was not sufficient proof in the record to justify a change of custody from the mother to the father of a 14-year-old boy, despite the child's preference for the paternal custody.[209] The boy's testimony that he feared and did not get along with his stepfather was discounted by the court.

> One social worker who interviewed [the child] testified that [the child] felt he was being placed in the position of having to prove his environment at home with his mother and stepfather unfit in order to get his wish to live with his father. The testimony indicated that [the setpfather and the boy] had some difficulties in getting along, we cannot say that they were to such an extent that a change of custody was called for.[210]

Similarly, in the Louisiana case of a 14-year-old boy who had lived with and been well-cared for by his mother for 6 years, the court found the child's preference insufficient to justify a change.[211] The court was influenced by the fact that the child, "had previously expressed a desire to live with his father but returned to his mother after a stay of six months with his father. A full consideration of all the testimony may have led the trial judge to believe [the boy's] present preference would be similarly short-lived."[212]

### Standards of Parental Fitness

In New York, as previously discussed, standards of parental fitness cover a broad range of subjective and objective standards, whose applications are difficult to forecast. This is generally true in most other jurisdictions.

In a Missouri decision, *Johnston* v. *Johnston,* the court held that the record did not support a change in custody of two children from the mother to the father,[213] The record balanced the following factors: The mother had served 60 days in jail and was currently serving 5 years probation for a felony narcotics conviction.[214] Other than that, her record was clean, she was gainfully employed, in good health, and had successfully maintained her child in a family unit with her two children of a previous marriage.[215] The court held that "nothing appears that would indicate it would be in [the child's] best interests that she be separated from her stepbrother and sister."[216] The father was remarried, had a young wife who was willing to care for the child, and was earning a very comfortable salary that made his economic circumstances superior to those of the mother.[217] The appellate court found that the trial court had abused its descretion in awarding custody to the father and had done so, in error, primarily based on the mother's narcotics conviction.[218]

> The law is clear that custody proceedings may not be used to punish a parent [citing cases]. . . . Particularly is this true in light of [the mother's] previous clean record, her work record and the fact, admitted by [the father] that she took good care of [the child] and her other children. The reason [other than the conviction and sentence] stated by the court that [the mother] would be under a five-year probation, is not convincing, since it is necessarily predicated upon the speculation that she would violate that probation.[219]

The Supreme Court of Georgia has held that a past history of mental illness on the part of the mother was insufficient grounds on which to base a change of custody, although in the case considered, there was sufficient evidence of *present* conditions that would justify the change.[220]

In *Vidrine* v. *Demourelle, supra,* the preference of the children for the father was an important factor, but there was also an element of relative fitness involved.[221] The father was at home on a regular basis as a result of his disability from a work-related accident.[222] He was deemed superior in his ability to provide a favorable environment for the children, compared with the mother.[223] The mother worked a night shift as a practical nurse, requiring her to sleep during the daylight hours.[224] In addition, the court pointed out (unfavorably) that she was living in a mobile home, as opposed to the father who maintained the children in a "family home."[225] The court also noted (unfavorably) that the mother suffered from arthritis, asthma, and allergies [226] The trial judge's decision, denying a change of custody in the mother's favor, was affirmed. It might be well to consider how many parents would be deprived of their children if arthritis, asthma, and allergy, coupled with a night job, are really sufficient disqualifications.

In *Lovko* v. *Lovko,* the court considered the case as an initial custody determination pursuant to a marital dissolution, although the children had de facto been living with the father pursuant to a separation agreement.[227] As such, the court hinted that its decision might have been different if the case had been considered a modification, which by statute required "a showing of changed circumstances so substantial and continuing as to make the existing order unreasonable."[228] (See Modification and Statutory Standards, *infra.*)

As an initial determination, however, the court found that it was in the children's best interests to go with the mother, as she "had developed a warm relationship" with them.[229] Moreover, although she had suffered from emotional problems in the past, her "mental health was restored to normal limits."[230] The court ruled that it was the best-interest test, and not the father's unfitness, that properly controlled the trial court's decision, and the said decision was affirmed.[231]

In an Oregon decision, *Strom* v. *Strom,* the mother had voluntarily left the child with the father for a number of months while she attempted to relocate.[232] The father sought a modification in his favor that was denied by the trial court.[233] The appellate court reversed, based on a record that demonstrated, among other things, the following:

1. The father had a steady job and moved from an apartment to a house to accommocate the child, whereas the mother worked intermittently, received welfare, and was always in debt.[234]
2. While residing with the mother, the child suffered from learning disabilities and hyperactivity and seemed to have trouble participating in group activities.[235] By contrast, the father gave the child considerable help at home in conquering his disabilities and had given more attention to his diet, all of which was credited with an improvement in the child's hyperactivity and learning deficiencies.[236]
3. The father had the support and assistance of his parents and fiancee, all of whom were apparently respectable people.[237] Again, by contrast, the mother's boyfriend, who cohabited with her on weekends, had twice been convicted of heroin-related felonies and "had recently violated parole by possessing heroin."[238]

The court, in reversing the trial court and ruling in the father's favor, was careful to characterize its decision as follows:

> This finding is not because of a judicial preference for the workaday life-style, higher income and more stable social environment of the father, as the mother's brief suggests, but rather because the mother was shown to be unable to help the child improve his personality habits, alleviate his learning disability, develop an ability to participate in activities with his peers, and find personal happiness and because no similar disadvantages have been shown in the father's home.[239]

It should be observed that the court did indeed spend considerable time detailing a great many factors that it then claimed played a minimal part in its decision.

In a Florida decision, *Rosenberg* v. *Rosenberg,* the appellate court affirmed a lower-court ruling transferring custody to the father.[240] ''The record supports the trial judge's finding that it was in the best interests of the child [in an effort to achieve a more stable environment] that the father have custody. This is amply demonstrated by the nomad type of existence the boy endured while in the custody of the mother.''[241]

It has been held in an Oregon decision, that where both parents were remarried, and the child accused her stepfather's son (by a previous marriage) of sexual abuse, the failure of the mother to banish the stepson from the home was not sufficient to justify transfer of custody to the father.[242] The court ruled that the mother's attitude was not inappropriate.[243]

> The facts are sufficient to present any parent with agonizing choices. Here, mother was faced with a child prone to fantasy and manipulation. . . . The stepbrother denied misconduct. . . . We do not believe that mother's decision to not immediately banish the stepson from the household was such a specific instance of parental misfeasance as to reflect a course of conduct or pattern of inadequate care which had had or threatens to have a discernible adverse effect upon the child [citing case].[244]

But having said all of this, the court conditions continued custody in the mother on the absence of the stepson from the home.

In *Caulkins* v. *Caulkins, supra,* the preference of the children was given weight, but it was not the deciding factor, in view of all the other facts and circumstances.[245] In *Caulkins,* the two minor children resided with their mother and stepfather. [246] The stepfather had had seven heart attacks, and the only income received by the couple was social security disability payments.[247] The disability of the stepfather apparently did not completely restrict his activities, as the household also included two younger children of his and the mother's.[248] In addition, the stepfather had an older son by a previous marriage, who, while visiting, had allegedly, but not conclusively, molested one of the subject children in the case under consideration.[249]

Further, there had been testimony that the stepfather had been severe in physically disciplining the children, although there was no evidence that severity had passed over into active abuse.[250] The court seemed to be more influenced by the emotional trauma that the children had apparently suffered, as evidenced by testimony of poor urination control in the two children, 8 and 9 years of age, respectively.[251]

The court seemed to be influenced even more by the physical conditions under which the children lived. The household had no indoor toilet or bathroom and the only running water in the house was in the kitchen. The children washed in the sink and used an outside toilet. The house had no telephone and was heated with a wood and coal burning stove. It was a distance of 2 miles through the woods to the nearest neighbor's house and the children had to walk 1¾ to 2 miles to catch the school bus.[252]

By contrast, the father had a regular job as a machinist, lived in a four-bedroom house with "bath, kitchen, living room, full basement and attached garage."[253]

The appellate court found sufficient evidence on the record to affirm the trial court's transfer of custody. The court found that while "factors such as remarriage and living quarters [were] not controlling," they were "sufficiently related to a child's welfare" to be considered in a determination.[254] Yet it is difficult to see why the court would outline the living conditions with such specificity if they had not, in fact, been a significant factor in the court's decision. The court gives itself away with the following statement:

> [N]either the mother nor the stepfather worked, leaving the children without role models to provide guidance and support toward becoming productive members of society. The only family income came from Social Security disability payments. The trial court's finding that the harm likely to be caused by the change of environment was outweighed by the advantages of such change was not contrary to the manifest weight of the evidence.[255]

## Modification and Statutory Standards

Generally, as in New York, the rule is that a substantial change in the circumstances is required to obtain a modification of custody after an initial determination has been made. The rationale behind the rule is generally couched in the same terms in all jurisdictions; that is, "to discourage repeated litigation of the same issues, and, more important, to provide young children with a stable environment."[256] However well-enshrined this general rule may be, its application to any given set of facts is likely to be as subjective as any initial determination. Surely that has been demonstrated by the brief review of random cases under Standards of Parental Fitness, *supra*.

It has been held that a failure to get along with a stepparent following the remarriage of the custodial parent is not by itself sufficient to justify a change of custody.[257] It has also been held that remarriage, and an attendant improvement in a parent's ability to care for the children on remarriage is also insufficient by itself to indicate a change of custody.[258] It has been held that the relative affluence of one parent over the other is not sufficient cause for transfer.[259] Yet relative affluence may be the single biggest factor in a court's view of what is a propitious, as opposed to an unfavorable overall environment, despite disclaimers to that effect.[260] Moreover, in terms of changing an overall environment, favorably or unfavorably, the remarriage of a parent may create a substantial difference. Whether a court will *see* it as substantial is unpredictable.

If the application of the standards of both initial determination and modification are hazy, the standards themselves are at least definitive. More and more jurisdictions have codified these standards, although the codifications do not usually work substantial changes in the case law that preceded them.

As noted under Standards of Parental Fitness, *supra,* [261] Indiana has a particularly stringent standard for modification, requiring "a showing of changed circumstances so substantial and continuing as to make the existing order unreasonable."[262] The modification statute is more demanding in its requirements than the statute governing initial determinations.[263]

Illinois also imposes a statutory requirement that modification be made only if "the child's present environment endangers seriously his physical, mental, moral or emotional health and the harm likely to be caused by a change of environment is outweighed by its advantages to him."[264] Again, the modification statute requires a firm showing of some negative effects, as contrasted with the more flexible guidelines of the statute governing initial determinations.[265]

As well-defined as the modification standards are relative to those governing initial determinations, it should be noted that language like "substantial" and "continuing" change of circumstances and "seriously endangers" the "moral and emotional health" leave a court with considerable room to exercise discretion. The very concepts these words define are *qualitative,* rather than *physical* or *quantitative* as are the concepts that may be found in a statutory definition of rape, adultery, or usury. At bottom, this is what makes the whole field of custody determination so constantly dynamic and sets it apart from other fields of law, even when statutory definitions are introduced.

**Notes**

1. See generally, chapter 2 *supra.*
2. See chapter 2, *supra.*
3. See chapter 2, *supra,* and chapter 2 note 4, *supra.*
4. *Saunders* v. *Saunders,* 60 A.D. 2d 701, 400 N.Y.S.2d 588 (3d Dept. 1977).
5. *Id.*

6. *Id.*

7. *Id.*

8. *Id.*

9. *Id.*

10. *Id.,* at 702. *See also Selbert* v. *Selbert,* 60 A.D.2d 692, 400 N.Y.S.2d 586 (3d Dept. 1977).

11. *S.* v. *J.,* 81 Misc. 2d 828, 367 N.Y.S.2d 405 (Sup. Ct. 1975).

12. *Id.*

13. *Id.,* at 831.

14. *Id.*

15. *Id.,* at 833.

16. *Id.,* citing *Rodolfo C.C.* v. *Susan C.C.,* 37 A.D.2d 657 (3d Dept. 1971).

17. *Id.,* at 832.

18. *Id.*

19. *Feldman* v. *Feldman,* 45 A.D.2d 320, 358 N.Y.S.2d 507 (2d Dept. 1974).

20. *Id.,* at 321.

21. *Id.*

22. *Id.,* at 322.

23. *Id.,* at 323.

24. *Repetti* v. *Repetti,* 50 A.D.2d 913, 914, 377 N.Y.S.2d 571.

25. *Id.,* at 914.

26. *Id.*

27. *Id.*

28. *Id.*

29. See chapter 2, *supra* and chapter 2, note 62 and 63, *supra.*

30. *Matter of Jane B.,* 85 Misc. 2d 515, 380 N.Y.S. 2d 848 (Sup. Ct. 1976).

31. *Weiss* v. *Weiss,* 53 Misc. 2d 262, 278 N.Y.S.2d 61 (Sup. Ct. 1967).

32. *Id.,* at 263.

33. *Id.*

34. *Id.*

35. *Id.*

36. *Romano* v. *Romano,* 54 Misc. 2d 969, 970–71, 288 N.Y.S.2d 138 (Fam. Ct. 1967). *See also Gluckstern* v. *Gluckstern,* 17 Misc. 2d 83, 158 N.Y.S.2d 504 (Sup. Ct. 1956), *aff'd,* 3 A.D.2d 999, 165 N.Y.S.2d 432, *aff'd,* 4 N.Y.2d 521, 176 N.Y.S.2d 352.

37. *Romano* v. *Romano,* 54 Misc. 2d, at 971.

38. *Id.,* at 973.

39. *Harrington* v. *Harrington,* 290 N.Y. 126, 130, 48 N.E.2d 290 (1943).

40. *Sheil* v. *Sheil,* 29 A.D.2d 950 (2d Dept. 1968).

41. *Id.* Also see chapter 2, *supra.*

42. *Id.*

43. *Id.*

44. *Repetti* v. *Repetti,* 50 A.D.2d 913, 377 N.Y.S.2d 571.

45. *Id.*

46. *Id.*

47. *Salk* v. *Salk,* 89 Misc. 2d 883, 887, 393 N.Y.S.2d 84 (Sup. Ct. 1975), *aff'd,* 53 A.D.2d 558, 385 N.Y.S.2d 1015 (1st Dept. 1976).

48. *Id.*

49. *Harrington* v. *Harrington,* 290 N.Y. 126, 48 N.E.2d 290 (1943).

50. *Foussier* v. *Uzielli,* 23 A.D.2d 260, 262, 264, 260 N.Y.S.2d 329 (1st Dept. 1965).

51. *Gluckstern* v. *Gluckstern,* 17 Misc. 2d, at 85. *See also* Chapter 2, Custody Disputes between Natural Parents, *supra,* and chapter 2, note 20, *supra.* "For I must conclude that as a man is to his wife in this regard, so he would be towards his children."

52. *Wasserberger* v. *Wasserberger,* 42 A.D.2d 93, 95, 345 N.Y.S.2d 46 (1st Dept. 1973), *aff'd,* 34 N.Y.2d 660, 335 N.Y.S.2d 580 (1974).

53. *Hughes* v. *Hughes,* 37 A.D.2d 606–607, 323 N.Y.S. 2d 621 (2d Dept. 1971).

54. *Calder* v. *Woolverton,* 50 A.D.2d 587, 375 N.Y.S.2d 150 (1975).

55. *Id.*

56. *Id., distinguishing Dintruff* v. *McGreevy,* 34 N.Y.2d 887, 316 N.E.2d 716 (1974).

57. *Pino* v. *Pino,* 57 A.D.2d 919, 395 N.Y.S.2d 210 (2d Dept. 1977).

58. *Mouscardy* v. *Mouscardy,* 63 A.D.2d 973, 974, 405 N.Y.S.2d 759 (2d Dept. 1978).

59. *Salk* v. *Salk,* 89 Misc. 2d, at 889.

60. *Repetti* v. *Repetti,* 50 A.D.2d, at 913.

61. *Pact* v. *Pact,* 70 Misc. 2d 100, 332 N.Y.S.2d 940 (Fam. Ct. 1972).

62. *Id.,* at 111.

63. *See generally Matter of Stuart,* 280 N.Y. 245, 20 N.E.2d 741 (1939); *Norwood* v. *Coffey,* 12 A.D.2d 579, 207 N.Y.S.2d 487 (1st Dept. 1960); *Mittenthal* v. *Dumpson,* 37 Misc. 2d 502, 235 N.Y.S.2d 729 (Fam. Ct. 1962).

64. *Pact* v. *Pact,* 70 Misc. 2d, at 109.

65. *Id., Hahn* v. *Falce,* 56 Misc. 2d 427, 435, 289 N.Y.S.2d 100 (Fam. Ct. 1968).

66. *See Pact* v. *Pact,* 70 Misc. 2d, at 109; *Hahn* v. *Falce,* 56 Misc. 2d, at 427; *Dintruff* v. *McGreevy,* 34 N.Y.2d, at 888.

67. *Pact* v. *Pact,* 70 Misc. 2d, at 109.

68. *Sandman* v. *Sandman,* 64 A.D.2d 698, 407 N.Y.S.2d 563 (2d Dept. 1978).

69. *Id.*

70. *Porges* v. *Porges,* 63 A.D.2d 712, 713, 405 N.Y.S.2d 115 (2d Dept. 1978).

71. *Id.*

72. *Pact* v. *Pact,* 70 Misc. 2d at 111.

73. *Repetti* v. *Repetti,* 50 A.D.2d, at 914.

74. *Ebert* v. *Ebert,* 38 N.Y.2d 700, 382 N.Y.S.2d 472 (1976).

75. *Id.,* at 704.

76. *Id.*

77. *Id.*

78. *Obey* v. *Degling,* 37 N.Y.2d 768, 375 N.Y.S.2d 91 (1975).

79. *Id.,* at 771.

80. *Lucey* v. *Lucey,* 60 A.D.2d 757, 400 N.Y.S.2d 610 (4th Dept. 1977).

81. See chapter 2, Custody Disputes between Natural Parents, *supra,* and chapter 3, Mores and Life-Styles of Parents Relative to Custody Award, *supra.*

82. *Zavasnik* v. *Zavasnik,* 59 A.D.2d 954, 955, 399 N.Y.S.2d 483 (3d Dept. 1977).

83. *Id.*

84. *Id.*

85. *Id.*

86. *Id.*

87. *Bishop* v. *Bishop,* 34 A.D.2d 834, 835 (2d Dept. 1970). *See also* chapter 2, Custody Disputes between Natural Parents, *supra,* chapter 2, note 62, *supra.*

88. *McAteer* v. *McAteer,* 55 A.D.2d 777, 389 N.Y.S.2d 491 (3d Dept. 1976).

89. *Id.*

90. *Harrison* v. *Harrison,* 54 A.D.2d 906, 388 N.Y.S.2d 26 (2d Dept. 1976).

91. *Id.*

92. *See* N.Y. Fam. Ct. Act art. 10 (McKinney 29A).

93. *Mouscardy* v. *Mouscardy,* 63 A.D.2d, at 974.

94. *Id.*

95. *Montagna* v. *Krok,* 62 A.D.2d 1039, 404 N.Y.S.2d 41 (2d Dept. 1978).

96. *Id.*

97. *Id.*

98. *Coleman* v. *Coleman,* 87 Misc. 2d 822, 386 N.Y.S.2d 928 (Fam. Ct. 1976).

99. *Id.,* at 823.

100. *Id.*

101. *Id.,* at 825.

102. *Id.*

103. *Id.*

104. *Id.*

105. *Id.,* at 882.

106. *Montagna* v. *Krok,* 62 A.D.2d, at 1039.

107. *Salk* v. *Salk,* 89 Misc. 2d, at 885.

108. *Id.,* at 887.

109. *Id.,* at 888.

110. *Id.,* at 892.

111. *Golden* v. *Golden,* 95 Misc. 2d 447, 449, 408 N.Y.S. 2d. 202 (Fam. Ct. 1978).

112. *Coleman* v. *Coleman,* 87 Misc. 2d, at 882.

113. *Id.*

114. *Montagna* v. *Krok,* 62 A.D.2d, at 1039.

115. *Bishop* v. *Bishop,* 34 A.D.2d, at 834.

116. *Bullotta* v. *Bullotta,* 43 A.D.2d 847, 351 N.Y.S.2d 704 (2d Dept. 1974).

117. *Id.*

118. *Rowe* v. *Rowe,* 42 A.D.2d 830, 345 N.Y.S.2d 811 (4th Dept. 1969).

119. *Snook* v. *Hall,* 33 A.D.2d 876, 307 N.Y.S.2d 679 (4th Dept. 1969).

120. *Id.*

121. *Salk* v. *Salk,* 89 Misc. 2d, at 888; *Lester* v. *Lester,* 178 A.D. 205, *aff'd,* 222 N.Y. 546 (2d Dept. 1917).

122. *Salk* v. *Salk,* 89 Misc. 2d, at 888.

123. *Id.,* at 887–888.

124. *Wasserberger* v. *Wasserberger,* 42 A.D.2d 93, 345 N.Y.S.2d 46 (1st Dept. 1973), *aff'd,* 34 N.Y.2d 660, 335 N.Y.S.2d 580 (1974); *Glendening* v. *Glendening,* 259 A.D. 384, 19 N.Y.S.2d 693 (1st Dept. 1940); *Kevin M.J.J.* v. *Alice A.J.J.,* 50 A.D.2d 959 (3d Dept. 1975).

125. *F.F.* v. *F.F.,* 37 A.D.2d 893, 894 (1st Dept. 1971).

126. *Hoffman* v. *Hoffman,* 224 A.D. 28 (1st Dept. 1928).

127. *Nehra* v. *Uhlar,* 43 N.Y.2d 242, 251, 401 N.Y.S.2d 168 (1977).

128. *Id.*

129. *Id.,* citing N.Y. Dom. Rel. Law § 75-i(2) (McKinney).

130. *Id.,* at 246.

131. *Id.*

132. *Id.*

133. *Id.,* at 250.

134. *Id.,* at 250–252.

135. *Nehra* v. *Uhlar,* 43 N.Y.2d, at 250, citing *Lang* v. *Lang,* 9 A.D.2d 401, 405, *aff'd,* N.Y.2d 1029 (1st Dept. 1959). *See also Golden* v. *Golden,* 95 Misc. 2d, at 449.

136. *Golden* v. *Golden,* 95 Misc. 2d, at 450.

137. *Id.,* at 448–449.

138. *Hood* v. *Munroe,* 62 A.D.2d 1058, 404 N.Y.S.2d 148 (2d Dept. 1978).

139. *Id.*

140. *Id.*

141. *Id.*

142. *Nehra* v. *Uhlar,* 43 N.Y.2d, at 251.

143. *Lang* v. *Lang,* 9 A.D.2d, at 401. *See Nehra* v. *Uhlar,* 43 N.Y.2d, at 250; *Nierenberg* v. *Nierenberg,* 43 A.D.2d 717 (2d Dept. 1973). *See also Dintruff* v. *McGreevy,* 34 N.Y.2d, at 888; *Aberbach* v. *Aberbach,* 33 N.Y.2d 592, 347 N.Y.S.2d 456 (1973); *Opferback* v. *Opferback,* 57 A.D.2d 1974, 395 N.Y.S.2d 831 (4th Dept. 1977).

144. *Lang* v. *Lang,* 9 A.D.2d, at 401.

145. *Nierenberg* v. *Nierenberg,* 43 A.D.2d, at 717.

146. *Id.,* at 718.

147. *Dintruff* v. *McGreevy,* 34 N.Y.2d, at 888. See chapter 3, Current Standards for Determination of Custody Disputes between Parents, *supra.*

148. *Id.*

149. *Id.*

150. *Pino* v. *Pino,* 57 A.D.2d 919, 395 N.Y.S.2d 210 (2d Dept. 1977); *Trampert* v. *Trampert,* 55 A.D.2d 838, 390 N.Y.S.2d 325 (4th Dept. 1976).

151. *Veronica M.* v. *Jacob N.,* 55 A.D.2d 689, 389 N.Y.S.2d 57 (3d Dept. 1976)

152. *Mantell* v. *Mantell,* 45 A.D.2d 918, 357 N.Y.S.2d 307 (4th Dept. 1974). *See also Aberbach* v. *Aberbach,* 33 N.Y.2d 592, 347 N.Y.S.2d 456 (1977); *Rothman* v. *Rothman,* 60 A.D.2d 625, 400 N.Y.S.2d 163 (2d Dept. 1977); *Goho* v. *Goho,* 59 A.D.2d 1045, 399 N.Y.S.2d 800 (4th Dept. 1977).

153. *Hood* v. *Munroe,* 62 A.D.2d 1058, 404 N.Y.S.2d 148 (2d Dept. 1978). See Effects of Contempt of Court Order of Violation of Prior Custody Agreement, *supra.* See chapter 6, Visitation, *infra.*

154. *Nehra* v. *Uhlar,* 43 N.Y.2d, at 251; *Kuleszo* v. *Kulesco,* 59 A.D.2d 1059, 1060 (4th Dept. 1977); *Goho* v. *Goho,* 59 A.D.2d 1045, 1046, 399 N.Y.S.2d 800 (4th Dept. 1977).

155. *Lisa* v. *Lisa,* 57 A.D.2d 919, 395 N.Y.S.2d 40 (2d Dept. 1977).

156. *Id.*

157. *Id.*

158. *Goho* v. *Goho,* 59 A.D.2d, at 1045.

159. *Id.*

160. *Id.*

161. See chapter 2, Custody Disputes between Natural Parents, *supra.*

162. See Mores and Life-Styles of Parents Relative to Custody Awards, *supra.*

163. *Arcarese* v. *Monachino,* 58 A.D.2d 1030, 397 N.Y.S.2d 384 (4th Dept. 1977).

164. *Id.,* at 1031.

165. *Id.*

166. *Id.*

167. *Id.*

168. *Lee* v.*Lee,* 92 Misc. 2d 551, 400 N.Y.S.2d 680 (Sup. Ct. 1977).

169. *Id.*

170. *Id.* at 681.

171. *Id.*

172. *Id.*

173. *Id.*

174. *Id.,* at 682.

175. *Id.,* at 683.

176. *Moore* v. *Moore,* 577 S.W.2d 613 (Ky. 1979).

177. *Id.,* at 613.

178. *Id.*

179. *Id.*

180. Ky. Rev. Stat. §403.270(2). *See Moore* v. *Moore,* 577 S.W.2d, at 613.

181. *Moore* v. *Moore,* 577 S.W.2d, at 613.

182. *In re Marriage of R.R.,* 575 S.W.2d 766 (1978).

183. *Id.,* at 768.

184. *Id.,* at 767.

185. *Id.,* at 768.

186. *Id.,* at 767, 768.

187. *Id.,* at 768–769.

188. *Id.,* at 768.

189. *Id.,* at 769.

190. *Myers* v. *Myers,* 468 Pa. 120, 360 A.2d 587 (1976).

191. *Id.,* at 589, 590.

192. *DeFranco* v. *DeFranco,* 67 Ill. App. 3d 760, 384 N.E.2d 997 (1978).

193. *Id.,* at 1003, citing Marriage and Dissolution of Marriage Act, Rev. Stat. ch. 40, § 602 par. 602b.

194. *Id.,* at 1002.

195. *Id.*

196. *Id.,* citing *Jarrett* v. *Jarrett,* 64 Ill. App. 3d 932, 382 N.E.2d 12 (1978).

197. *Id.,* at 1002.

198. *DeFranco* v. *DeFranco, supra,* 384 N.E.2d at 1002.

199. *Jarrett* v. *Jarrett,* 382 N.E.2d, at 16.

200. *Vidrine* v. *Demourelle,* 363 So. 2d 943 (La. Ct. App. 1978).

201. *Carroll* v. *Carroll,* 64 Ill. App. 3d 925, 382 N.E.2d 7, 11 (1978); *Caulkins* v. *Caulkins,* 68 Ill. App. 3d 284, 385 N.E.2d 1117 (1979).

202. *Cameron* v. *Cameron,* 137 Vt. 16, 398 A.2d 294, 296 (1979), citing Vt. Stat. Ann. §§ 14, 2650.

203. *Id.,* at 296.

204. *Id.,* at 295.

205. Wash. Rev. Code § 26.09.190. *See Marriage of Croley,* Wash. 2d 288, 588 P.2d 738 (1978).

206. *Harbin* v. *Harbin,* 238 Ga. 109, 230 S.E.2d 889, 890 (1976).

207. *Id.,* at 890.

208. *Id.,* at 891.

209. *Saure* v. *Saure,* 61 Ill. App. 3d 11, 377 N.E.2d 850 (1978).

210. *Id.,* at 852.

211. *Wyerman* v. *Carter,* 365 S.2d 1147 (La. App. 1978).

212. *Id.,* at 1148.

213. *Johnston* v. *Johnston,* 573 S.W.2d 406 (Mo. Ct. App. 1978).

214. *Id.,* at 409.

215. *Id.,* at 410.

216. *Id.*

217. *Id.*

218. *Id.,* at 413.

219. *Id.*

220. *McNair* v. *McNair,* 242 Ga. 105, 249 S.E.2d 573 (1978).

221. *Vindrine* v. *Demourelle,* 363 So. 2d, at 943.

222. *Id.,* at 945.

223. *Id.*

224. *Id.*

225. *Id.*

226. *Id.*

227. *Lovko* v. *Lovko,* 387 N.E.2d 166 (Ind. Ct. App. 1978).

228. *Id.,* at 171.

229. *Id.,* at 175.

230. *Id.*

231. *Id.*

232. *Strom* v. *Strom,* 37 Or. App. 767, 590 P.2d 238 (1978).

233. *Id.*, at 239.

234. *Id.*

235. *Id.*

236. *Id.*

237. *Id.*

238. *Id.*, at 239–240.

239. *Id.*, at 240.

240. *Rosenberg* v. *Rosenberg,* 365 So. 2d 185 (Fla. Dist. Ct. App. 1978).

241. *Id.*, at 186.

242. *Marriage of Reynolds,* 38 Or. App. 291, 587 P.2d 480 (1978).

243. *Id.*, at 482.

244. *Id.*

245. *Caulkins* v. *Caulkins,* 385 N.E.2d, at 1117.

246. *Id.*, at 1118.

247. *Id.*

248. *Id.*

249. *Id.*, at 1118–1119.

250. *Id.*

251. *Id.*

252. *Id.*, at 1118.

253. *Id.*

254. *Id.*, at 1120.

255. *Id.*, at 1120–1121.

256. *Marriage of Reynolds,* 387 Or. App., at 291.

257. *Marriage of Atkinson,* 38 Or. App. 375, 590 P.2d. 279 (1979).

258. *Davis* v. *Davis,* 365 So.2d 81 (Ala. Civ. App. 19).

259. *Carroll* v. *Carroll,* 382 N.E.2d, at 11.

260. *Compare Carroll* v. *Carroll,* 382 N.E.2d, at 11 *with Strom* v. *Strom,* 590 P.2d, at 238; *Caulkins* v. *Caulkins,* 385 N.E.2d, at 1117.

261. See chapter 3, *supra.* See note 225 *supra,* citing *Lovko* v. *Lovko,* 384 N.E.2d, at 166.

262. Ind. Code § 31–1–11.5–22(d).

263. *Lovko* v. *Lovko,* 384 N.E.2d, at 166. *Compare* Ind. Code § 31–1–11.5–22 *with* Ind. Code § 31–1–11.5–21.

264. Ill Rev. Stat. ch. 40 § 610. *See Drury* v. *Drury,* 65 Ill. App. 3d 290, 382 N.E.2d 608; *Jarrett* v. *Jarrett* 382 N.E.2d, at 16.

265. Ill. Rev. Stat. ch. 40 § 602, as discussed in *Drury* v. *Drury* 65 Ill. App. 3d, at 290.

# 4 Effect of Illegitimacy

## Theoretical Development

It is an ancient rule in New York that the natural father of an illegitimate child has a superior right to his custody and control as against all parties except for the mother of the child.[1]

> The rule is that the mother has the right to the custody of an illegitimate child as against the father, though the father has the right to the custody as against a stranger [citing cases]. . . . The proper statement of the rule is that the mother of an illegitimate child is *prima facie* entitled to its custody and, when she is a proper and suitable person, the court will award its custody to her as against the father or anyone else.[2]

In the days of the ancient common-law rule that bestowed a *prima facie* right to custody on the father generally (see chapter 2, Custody Disputes between Natural Parents, *supra*), the mother of an *illegitimate* child enjoyed a superior *prima facie* right to custody.[3] With the advent of the Tender Years Doctrine, which established a tacit presumption in favor of maternal custody in cases wherein the child was not illegitimate, the courts could enhance the unwed mother's superior right to her child as against the unwed father. A theoretical distinction still was retained by the courts, however. It must be recalled (see chapter 2, Custody Disputes between Natural Parents, *supra*), that the Tender Years Doctrine was always expressed by the courts in equivocal terms, and the courts generally continued to maintain the fiction that there was no distinction in custody cases between the rights of married parents. The preference for maternal custody in disputes involving children born *in* wedlock could be referred to only obliquely in terms of a rebuttable presumption because of the limitations imposed by statute.[4] In the case of out-of-wedlock children, the courts could openly assert the preference for maternal custody as a *prima facie* right.

> While the welfare of the child is the paramount and, indeed, the only proper consideration for the determination of the custody of a child whether legitimate or illegitimate [citing cases], nevertheless, in the case of an illegitimate child the rules for making that determination are different

than in the case of a legitimate child. In the case of the legitimate child there is no *prima facie* right to the custody of the child in either parent [citing statute]. However, in the case of an illegitimate child, the mother of the child is in a favored position.[5]

Bearing in mind that the application of the doctrine established in Domestic Relations Law Sections 70 and 240, (the statutes cited in the immediately preceding excerpt) was so often subordinated to the Tender Years Doctrine (see chapter 2, Custody Disputes between Natural Parents, *supra*), it is questionable as to how much genuine difference was made by maintaining a separate rule for out-of-wedlock children. It is likely that the effect of the rule was to add weight to the decision of the court when it would have been inclined to apply the Tender Years Doctrine whether the parents had been married or not. With or without the prevalence of the Tender Years Doctrine, however, the courts "have not hesitated to award the custody of an illegitimate child to its father to the exclusion of the mother where the mother was shown to be unfit and the court was satisfied that the welfare of the child required such a determination."[6]

In *People ex rel. Meredith* v. *Meredith,* the court considered the mother's qualifications as to fitness. At the age of 24 she had one child born out of wedlock, at least one paramour, three exhusbands, one conviction for bigamy, and an impending fourth marriage.[7] Further, there was testimony that she has been neglectful of the child and was often intoxicated.[8] Moreover, the mother resided with the maternal grandmother, who herself lived with a paramour and three of her own out-of-wedlock children.[9]

The father, however, lived with his own parents (who were married to each other) in a home in Florida, earned a respectable income at a respectable job, and had always conducted himself toward the child with an attitude of concern, affection, and responsibility.[10] The appellate division held that the record led to an "inevitable" decision in the father's favor that should not be disturbed on appeal.[11]

In *In re Cornell* v. *Hartley,* however, the court required the father to "rebut the mother's *prima facie* entitlement to the custody of her illegitimate child" by demonstrating her unfitness.[12] The anecdotal evidence, provided solely by the father, as to the mother's frequenting of taverns and her predilection toward frequent intoxication was not considered sufficient to warrant a transfer of custody to the father.[13] The court's coup de grace for the father's position came with its invocation of the Tender Years Doctrine and its citation of the classic language in *Ullman* v. *Ullman:* "The child at tender age is entitled to have such care, love and discipline as only a good and devoted mother can usually give."[14]

This points up the inescapable philosophical tie between the Tender Years Doctrine as applied to the married parents of children in custody disputes and the *prima facie* presumption in the mother's favor for children born out of wedlock. If the rationale behind the Tender Years Doctrine can no longer be sustained; that is, that the mother is *naturally* a more suitable parent, then it must, of necessity, downgrade the presumption with regard to out-of-wedlock children.

### Criticism and Abandonment of the Maternal *Prima Facie* Right to Custody of Out-of-Wedlock Children

The doctrine that holds that a mother has a *prima facie* right to the custody of an out-of-wedlock child was criticized as long ago as 1931, even as the same decision cited *Ullman* v. *Ullman* and approved the Tender Years Doctrine generally.[15] In referring to Section 70 of the New York Domestic Relations law, providing in part that, "there shall be no *prima facie* right to the custody of the child in either parent," the court held, "[The Section] it is true, probably has relation only to children born in wedlock, but I perceive no reason why, if the parents are not married, the guiding principle should not be the same."[16]

Some 35 years later, in *Godinez* v. *Russo,* the court took the view that Section 70 of the Domestic Relations Law was, in fact, applicable to out-of-wedlock children after all.

> It further appears to the court, however, that the distinction between legitimate and illegitimate children insofar as the latter, in matters of custody, carries with it the presumption of custody in favor of the natural mother, should be reconsidered and abolished. . . . It is submitted that the proper standard is that which is enumerated in section 70 of the Domestic Relations Law hereinabove quoted regardless of the manner of birth of the child involved. This court should be granted the same privileges and powers in determining the custody of a child born out of wedlock as between the putative father and the natural mother as exist in the case of legitimate children. The harsh view of the common law that a natural child is nobody's child no longer prevails. To continue the presumption of custody in favor of the natural mother is in a sense a continuation of a stigma which attaches to an illegitimate child. The [court] should have the powers, both as to the illegitimate as well as the legitimate child, only the duty to seek a determination required for the welfare and best interest of the child.[17]

This doctrine of the mother's *prima facie* right, as expressed in *Meredith* v. *Meredith,* [18] was criticized with the greatest of weight in the dissenting opinion of Judge Scileppe in *Anonymous* v. *Anonymous.* [19] It was further held worthy of abolition in a 1977 miscellaneous decision, *Boatwright* v. *Otero.* [20] The court said that "blind adherence to an approach which mandates *prima facie* custody in the natural mother inhibits adequate consideration of the best interests of the child.''[21] Further, ''[t]his court holds that the present state of rights of the unwed father, who has openly acknowledged paternity and has maintained an on-going relationship with his child, has evolved to the point where the proper standard to be used in a custody proceeding should be the 'best interests of the child.' ''[22] The court then proceeded to evaluate the relative merits of the parents according to the standards of best interests.[23]

Considering, however, the flagrantly immoral state of the mother's sexual affairs, her voluntary abandonment of the children in question, her production of a total of four illegitimate children by the age of 26—all compared to the father's loving and supportive role in the lives of the children—it is doubtful if the court would have reached any other conclusion in spite of the rule.[24] If one compares *Boatwright* with *Meredith,* there is little difference in the factual circumstances or in the outcome of the cases. The only distinction is that one case (*Meredith*) is decided as an exception to the general rule, and the other (*Boatwright*) is decided as good reason for abandoning the rule altogether.

It has been amply demonstrated in our examination of the Tender Years Doctrine[25] that the rules granting *prima facie* rights to one parent or another were never so rigidly enforced as to admit of no exception when the sensibilities of the court, in the context of the prevailing mores, were sufficiently outraged by a particular set of facts. It was inevitable that, as the philosophical basis behind the Tender Years Doctrine fell into disrepute, so would the *prima facie* right of an unwed mother to custody. They are both, necessarily, based on the same premise.

It should be borne in mind that there has never been a clear rejection or reversal of the New York Court of Appeals decision in *Anonymous* v. *Anonymous*[26] and that it is the dissenting opinion that is quoted so liberally as authority for the abolition of the *prima facie* right of the unwed mother.[27] But in view of the general disapproval now accorded to the Tender Years Doctrine to be applied to *married* parents, it seems safe to assume that the father of an out-of-wedlock child will not be placed in a more adverse position than one who has been married to the mother.

**Effect of Federal Decisions**

In helping to establish, in a general sense, equality of rights for an unwed father, the U.S. Supreme Court has played a significant role in its rulings in what have come to be considered landmark decisions. Foremost among these are *Stanley* v. *Illinois,* wherein it was held that an unwed father must be given the same right as a married father to show that he is a fit custodian for his children.[28] Moreover, his children cannot arbitrarily be made wards of the state without a hearing and proof of parental unfitness and neglect, wherein, as in *Stanley,* the mother was deceased, and the unwed father had de facto custody.[29]

*Stanley* v. *Illinois* has thus given impetus to many decisions expanding the rights of unwed fathers. The decision's implicit recognition of the right of an unwed father to equality of treatment with a married father was cited in those cases wherein unwed fathers sought visitation and in those jurisdictions wherein it was denied to them as a matter of course.[30] In New York, however, the courts generally recognized visitation rights in unwed fathers, even during the period where the *prima facie* right of the mother to actual custody was still unequivocally recognized.[31]

*Stanley* v. *Illinois* has been cited in cases wherein the right of the unwed father to custody has been upheld against the mother on a determination of "the parameters for the rights of an unwed father under the due process and equal protection clauses of the Federal Constitution."[32] It has also been cited wherein the father's right to custody of his illegitimate child has been upheld, so long as he is fit, against the maternal relatives of the child, subsequent to the mother's death: "The [Supreme C]ourt recognized that the interests of a father of an illegitimate child are not different from those of other parents."[33]

Starting with the premise that the rights of an out-of-wedlock father are now established as equal to those of any father (bolstered by the decision in *Stanley* v. *Illinois*), the effect of this newly recognized status raised the question of the unwed father's right relative to those of third-party claimants for the child's custody. If the unwed father's rights are now equal to a married father's rights, are they merely equal to, or superior to, the rights of third parties? This issue will be dealt with in chapter 5, Custody Disputes between Natural Parents and Third Parties, *infra.* The effect of illegitimacy on visitation is outlined in chapter 6, Visitation, *infra.* With regard to contests between natural parents, in light of the new status of out-of-wedlock fathers, reference should be made to chapter 3, Current Standards of Custody Determination Between Natural Parents, *supra.* The effect of illegitimacy on adoption and termination of parental rights was addressed in the U.S. Supreme Court decision in *Caban* v. *Mohammad.*

In *Caban* v. *Mohammad,*[34] the Supreme Court held that the necessity of the consent of a father to the adoption of his child by another could not be held, under the law, to be of more or less importance than the consent of the mother, whether or not the parents had ever been married.[35] The Court held further that the distinction in the applicable statute between the consent required of unmarried mothers and the dispensation of such consent by unmarried fathers "does not bear a substantial relation to the State's interest in providing adoptive homes for its illegitimate children."[36]

In sum we believe that [the New York Statute] is another example of "over-broad generalization" in gender-based classifications [citing cases]. The effect of New York's classification is to discriminate against unwed fathers even when their identity is known and they have manifested a significant paternal interest in the child. The facts of this case illustrate the harshness of classifying unwed fathers as being invariably less qualified and entitled than mothers to exercise a concerned judgment as to the fate of their children. [The statute] excludes some loving fathers from full participation in the decision whether their children will be adopted and, at the same time, enables some alienated mothers arbitrarily to cut off the paternal rights of fathers. We conclude that this undifferentiated distinction between unwed mothers and unwed fathers . . . does not bear a substantial relationship to the State's asserted interests.[37]

It has been observed that, by and large, the U.S. courts take very little cognizance of custody issues in particular, and matrimonial issues in general, leaving these matters to the discretion of the individual states. The exceptions have been those cases wherein a constitutional issue, a conflict of law issue, or an issue involving a specific federal statute are involved.[38] In finding substantial constitutional impediments in gender-based discrimination against unwed fathers, as was done in *Caban* and *Stanley,* the federal courts have potentially revolutionized the role of unwed fathers in the entire scheme of custody law. This development creates fertile ground for speculation as to the intervention of the federal courts in those situations wherein the Tender Years Doctrine has remained the established rule, and a *prima facie* right to custody is founded on gender.

**Proving Paternity as Prerequisite to Rights of Father**

Although questions of evidence and proof in custody disputes are generally beyond the scope of this text, it is worth noting that when illegitimacy is a factor in determining the custody or visitation rights of a parent, proof of paternity may become the threshold issue before the other substantive issues can be reached. Thus if (as in earlier cases) the unwed father had a right to custody inferior to the mother's, but superior to third parties, then he would have been required to prove that he was indeed the natural father in order to enjoy such standing. Even under current standards, wherein the unwed father's right is *equal* to that of the mother but may be superior to that of third parties, or where his consent may be required for adoption, as is now mandated under *Caban* v. *Mohammad,*[39] the issue of actual paternity might still be disputed.

These circumstances raise the possibility of an unwed father placing himself in the position of asserting paternity in order to enjoy custody and/or visitation, as opposed to the more commonplace scenario whereby the father denies paternity in order to escape support obligations. Proof or disproof of paternity is a book-length issue in itself, which is already covered by one of the most authoritative and respected treatises in the field of domestic relations.[40] This subsection will offer a few examples from miscellaneous decisions in order to illustrate some of the exotic legal issues that can arise when paternity itself becomes the issue in a custody dispute.

In a 1974 New York miscellaneous decision, the unwed mother had died, and the unwed father was contesting a custody claim against the maternal grandmother and maternal great-aunt of the subject child.[41] The law at the time was more clearly established than it is today: that is, that the right of a natural unwed father to custody of his child [barring unfitness] was superior to that of a third party.[42] The grandmother and great-aunt sought to prove that the alleged father had not, in fact, sired the child at all and thus deprive him of the legal advantages consistent with that status.[43]

The maternal relatives, in support of their contentions, sought to introduce the child's birth certificate showing a blank in the space reserved for the name of the father.[44] The court refused to allow the introduction of the birth certificate as evidence that the deletion proved such a fact.[45] The admissibility of a birth certificate under New York evidentiary rules is limited to show only the fact of birth, and cannot be admitted to show any other facts contained therein.[46]

The alleged father sought to retain his legal advantage by offering his own testimony as to his course of sexual relations with the deceased mother that preceded the birth of the subject child.[47] In considering this offer of proof, the court found itself facing the objection arising from a New York statute that prohibits the testimony of an interested party in a cause of action as to transactions or conversations with a decedent (the "dead-man's statute").[48]

The court found at the outset that the illegal father was clearly a party in interest within the meaning of the statute and further found "[t]hat the acts of intercourse and cohabitation are transactions within the meaning of the statute. . . ."[49]

The court, however, distinguished this particular case and allowed the father to testify as to his relations with the mother in order to establish his paternity.[50]

This court holds that testimony as to acts of intercourse and cohabitation between respondent and decedent are admissible, and that such testimony does not come within the prohibition of [the statute]. It is the opinion of this court that the "deadman's statute" as it is popularly known, is, and has been, designed to protect a decedent's estate from the prejudice of uncontroverted or perjured testimony where there is a pecuniary or property interest involved. There is no such pecuniary or property interest in this case. The issue to be determined is one of status; i.e., the blood relationship between respondent and child rather than the right to property. The object of the litigation in the case at bar is not property or money or tangible economic benefit, but the custody of a defenseless child, whose best interests must be held paramount.[51]

The court found the weight of the evidence to establish the paternity of the alleged father and that the best interests of the child lay with continued maintenance in the father's care.[52]

In another 1974 miscellaneous decision, the parties had been married some 4 months after the mother had conceived a child.[53] The mother gave birth, and the parties and the child lived together for about 1 year prior to separation. The respondent father sought to enforce his rights to visit the child following separation and a court order of support and visitation.[54] During enforcement proceedings, the mother abruptly decided that she wanted neither the support nor the father's visitation.[55] She then testified, under oath, that he was not the father of the child, therefore putting herself in the position of having perjured herself when she filed the original petition for support.[56] During the enforcement proceedings, she denied that her husband was the father of the child, thus placing herself in the position of an admitted perjurer by the diametrical reversal of her previous testimony.[57] The court was thus faced with the necessity of relieving the father of his support obligations and the mother of her concomitant visitation obligation, for the benefit of the child. "[T]his court does not see where it would be in the best interests of the child to saddle him with a grudging father who, formerly concerned and loving, is now understandably hurt, confused and hostile in view of the [mother's] recent admissions'."[58]

In order to reverse its previous decree, the court had to overcome the presumption of legitimacy of a child born in wedlock, a presumption "well settled, almost to the point of cliche [and] . . . 'one of the strongest and most persuasive known to the law.' "[58] "This presumption is, according to most of the cases, equally as potent where the child is conceived before marriage."[59] The court concluded that under the circumstances, the presumption was overcome by the sway of reason, that the subject was *not* the offspring of the respondent-husband, and that both the support and the visitation provisions of its previous order could properly be reversed.[60] The court's language is enlightening.

This court believes that common sense and reason require a recognition that the mores of society have altered since the presumption was first promulgated. . . . We can no longer take the view that it is only the rare, immoral woman who does not remain chaste until marriage. Further, we cannot maintain the fiction that where the poor misguided soul does yield, after much protest, to the ways of the flesh, she waits faithfully and fervently for her one true love to make an honest woman of her.

It is perfectly reasonable and sensible to believe that where a woman has engaged in antenuptial relations with one man, that she is capable of doing so with others. Where this probability is coupled with the [mother's] in-court admissions in the face of consequences of a perjury prosecution, loss of support for her child, providing her husband with grounds for annulment, not to mention the embarrassment and ignominy involved, this court believes that the presumption of legitimacy is sufficiently overcome.[61]

## Other Juridictions

### New Hampshire

New Hampshire has a statute whereby a putative father of a child born out of wedlock may apply to have such child legitimized.[62] The effect of a declaration under the statute is "to impose upon the father all the obligations which fathers owe to their lawful issue" and "to entitle such child by succession, inheritance or distribution to real and personal property by, through, and from his father and mother as if such child had been born in lawful wedlock."[63] The New Hampshire Supreme Court, in construing all relevant statutes strictly, concluded that its court had no statutory authority to pass on questions of visitation and custody with regard to children born out of wedlock.[64] The court castigated the legislature for its failure to deal with the "problems resulting from the separation of the increasing number of unwed parents who have been living together for a period of time as man and wife."[65]

In spite of its strict construction of applicable statutes, the court concluded that the rights of the father and child to each other's company, through visitation, were so basic as not to require specific statutory grants of powers.[66]

We hold therefore, that following legitimation of the child under RSA 460:29 (Supp. 1977), the superior court has the authority in its discretion to make orders relating to visitations between the plaintiff and his child.[67]

The rationale was stated in the following terms:

This court has held that visitation rights of parents are important rights that should not be denied without good cause [citing case]. These rights are based on factors unrelated to marriage between the parents of a legitimated child, and should not depend upon the existence of divorce proceedings where there never was a lawful marriage to be dissolved. . . .[68] [T]he right of the child and father to a continuing relationship should not depend upon legislative enactment. It is a right that has its foundation among those "natural essential and inherent rights" that are recognized in [the New Hampshire Constitution].[69]

Although in this particular case, the court dealt only with an application for visitation, its characteristization of the importance of the parent-child relationship, regardless of out-of-wedlock status, implies that it might easily traverse the short distance necessary to include custody among the "essential" rights that are inherent of disposition by the judiciary. The tone of the decision is altogether reminiscent of the *parens patriae* doctrine, long recognized in New York and in ancient English decisions.[70] There is no mistaking the court's intention to raise the status of an out-of-wedlock father to the same level as a married father in relationship to his children.

## Connecticut

The Supreme Court of Connecticut has also upheld the right of an unwed father to bring a *habeas corpus* proceeding to determine the custody of illegitimate children under the *parens patriae* theory.[71] The Connecticut Supreme Court distinguished the Stanley case as follows:[72]

> [R]ecent decisions of the United States Supreme Court regarding the rights of unwed fathers do not compel us to affirm the action of the trial court in the present case by concluding that standing is acquired only when a period of cohabitation and support is alleged in conjunction with the allegation of fatherhood.[73]

The court observed as follows, with implicit approval:

> In recognition of the well-established principle that a determination of custody should be premised upon the paramount consideration of what would be in the best interests of the children, a number of jurisdictions have recently taken the view that the natural father of illegitimate children has custodial rights similar to those of a father of legitimate children upon a dissolution of a marriage.[74]

The court concluded, in reversing the decision below, that

> [I]n accordance with this court's constant emphasis upon consideration for the welfare of minor children, legitimate or not, we perceive no valid reason for denying the admitted natural father of an illegitimate child at the least the opportunity to obtain judicial determination of custody. . . .[75]

## Utah

Utah has an approach to the custodial rights of unwed fathers that is more dependent on statute than on the *parens patriae* doctrine. Under Utah statutes, the mother of an out-of-wedlock child is entitled to exclusive custody and control until the child reaches the age of 10 years, unless, on petition to an appropriate court, she is shown to be unfit.[76] Therefore, it would appear that Utah's statutory scheme is violative of the general principles enunciated in *Stanley* v. *Illinois,* which condemns wholly gender-based favoritism in custody disputes.

Utah has another statute, however, that enables the father of an out-of-wedlock child to legitimize such child by acknowledging paternity and "otherwise treating it as if it were a legitimate child."[77] In a visitation dispute between the parents of an out-of-wedlock child, the Utah Supreme Court has ruled that once a father has complied with the appropriate statute, his "child is thereupon deemed for all purposes legitimate from the time of its birth."[78] "Thus, once a child has been legitimated under [the statute], a dispute between mother and father as to the father's visitation rights will be resolved by applying the law governing visitation of a legitimate child. . . ."[79] In other words, the dispute would be decided under the same statute that applies to disputes between parents who are or had been married. The out-of-wedlock father is thus given parity with a married father as to visitation, and, although the facts of the decision were limited to visitation, the application of the same reasoning to a custody dispute is certainly a logical next step.

## Notes

1. *Trainer* v. *Cooper,* 8 How. Pr. 288, 292 (1853).

2. *Meredith* v. *Meredith,* 272 A.D. 79, 82, 69 N.Y.S.2d 462, aff'd 297 N.Y. 692 (1947).

3. *Trainer* v. *Cooper,* 8 How. Pr., at 293.

4. N.Y. Dom. Rel. Law §§ 70, 240 (McKinney). See chapter 2, Custody Disputes between Natural Parents, *supra;* see chapter 2, Custody Disputes between Natural Parents, notes 9 and 71, *supra.*

5. *Cornell* v. *Hartley,* 54 Misc. 2d 732, 283 N.Y.S.2d 318 (Sup. Ct. 1967).

6. *Id.,* at 735.

7. *Meredith* v. *Meredith,* 272 A.D., at 84.

8. *Id.*

9. *Id.,* at 85.

10. *Id.,* at 86.

11. *Id.*

12. *Cornell* v. *Hartley,* 54 Misc. 2d, at 732.

13. *Id.,* at 736–737.

14. *Id.,* at 737, citing *Ullman* v. *Ullman* 151 A.D. 419, 135 N.Y.S. 1080

(2d Dept. 1912). See also chapter 2, Custody Disputes between Natural Parents, *supra*.

15. *Mahoff* v. *Matsoui,* 139 Misc. 21, 23, 247 N.Y.S. 112 (Sup. Ct. 1931), citing N.Y. Dom. Rel. Law § 170 (McKinney) *as amended by* 1923 N.Y. Laws ch. 235.

16. *Id.,* at 26.

17. *Godinez* v. *Russo,* 49 Misc. 2d 66, 266 N.Y.S.2d 636 (Fam. Ct. 1966).

18. *Meredith* v. *Meredith,* 272 A.D., at 79.

19. *Anonymous* v. *Anonymous,* 26 N.Y.2d 740, 745, 309 N.Y.S.2d 40 (1970).

20. *Boatwright* v. *Otero,* 91 Misc. 2d 653, 398 N.Y.S.2d 391 (Fam. Ct. 1977).

21. *Id.,* at 656.

22. *Id.,* at 657.

23. *Id.*

24. *Id.*

25. See chapters 2, Custody Disputes between Natural Parents and 3, Current Standards for Determination of Custody Disputes between Parents, *supra*.

26. *Anonymous* v. *Anonymous,* 26 N.Y.2d, at 740.

27. *Id. See Boatwright* v. *Otero,* 91 Misc. 2d, at 656.

28. *Stanley* v. *Illinois,* 405 U.S. 645 (1972).

29. *Id.*

30. See chapter 6, Visitation, *infra*.

31. See chapter 6, Visitation, *infra*.

32. *Boatwright* v. *Otero,* 91 Misc. 2d, at 656.

33. *Blake* v. *Charger,* 76 Misc. 2d 577, 351 N.Y.S.2d 322 (Fam. Ct. 1974).

34. *Caban* v. *Mohammad,* 441 U.S. 380 (1979).

35. *Id.*

36. *Id.*

37. *Id.*

38. See chapter 1, Jurisdiction, *supra*.

39. See generally cases cited notes 34–37, *supra*.

40. S. Schatkin, Proof of Disputed Paternity Proceedings Rev. ed. (1980).

41. *Blake* v. *Charger,* 76 Misc. 2d, at 577.

42. *Id. See Trainer* v. *Cooper,* 8 How Prac., at 292; *Meredith* v. *Meredith,* 272 A.D., at 79; *Cornell* v. *Hartley,* 54 Misc. 2d, at 732.

43. *Blake* v. *Charger,* 76 Misc. 2d, at 577.

44. *Id.,* at 579.

45. *Id.*

46. *Id. See* J. Prince, Richardson on Evidence § 345 10th ed. (1973).

47. *Blake* v. *Charger,* 76 Misc. 2d, at 578.

48. *Id. See* N.Y. Civ. Prac. Law § 4519 (McKinney).

49. *Blake* v. *Charger,* at 578. *See Matter of Kelley,* 238 N.Y. 71 (1924); *Matter of Christie,* 167 Misc. 484, 4 N.Y.S.2d 484 (1938).

50. *Blake* v. *Charger,* 76 Misc. 2d, at 578.

51. *Id. See also Colon* v. *Tristani,* 45 P. R. 219.

52. *Blake* v. *Charger,* 76 Misc. 2d, at 582.

53. *London* v. *London,* 78 Misc. 2d 535, 356 N.Y.S.2d 1000 (Fam. Ct. 1974).

54. *Id.*

55. *Id.*

56. *Id.,* at 536.

57. *Id.,* at 537.

58. *Id.,* at 536.

59. *Id.*

60. *Id.,* at 537.

61. *Id.*

62. N.H. Rev. Stat. Ann. § 460.29. *See Locke* v. *Ladd,* 399 A.2d 962, 963 (N.H. 1979).

63. *Locke* v. *Ladd,* 399 A.2d, at 963–964.

64. *Id.,* at. 964–965.

65. *Id.,* at 965.

66. *Id.*

67. *Id.*

68. *Id.*

69. *Id.*

70. See chapter 1, Jurisdiction, *supra.*

71. *Pi* v. *Delta,* 175 Conn. 527, 400 A.2d 709, 710 (1978). See chapter 1, Jurisdiction, *supra.*

72. *Id.* 175 Conn., at 527, citing *Stanley* v. *Illinois,* 405 U.S. 654.

73. *Id.,* 400 A.2d, at 711.

74. *Id. See also Orezza* v. *Ramirez,* 19 Ariz. App. 405, 507 P.2d 1017 (1973); *Brown* v. *Bray,* 300 So. 2d 668 (Fla. 1974); *Irby* v. *DuBois,* 41 Ill. App. 3d 609, 354 N.E.2d 562 (1976); *Marshall* v. *Stefanider,* 17 Md. App. 364, 302 A.2d 682 (1973); *Boatwright* v. *Otero,* 19 Misc. 2d 653, 398 N.Y.S.2d 391 (Fam. Ct. 1977); *Sparks* v. *Phelps,* 22 Or. App. 570, 540 P.2d 397 (1975).

75. *Pi* v. *Delta,* 400 A.2d, at 712.

76. Utah Code Ann. § 77-60-12. *See Slade* v. *Dennis,* 594 P.2d 898 (Utah 1979).

77.  Utah Code Ann. § 78-30-12. *See Slade* v. *Dennis,* 594 P.2d, at 899.
78.  *Slade* v. *Dennis,* 594 P.2d, at 901.
79.  *Id.,* at 901.

# 5 Custody Disputes between Natural Parents and Third Parties

## General Considerations

Few issues affect more closely the intimate lives of people than the regulation of child care and marital-sexual relationships. Not surprisingly, few legal questions generate as much passionate debate and disagreement among both lawyers and lay social commentators. Of all these issues of love, sex, marriage, and child care that a court of law may have occasion to consider, possibly the most volatile is that of justifying the removal of a child from the care and custody of its natural parent. The status accorded to motherhood and the intimacy of the parent-child relationship as experienced in Western society greatly enhance the enormity of the judge's responsibility in deciding to remove a child from a natural parent.

In attempting to develop criteria for the resolution of this sensitive issue, two schools of thought have developed. Each has maintained outspoken followings among laymen, the legal community, and the community of professional behavioral scientists including psychiatrists, psychologists, social workers, and so forth. The two philosophies can be categorized as follows: (1) the traditional natural-rights school, which recognizes a superior right of the natural parent to the custody of his or her child against any third party, and which can only be defeated by the most overwhelming demonstration of unfitness or by abandonment and (2) the best-interests-of-the-child school, which does not recognize the primacy of a natural parent's rights and advocates a judicial determination based on a balancing of such factors as environment, material benefits, and emotional and psychological adjustment. This chapter will analyze the development of the law—first in New York and then in other selected jurisdictions—in terms of the relative prevalence of the two competing doctrines.

## The Parental Right Doctrine

There is little question that the Parental Right Doctrine, recognizing the superior right of a natural parent to the custody of a child against third parties, was the prevailing rule in New York throughout all of its legal history. It is only since the late 1970s that the rule has been modified to any extent.

The leading case upholding the primacy of the natural parent's rights was decided by the Court of Appeals in 1952.[1] The court found that, up until that time, "the several counsel who have filed briefs on this appeal have found no reported New York case, where, for any reason, a small child has been ordered delivered from the custody of a decent parent in a decent home into the hands of others."[2] In this principal decision, *People ex rel. Portnoy* v. *Strasser*,[3] the Court of Appeals returned a 7-year-old girl to the custody of her natural mother by unanimously reversing the appellate division.[4] The appellate division had, in turn, unanimously affirmed the trial court is sustaining a writ of *habeas corpus* and directing that custody of the child be delivered to her maternal grandmother.[5]

Robin Strasser, the subject of this *habeas corpus* proceeding, was the child of white Jewish parents who separated and eventually divorced during the years immediately following her birth.[6] The child thereupon lived part of the time with her maternal grandmother, Mollie Portnoy, and the remainder of the time with her mother in the years immediately preceding the commencement of the cause of action.[7] Robin was in her grandmother's care when, in 1949, her mother remarried a Black man of blameless reputation and prosperous circumstances.[8] The mother regained de facto custody of Robin, and the grandmother then brought a *habeas corpus* proceeding in order to obtain permanent custody of the child.[9]

The grandmother, in seeking to obtain custody, charged her daughter with unfitness as a mother. Mrs. Portnoy's complaint as to her daughter's fitness was based on the latter's left-wing political activities, her outside employment and use of a day-care nursery for the child, her failure to train Robin in the Jewish faith of her ancestors, and her deficiencies as a housekeeper.[10] The court, at the outset, distinguished this type of case from those involving competing natural parents[11] and then went on to hold that the facts and circumstances did not amount to such unfitness as would justify removal of the child from her mother.

> We do not have here one of those unhappily frequent cases where the contest is between parents and the courts must make the best available choice. Nor is this a case where a parent has left a child with relatives for a long time, then seeks it back [citing case]. Here a grandparent has assumed the very heavy burden of proving that a little girl should, by court order, be separated from her own and her mother's home. To sustain that burden, relator must do more than prevail on a simple factual issue as to which are the better surroundings or as to which party is better equipped to raise the child. . . . "[The mother's] right as a parent . . . to the care and custody of the child becomes superior to that of all others unless it should be shown . . . that she is an unfit person to exercise such guardianship [citing case]."[12]

In fact, *Portnoy* v. *Strasser* is a composite holding of what was the law in most American jurisdictions until the 1960s; that is, that the right of a natural parent to the custody of his child is paramount against the right of all other claimants unless such natural parent is proved unfit.

This position was bolstered by the Court of Appeals with a citation to the U.S. Supreme Court decision in *Meyer* v. *Nebraska,* [13] which is often cited in cases reaching a similar conclusion. *Meyer* v. *Nebraska* held in part that the right to "marry, establish a home and bring up children" are among "those privileges long recognized at common law as essential to the orderly pursuit of happiness by free men."[14] The Court of Appeals, referring to *Meyer* v. *Nebraska* in its *Portnoy* decision, read *Meyer* as authority for its holding that "the right of a parent, under natural law, to establish a home and bring up children is a fundamental one and beyond the reach of any court [citing case]."[15]

The clarity and tone of the language used in *Meyer* and *Portnoy* is significant. References to the right of a biological parent to its child's custody as "fundamental" under "natural law" and "beyond the reach of any court" as "essential to the orderly pursuit of happiness by free men" raise the parental-right doctrine to the level of an axiom equal to the "self-evident" truths and "inalienable rights" reminiscent of the Declaration of Independence. The biological parent-child relationship is nothing less than enshrined by the language in *Portnoy.* As such, it is not surprising that the Parental Right Doctrine has resisted attack so steadfastly for so long and even now, though modified in recent decisions, continues to carry considerable weight.[16]

## Continued Prevalence of the Natural Right Doctrine in New York

The strong expression of support for natural rights of parents in the absence of unfitness, as held in *Portnoy,* was followed in 1953 by the decision in *People ex rel. Kropp* v. *Shepsky.* [17] The decision was rendered in a *habeas corpus* proceeding brought by the natural mother to regain custody of her out-of-wedlock child.[18] The 18-year-old mother, alone and without help from family or friends, managed to care adequately for her baby until about 18 months after its birth.[19] At that time, in difficult circumstances, she entrusted the child to the respondent and signed a consent to adoption.[20] Two weeks later she requested the return of the child and hired attorneys for the purpose of securing its return.[21]

The Court of Appeals ruled in favor of the natural mother's right to the return of her child, in light of the principles enunciated in *People ex rel. Portnoy* v. *Strasser*[22] and *Meyer* v. *Nebraska.* [23] "[W]e find no basis for denying custody of the child to [the] natural parent, who did not abandon it and against whom no showing of present unfitness has been made."[24]

The court further elaborated on the "natural right" presumption as follows:

> It has often been said that a child's welfare is the first concern of the court. . . . *However valid this statement may be in a contest involving the parents alone, it cannot stand without qualification in a contest between parents and non-parents* [emphasis added]. The mother or father has a right to the care and custody of a child, superior to that of all others unless he or she has abandoned that right or is proved unfit to assume the duties and privileges of parenthood [citing cases].[25]

The court distinguished the instant case from those falling within the exception to the rule

> Accordingly, we have sanctioned withholding the child from the custody of a parent who has abandoned or transferred the parental right, either expressly or by implication [citing case], may have the child taken from him.[26]

The court hastened to add, however, that the instant case fell "within the rule and not within the exception" wherein "consent initially given to a child's adoption, often under the pressure of circumstances, is thereafter withdrawn."[27] The court placed the burden of proof, "not, for instance, upon the mother to show that the child's welfare would be advanced by being returned to her, but rather upon the non-parents to prove that the mother is unfit to have her child. . . ."[28]

> In view of the mother's way of life during the past several years, her manifest devotion to her child, her persistent efforts to regain its custody in the face of great obstacles, her steady employment and her provision for a suitable home in which to rear the child, a finding that she was other than fit to assume the child's custody would be erroneous as a matter of law, and nothing in the record supports even an inference that the child's welfare would be promoted by being kept from the mother. In a word, there was no warrant for denying the mother's petition.[29]

Probably the most publicized or notorious case in this field, and the most familiar to the layman, is *Scarpetta* v. *Spence Chapin Adoption Service,* or the "Baby Lenore" case.[30] The media treatment of the Baby Lenore case turned it into a soap opera with the "good guys" versus the "bad guys" alternately winning rounds in the legal proceedings. Most laymen who followed the case remember that the foster parents ultimately retained custody of the child and presumably lived happily ever after. What is readily forgotten is that the foster parents ultimately retained custody because they flouted the jurisdiction of the New York courts by removing themselves and the child to Florida, following an adverse ruling by the Court of Appeals.[31] The court's ruling was clearly in favor of the rights of the natural mother.

Olga Scarpetta, the biological mother, found herself alone and destitute in New York, and, having given birth to an out-of-wedlock child, surrendered the child for boarding care with the defendant adoption service.[32] Only 5 days after the surrender, the "mother repented her action and requested the child's return."[33] The Court of Appeals unanimously affirmed the appellate division, which had, in turn, affirmed the trial court's award of custody to the natural mother.[34] In upholding once again the primacy of the natural parent's right to custody in the absence of unfitness or abandonment, the court commented at length.

> It has been repeatedly determined, in so far as the best interests of the child are concerned, that the "mother or father has a right to the care and custody of a child superior to that of all others, unless he or she has abandoned that right or is proved unfit to assume the duties and privileges of parenthood [citing cases]." It has been well said that "the status of a natural parent," is so important, "[t]hat in determining the best interests of the child, it may counter-balance, even outweigh, superior material and cultural advantages which may be afforded by adoptive parents. For experience teaches that a mather's love is one factor which will endure, possibly endure after other claimed material advantages and emotional attachments may have proven transient [citing cases]."

> The primacy of status thus accorded the natural parent is not materially altered or diminished by the mere fact of surrender under the statute, although it is a factor to be considered by the court. To hold, as the agency suggests—that a surrender to an authorized agency constitutes, as a matter of law, an abandonment—would frustrate the policy underlying our legislation [citation omitted], which allows a mother to regain custody of her child, notwithstanding the surrender to the agency, provided, of course, that there is some showing of improvidence in the making of the surrender, that the interest of such child will be promoted and "that such parent is fit, competent and able to duly maintain, support and educate such child." Nor do we perceive any distinction, in principle, between the effect of a surrender to an authorized agency and of a surrender to an individual. "The policy urged that, if surrender may be undone, authorized agencies will be inconvenienced or even frustrated in their placement of children is not a sufficient counterweight. The fact of relationship between a natural parent and child ought not to be subordinated to such considerations, important as they are [citation omitted]."

> Consequently, to give the fundamental principle meaning and vitality, we have explicitly declared that "except where a nonparent has obtained legal and permanent custody of a child by adoption, guardianship, or otherwise, he who would take or withhold a child from mother or father must sustain

the burden of establishing that the parent is unfit and that the child's welfare compels awarding its custody to the nonparent [citation omitted].[35]

Cases in which the improvidence of the natural mother's surrender are held to be insufficient reason to order the return of the child are, for the most part, distinguishable by the mother's tardy or halfhearted interest in regaining custody. This distinction is in the nature of finding a constructive abandonment and does not vitiate the vitality of the Natural Right Doctrine as decisional law in New York.[36]

Not long after the Baby Lenore case, the decisional law in favor of the rights of natural parents was once again reaffirmed by the Court of Appeals in *Spence Chapin Adoption Service* v. *Polk*.[37] In *Polk,* the natural parent had surrendered the child to the agency to be placed for foster care.[38] The child was never placed for adoption. There was no attempt to prove nor was there any proof that the natural parent was unfit.[39] Moreover, the agency and the New York City Department of Social Services consented to a return to the mother's custody, thus nullifying the surrender.[40]

> These salient circumstances distinguish this case from others in which a child has been surrendered and the surrendering parent has sought judicial assistance in undoing the surrender [citing case], or where prospective adoptive parents have had custody looking to adoption and have sought to retain the child against the wishes of a mother who has changed her mind [citing case].[41]

The Court of Appeals in *Polk* is, if anything, more emphatic and precise in its support of natural rights of biological parents than in its earlier decisions.

> Thus, the issue is not . . . whether one choice of custody or another is better for the child, or, put another way, whether [the adoptive parents] would raise the child better than would the unwed mother, or which cultural or family background would be best for the child. Least of all is the issue that of comparing the quality and depth of love and affection between the child and those who would compete for its custody. Nor is the issue whether natural parents or adoptive parents make ''better'' parents, whatever that may mean. The power of the State, let alone its courts, is much narrower. Child and parent are entitled to be together unless *compelling reason stemming from dire circumstances or gross misconduct forbid it in the paramount interest of the child,* or there is abandonment or surrender by the parent [emphasis added]. The Family Court misconceived the nature of the proceedings and considered itself free to determine conscientiously in whose custody the child would fare best, the foster care custodians, the natural mother, or some future adoptive couple. . . .

> The Appellate Division correctly determined that the court was without power, absent abandonment of the child, statutory surrender outstanding

or the established unfitness of the mother, to deprive the mother of custody. Since none of these factors was present the natural mother was entitled to obtain the custody of her child, and the child was entitled to be returned to its mother.[42]

The plain, direct language in *Polk* makes it apparent that the publicity generated by the Baby Lenore case[43] and the generally sympathetic treatment that the foster parents received in the media had little effect on the decisional law in New York. At least up until the time of the decision in *Polk,* the law in New York did not recognize a simple test of "in whose custody the child would fare best" or, in other words, the best-interests-of-the-child test in any contest between parent and nonparent.

## The Natural Right Doctrine under Attack

*Legislative Reaction*

The publicity generated by Baby Lenore, although it had no effect on the Court of Appeals, had a considerable effect on the New York legislature. The public controversy resulting from the decision was at least partly responsible for the following amendment to the New York Social Services Law, passed with an effective date of May 30, 1972:

> In an action or proceeding to determine the custody of a child surrendered for adoption and placed in an adoptive home or to revoke or annul a surrender instrument in the case of a child placed in an adoptive home, the parent or parents who surrendered such child shall have no right to the custody of such child superior to that of the adoptive parents, notwithstanding that the parent or parents who surrendered the child are fit, competent and able to duly maintain, support and educate the child. The custody of such child shall be awarded solely on the basis of the best interests of the child, and there shall be no presumption that such interests will be promoted by any particular custodial disposition.[44]

The extent to which this statute changed the decisional law should not be overestimated. First, it deals only with cases specifically involving children surrendered for adoption or placed in an adoptive home. Not every custody dispute between parents and third parties involves a formal, or even informal, surrender for adoption or a placement with the prospect of adoption. Second, even though "presumption" in favor of the natural parent is specifically forbidden for the purpose of this statute, it remains to be seen to what extent courts will be influenced by prior decisional law in finding that the child's best interests are in fact synonymous with custody in a natural parent who is fit.

A tendency to blend the language of the Best Interests Doctrine with the Natural Right doctrine may be seen in some of the language used in *Scarpetta* (Baby Lenore).[45] A look at later cases in chapter 6, Visitation, *infra,* will indicate the extent to which this line of reasoning has been followed.


*Decisional Reaction*

The first direct decisional attack on the Natural Rights Doctrine was a miscellaneous decision that appeared in 1973, *In the Matter of Catherine S.*[46] The natural parents of Catherine and her sister Darlene were both former drug addicts.[47] They petitioned the court for the return of Darlene, having already obtained de facto custody of Catherine.[48] Darlene had been placed, unofficially, with an aunt who had been her foster parent for 18 months; the child was 3 years old at the time of the decision.[49]

The court heard testimony from its psychiatrist that the natural mother "has little emotional response to offer a child," and "she cannot benefit her daughter" and that the natural father was "in need of therapy" and "not adequate to give emotional support."[50] The family court judge, who decided against the natural parents, stated the question as follows: "Are the parents entitled to the immediate return of the child because they are the natural parents regardless of the effect of such return upon the child?"[51]

The judge conceded that prior Court of Appeals decisions[52] "reaffirmed that the primacy of parental rights may not be ignored and that a dispute between a parent and non-parent may not be resolved simply by determining which party can provide or afford better surroundings in order to raise the child," but "this does not mean the child's interests are subordinated. . . ."[53]

The court continued

> If we are not to completely subordinate the child's rights and interests, we must also consider his emotional well-being and the effect of an immediate or even eventual return to the natural parents.[54]

The decision in *Catherine S.* ultimately awarded custody to the foster parents because "the court is unwilling to risk the welfare of the child by granting a change in custody without first establishing that the child will not be emotionally damaged thereby."[55] The decision, while conceding that, "New York has been more oriented toward the principle of parental right,"[56] apparently rejected that principle and substituted instead the principle that a custody award should be based on which contestant can provide the superior emotional climate. This determination is apparently to be made on the basis of expert opinion as to what is best for the child with reference to the theories and practices of the behavioral sciences.

The position taken by the court in *Catherine S.* may well have been, even then, "clearly in accord with the philosophy and social interest predominant in the Twentieth Century."[57] But it was clearly *not* in accord with the decisional law in New York at the time it was rendered, according to the Court of Appeals.[58] Still, this was the first open rebellion from the lower courts, and for that reason, its importance as a landmark case in the train of events that led to a modification of the "natural right" doctrine cannot be understated.[59]

In *Matter of Confessora B.,* custody of the subject child was awarded to the "psychological parent," in accord with the reasoning laid down in *Catherine S.* and as against the natural parent.[60] The biological parent was neither claimed to be, nor proved to be, unfit. In *Confessora B.,* the subject child had been shuttled back and forth between his foster parents and his natural mother (who were cousins) on numerous occasions.[61] Between the time that the child was 3 years of age and the date of the family court's decision in 1973, he had lived with his natural mother for a continuous period of only 2 years (1967–1969).[62] The court found neither unfitness nor abandonment on the part of the natural mother, but, in echoing *Catherine S.,* it held as follows:

A child is not a piece of furniture which can be put in storage for an indefinite period of time, and reclaimed at the owner's convenience. A child is affected by, and reacts, physically, morally and psychologically, to his environment and the persons who surround him. These are the factors that mold him, teach him, and in general affect the total being of the child.[63]

The court, in *Confessora B.,* unequivocally concurred with *Catherine S.* and held the "best interests" of the child to be "paramount" over the rights of the natural mother, which were relegated to the status of "the highest significance."[64]

*Confessora B., subnom Benitez* v. *Llano* was affirmed by the appellate division without opinion.[65] A strong dissent, however, was registered by a dissenting justice, who held as follows, citing *Spence Chapin* v. *Polk* and *People ex rel. Kropp* v. *Shepsky:*[66]

It is well-established that in a contest between a parent and non-parent for the custody of a child, the natural parent has a paramount right to raise the child and may not be deprived of that right absent a showing of unfitness or abandonment [citing cases]. It was an abuse of discretion for the Family Court to award custody to respondents because of the length of time the child lived with respondents, his age and his expressed desires to remain with them. The child's natural mother was not unfit to care for him and had not abandoned him.[67]

At this stage in the development of the law, the struggle between the two opposing doctrines ascended to the level of high drama.

## The Waning of the Natural Right Doctrine

In *Matter of Bennett* v. *Jeffreys,* the New York Court of Appeals significantly modified the principles in the line of cases discussed in this chapter.[68] In *Bennett,* a 15-year-old girl had given birth out of wedlock to a baby girl. In the court's statement of facts, the young mother, "[u]nder pressure from her [own] mother . . . reluctantly acquiesced in the transfer of the newborn infant to an older woman, Mrs. Jeffreys, a former classmate of the [infant's] grandmother."[69]

Eight years later, the natural mother, on the verge of college graduation, sought to regain custody of her child.[70] In this endeavor, she was supported by her own parents, who, in a reversal of their previous attitude, offered their own home and resources for the benefit of the infant's care.[71] No formal adoption had ever been sought nor granted in Mrs. Jeffrey's favor, nor had there ever been any formal statutory surrender or placement of the child involving an authorized agency.[72]

The trial court ruled that "although the mother had not surrendered or abandoned the child and was not unfit, the child should remain with the present custodian. . . ."[73] The appellate division reversed the trial court, and was, in turn reversed by the Court of Appeals.[74]

The Court of Appeals clearly sought to eliminate all possible distinguishing circumstances from its decision and deal strictly with the common-law principles for the determination of child custody as enunciated in its previous decision, discussed *supra.*

> At the outset, it is emphasized that not involved is an attempted revocation of a voluntary surrender to an agency or private individual for adoption [citations omitted]. Nor is abandonment involved [citation omitted]. Nor does the proceeding involve an attempted permanent termination of custody [citations omitted]. Nor is there involved the temporary placement into foster care by an authorized agency . . . [citations omitted]. Instead, this proceeding was brought by an unwed mother to obtain custody of her daughter from a custodian to whom the child had been voluntarily, although not formally, entrusted by the mother's parents, when the mother was only 15 years old. Thus, as an unsupervised private placement no statute is directly applicable, and the analysis must proceed from common-law principles.[75]

The court went on to pay lip service to the general principle that "[t]he parent has a "right" to rear its child and the child has a "right" to be reared by its parent.''[76] The court's fervor for this principle, once so explicit and consistent,[77] was not, however, significantly qualified and excepted. The court introduced the "extraordinary circumstances" test to supplant the "unfitness" test.[78] Thus the court brought the law, as expressed in *Bennett,* one step beyond the "compelling reason stemming from dire circumstances" criterion, as enunciated in *Spence Chapin* v. *Polk.*[79] Yet the court does not go so far as to unequivocally adopt the best-interests test.

> But neither decisional rule nor statute can displace a fit parent because someone else could do a "better job" of raising the child in the view of the court (or the Legislature), so long as the parent or parents have not forfeited their "rights" by surrender, abandonment, unfitness, persisting neglect or other extraordinary circumstances. These "rights" are not so much rights, but responsibilities which reflect the view, noted earlier, that, except when disqualified or displaced by extraordinary circumstances, parents are generally best qualified to care for their own children and therefore entitled to do so (*Matter of Spence Chapin Adoption Service* v. *Polk,* 29 N.Y. 196, 204, *supra*).[80]

The extraordinary-circumstances test, however, was specifically distinguished from the best-interests test in *Bennett.*[81] The test is deemed by the court to "trigger" the "best interests of the child" test and does not mean that "parental rights or responsibilities may be relegated to a party with all the other surrounding circumstances in the analysis of what is best for the child."[82]

Most importantly, the court made the following significant distinction in announcing the extraordinary-circumstances trigger test: "The child's 'best interest' is not controlled by whether the natural parent or the nonparent would make a 'better' parent. . . ."[83]

The rule, post-*Bennett,* was encapsulated by the court as follows:

> To recapitulate: intervention by the State in the right and responsibility of a natural parent to custody of his or her child is warranted if there is first a judicial finding of surrender, abandonment, unfitness, persistent neglect, unfortunate or involuntary extended disruption of custody, or other equivalent but rare extraordinary circumstances which would drastically affect the welfare of the child. It is only on such a premise that the court may then proceed to inquire into the best interests of the child and to order a custodial disposition on that ground.[84]

Inevitably, the decision in *Bennett* v. *Jeffreys* was, and will continue to be, hailed as the decision that brought New York into the best-interests column with those jurisdictions more aggressively committed to that particular point of view.[85]

This would, in our opinion, be reading more into the decision than was intended, although it is plain that the Natural Right Theory was significantly and undisputedly modified. Certainly, *Bennett* has sufficient best-interest catch phrases in it to lend credence to any potential misinterpretation of its intent. "The day is long past in this State . . . when the right of a parent to the custody of his or her child . . . would be enforced inexorably . . . on the theory solely of an absolute legal right."[86] Reference is made to "the modern principle that a child is a person, and not a subperson over whom the parent has an absolute possessory interest."[87]

The Court of Appeals, in a subsequent memorandum decision, was careful not to overstate its own modification in *Bennett* v. *Jeffreys*. In reversing the decision of the appellate division in *Gomez* v. *Lozado*,[88] the Court of Appeals admonished the appellate division as follows: "The appellate court seems to have accorded a parental primacy, which, as developed in the *Bennett* case . . . is not as absolute as argued by the father."[89]

The language in *Bennett* was also delicately and judiciously interpreted and applied in *Raysor* v. *Gabbey,* among the later cases applying its principles.[90] In *Tyrrell* v. *Tyrrell,* the appellate division, in restoring custody of an infant to the natural mother and thus ruling against an adversary stepmother (subsequent to the father's death) distinguished the case so as to delineate what were not "extraordinary circumstances."[91] "In all cases wherein extraordinary circumstances have been found to exist, there has been clear evidence of unfitness or proof of an intention to surrender all parental responsibilities or of a lack of interest in the child combined with acquiescence in custody by a nonparent."[92] In *Matter of Patricia A.W.,* the trial court gave in to the overwhelming temptation to perceive in *Bennett* the adoption of the "best parent as best interests rule," which the Court of Appeals had specifically sought to avoid.[93] *Bennett* v. *Jeffreys* and *Gomez* v. *Lozado*[94] were cited as the long-awaited recognition of the "best interests" criteria and the psychological parent school of thought, as the overwhelming and, perhaps, in practical application, the only factor in deciding any case in which the future of a child is at stake.[95] The court further commented on *Bennett* as the final recognition of the point of view first expressed in *Matter of Catherine S.,*[96] complete with a memorial footnote to the foresight of the judge who wrote that decision.[97]

In *Matter of Sanjavini K.,*[98] the Court of Appeals recorded the following language, in returning a child to its natural mother, from which, if the most sensational inference is drawn, the *Bennett* v. *Jeffreys* decision must be perceived as overruled:[99] "[I]t is fundamental to our legal and social system, that it is in the best interest of a child to be raised by his parents unless the parents are unfit . . ."[100]

There is no indication, however, that the Court of Appeals sought to do more than distinguish the facts in *Sanjavini K.* from those in *Bennett,* and leave in effect the current rule, as recorded in *Bennett,* will all the equivocations originally included. *Tyrell* v. *Tyrell,* [101] decided at the same time as *Sanjavini K.,* cited *Bennett* v. *Jeffreys* as current authority while also distinguishing the case on its facts. [102]

Whatever else *Bennett* v. *Jeffreys* may have done—and it has done much to modify the Natural Right Doctrine—a careful reading of it ought to establish that it has not adopted the Best Interests Theory categorically nor has it ratified the point of view advocated in *Matter of Catherine S.* [103] or *Matter of Confessora B.* [104]

That wholehearted belief in the ability of judges and behaviorists to settle the best interests of a child between themselves by deciding who is the best parent or who provides the best environment is not yet the law in the jurisdiction of New York. Where that view has been adopted, the fervor with which it *is* expressed is usually unequivocal.

**Other Jurisdictions**

The state of the law in New York, as demonstrated in the foregoing sections, has evolved from a relatively clear rule in favor of the Natural Right Doctrine into a modified version that may or may not signal its complete abandonment.

The law in most other jurisdictions is in no less of a state of flux. It is no news to anyone—lawyer or layman—with a realistic point of view that courts will be influenced by trends in social views. Their decisions will evolve accordingly.

The only generalization that can be made is that it is not possible to stereotype or predict a particular jurisdiction's position on best interests or natural right by looking at its socioeconomic profile. The courts of populous, industrial, "progressive" New York were wedded to the allegedly archaic view embodied in the Natural Right Doctrine, while rural, conservative, Middle-American Iowa, had gone further than any other jurisdiction in the literal application of the Best Interests Criterion.

Generally, the Natural Right Doctrine is on the defensive. Yet courts, while pushing natural right into the background, hesitate to administer the coup de grace.

*Arizona*

In an intermediate appellate decision in 1972, the Arizona Court of Appeals made a plain and distinct pronouncement in favor of the Natural Right Doctrine in *LeRoy* v. *Odgers.* [105] In analyzing the legislative policy on the subject, up to that time, the court commented thus:

Our legislature has expressed itself with respect to child custody. In the chapter on divorce, the court is directed to order that which is "most expedient under all circumstances for . . . present comfort and future well-being" of the minor child [citation omitted]. This legislative pronouncement is known as the "best interest of the child" standard. On the other hand, in the chapter on guardianship, the legislature has declared that either parent, not otherwise unsuitable, shall be entitled to the guardianship of a minor in preference to others [citation omitted].[106]

Yet the court concludes that is it the Natural Right Doctrine that, in fact, prevails. "Reading these statutes together, they create at the very least, a rebuttable presumption that a fit parent is to be preferred over nonparents with respect to child custody."[107]

The court goes further in pronouncing all the key natural-right phrases.

Nothing to the contrary appearing, the law presumes parental fitness [citation omitted]. Unless there is a finding of parental unfitness, a parent is entitled to custody as against a grandparent [citations omitted]. In the absence of evidence to the contrary, there is a presumption that a child's welfare will best be served by giving custody to a parent, and parental rights should never be denied except for the most cogent reasons and unless parental unfitness is clearly established by the evidence.[108]

In *LeRoy,* the trial court granted custody to the maternal grandmother and removed the children from their mother's custody on evidence presented that they were not attending public school.[109] Instead, they were being instructed at home on a daily basis by a tutor.[110] "Whether this mode of education had been approved by the appropriate school authorities pursuant to [statute] so as to excuse the children's attendance in public schools as mandated by [statute], was not inquired into, nor was any evidence relative thereto presented. Furthermore, there was no evidence that his home instruction was detrimental to the children's best interests."[111]

The court concluded that, on the record, there was no finding of parental unfitness, and, hence, the trial court's decision could be upheld under prevailing criteria.

In fact, it would appear that the primary reason for the custodial order was a conclusion that a public school education was preferable. . . . We [have] indicated that courts should not interfere with parental custody merely because a child's "lifestyle" does not comport with the standards of others, in absence of a showing of serious adverse effects upon the child. In the case at bench, there was no showing whatsoever that the home education program was detrimental to the children—in fact the contrary appears.[112]

*Gowland* v. *Martin,* decided in 1974 by an intermediate Arizona appellate court, affirmed Arizona's continued adherence to the Natural Right

Doctrine in finding against the natural father as unfit.[113] Thus the rule was affirmed by the application of its most important exception.

The natural parents of the infant, Troy Gowland, were both 14 years old when they married.[114] Their baby was born soon after the ceremony, and the couple lived together for the next 2 years, at all times dependent on both sets of grandparents for support and aid in rearing their infant.[115]

After the couple parted, the maternal grandparents, Mr. and Mrs. Martin, assumed full responsibility for the care of the infant, while their daughter traveled to and from California with a new male companion.[116] The father continued to live with his own parents throughout this period.[117] He subsequently graduated from high school, obtained a job, filed for divorce, and sought to regain the custody of his infant child from his former in-laws.[118]

The trial court granted custody to the maternal grandparents and was thereafter affirmed by the appellate court.[119] "While early decisions in this jurisdiction have spoken of the right of the natural parent to have custody of his own children as against anyone else [citations omitted], our Supreme Court has made it clear that the parental right to custody can and should be ignored if the best interests of the child demand otherwise [citations omitted]."[120]

The best-interests language in the just-quoted paragraph is misleading. The award was clearly made on the facts of the case that showed the father to be unfit and "[in]capable of assuming complete responsibility at this time due to his lack of experience in the father role and his need to finish preparing his own life."[121]

The court's grounding of its decision on the father's unfitness and, hence, its affirmation of the Natural Right Doctrine is clarified in its holding that "[w]hatever the validity of the parental right doctrine, the authorities are unanimous that it has no application when the parent is proven to be unfit."[122]

The language in *Gowland* referring to the child's "best interests"[123] provides sufficient raw material for a subsequent decision enlarging the best-interest language and conveniently ignoring the fact that the decision affirmed the Natural Right Doctrine. This appears to be the bottom line of the decision in *In re Arias,* also decided in 1974.[124]

In *Arias,* the natural father of two infants who were born out of wedlock sought to regain custody from a maternal aunt who had received letters of guardianship following the death of the natural mother.[125] The court in *Arias* expresses the general rule in the following terms, citing *Gowland* v. *Martin* as authority.[126]

It has long been the law of this State that a natural parent is entitled to custody as against anyone else, in the absence of a showing of unfitness. This ruling is subject to the provision that parental right to custody can and should be ignored if the best interests of the child demand otherwise.[127]

What the court *did* ignore, in this particular passage is that *Gowland* v. *Martin* did not modify the Natural Right Doctrine as the paragraph implies. Moreover, the facts in *Arias* furnish sufficient substance for a ruling against the father based on his unfitness.[128] Among the reasons cited by the court for its affirmation of the trial-court decision are facts that amount to a constructive abandonment of the children by the father, compounded by an unstable home environment that would be inimical to the children's best interests.[129] The decision could clearly have been made on the basis of the unfitness under the Natural Right Doctrine without resorting to the Best Interests Rule. The fact that the court in *Arias* chose to go further may be a herald of coming modification. The Natural Right Doctrine is generally under attack on many fronts, but it is not yet defeated.

## Iowa: Bastion of Best Interests

If there is a stereotypical image of the state of Iowa, in the general sense, it is no doubt one that is middle-west, middle-class, middle-American, rural and conservative. Perhaps this image is true, perhaps not, but, if one is wedded to it, then it may come as some source of surprise that the Natural Right Doctrine, the traditionalist view, has met its most resounding defeat in the courts of Iowa.

Iowa decisions on child-custody cases represent what is perhaps the most unequivocal rejection of blood ties and the most unabashed adoption of a subjective moral standard as criteria for an award. In *Painter* v. *Bannister,*[130] the court awarded custody to the maternal grandparents in recognition of their approved middle-western, middle-class life-style. The natural father, although acknowledged to be "fit," was rejected as custodian because of his "arty" life-style as a northern California free-lance photographer.

While conceding the natural father's fitness on all counts and the fitness and concerned attitude of the father's current wife, the court nevertheless awarded custody to the grandparents.[131]

> The [grandparents'] home provides [the child] with a stable, dependable conventional middle-class, middle-west background and an opportunity for a college education and profession, if he desires it. It provides a solid foundation and secure atmosphere. In the [father's] home, [the child] would have more freedom of conduct and thought with an opportunity to develop his individual talents. It would be more exciting and challenging in many respects, but romantic, impractical and unstable.[132]

All of the factors enumerated by the court in reaching its decision as to the child's best interests indicate a concern for matters of life-style, wherein there is no attempt to hide the prejudices of the culturally dominant forces.

Our conclusion as to the type of home [the father] would offer is based upon his Bohemian approach to finances and life in general. . . . [The father] is either an agnostic or athiest, and has no concern for formal religious training. He has read a lot of Zen Buddhism and "has been very much influenced by it." [His present wife] is a Roman Catholic. They plan to send [the child] to a Congregational Church, near the Catholic Church, on an irregular schedule. . . .

He is a political liberal and got into difficulty in a job at the University of Washington for his support of the activities of the American Civil Liberties Union in the university news bulletin. . . .

There were "two funerals" for his [late] wife. One in the basement of his home in which he alone was present. He conducted the service and wrote her a long letter. The second at a church in Pullman was for the gratification of her friends. He attended in a sport shirt and sweater.[133]

If formality of dress at funerals is a relevant factor to consider, then it will come as no shock that the court went on the compare the exterior paint jobs on the respective homes of the adversaries. Its conclusion was, not surprisingly, in favor of the grandparents.[134] The decision in *Painter* v. *Bannister* is remarkable in its forthright, totally unembarrassed equation of the best interests of children with their maintenance in a culturally conforming environment. The decision does not require a great deal of explanation and analysis. It explains itself with little difficulty or hesitation, and this, to some extent, is what makes it unique. The language of the decision leaves small room for subsequent evolutionary modification. The Best Interests Doctrine, due to this decision, is as well established in the state of Iowa as its proponents could hope it to be.

*Painter* v. *Bannister* has to date not been overruled nor seriously criticized by an Iowa court. Subsequent decisions reinforced the principles laid down in *Painter* with the same straightforward, unequivocal partisanship. In *Halstead* v. *Halstead*,[135] the Iowa Supreme Court describes the law of child custody in terms of "our relatively broad best interest of the child principle."[136] *Halstead* goes further to the point of citing, with approval, the model custody act adopted by the Family Law Section of The American Bar Association in 1963.[137] The model statute provides that "Custody may be awarded to persons other than the father or mother whenever such award serves the best interests of the child. Any person who has had de facto custody of the child in a stable and wholesome home and is a fit and proper person shall *prima facie* be entitled to an award of custody."[138] Although the court obviously cannot adopt legislation, it uses the model statute as a concise expression of its decisional policy.

The court in *Halstead* appears to go so far as to weigh the relative material advantages offered by each of the competing custodians in the process of making its decision.[139] This approach has been rejected by other vigorous proponents of the Best Interests Doctrine, although comparative evaluation of "cultural" advantages is a basic and approved principle of the Best Interests Doctrine.[140]

If there can be any doubt as to the court's total commitment to best interests at the time of the decision, that doubt is dispelled by the dissenting opinion of Justice Becker. In stating the majority rule as a prelude to his critique, Justice Becker conceded the law to be "that the first and governing consideration must be the best interest of the child. . . . Further, it is not necessary that a parent be found unfit to care for the child in order that custody be awarded to another. This rule is not announced in either *Painter* v. *Bannister* . . . or in this case, but it is implicit in the results of both."[141]

In *Garvin* v. *Garvin* the court apparently was so committed to the Best Interests Doctrine as to find it unnecessary to continue to cite authority.[142] What makes the *Garvin* case most significant, however, is the formal recognition given by the court to the influence of the behavioral sciences.

> In keeping pace with apparent advances by the behavioral sciences concerning benefits to children of a wholesome, loving and secure home life, free from the trauma of needless transplantation, a majority of the courts hold there should be no automatic determination in favor of a parent. . . . and it has been said the "natural right" concept restricts thoughtful inquiry into latent problems of child development and should not be permitted to control, especially when the non-parent has occupied a *loco parentis* position for such a time as to become the true parent by association.[143]

A dissenting opinion in *Garvin* criticized the majority's commitment to the principles of *Painter* and *Halstead* as being, in its own way, as inflexible and undesirable as the Parental Rights Doctrine.[144] But this view was not a harbinger of change in the majority opinion. The policy of *Painter, Halstead,* and *Garvin* was reaffirmed 3 years later in *Hulbert* v. *Hines.*[145]

The commitment to best interests does not, invariably, mean that a natural parent will never prevail. Indeed, in *Hulbert* v. *Hines* and many subsequent cases, the Iowa courts awarded natural parents de novo custody or returned custody to them. But the principle of best interests had to be satisfied as a prerequisite to such an award. The Iowa decisions, in fact, pay lip service to the "rebuttable presumption" that a child is better off with a natural parent.[146] But it is made clear time and again, at least as late as 1970, that this presumption is rebutted by a showing that the child's best interests preclude parental custody. A showing of parental unfitness is not necessary to rebut the presumption.[147]

Later cases drift in the opposite direction slightly but never repudiate the principles of *Painter* and *Halstead*. In *Doan Thi Hoang Anh* v. *Nelson,*[148] the court affirmed the principle established in *Halstead* v. *Halstead*[149] that when a nonparent with lawful custody of a child has provided for the child's needs for a substantial period of time, and when the child is attached to the status quo, "a court is not justified in transferring that custody to another except for the most cogent reasons."[150]

Despite this general rule, the child was restored to the custody of the natural mother because "[t]here is no showing of parental unfitness to overcome the presumption in her favor."[151] These are certainly surprising words for a jurisdiction that has totally repudiated the Natural Right Doctrine.

A more impressive indication of coming change in Iowa doctrine can be found in a 1977 decision, *Matter of Burney.* [152] In what appears to be a modification of the most extreme application of best interests, the court, at least, goes on record in eschewing material and cultural advantages as factors in determination.[153] The comparison of relative *emotional* advantages, however, is not repudiated, and there is no showing that the more solid standard of unfitness will replace best interests as the grounds on which the natural parent preference can be rebutted.[154]

Interestingly, the *Burney* decision cites the New York case of *Bennett* v. *Jeffreys* with approval.[155] This may be the most meaningful herald of all, showing that modification of Iowa's extreme Best Interests Doctrine is incubating in judicial minds. *Bennett* was the case that clearly modified New York decisional law in moving it away from complete commitment to the Natural Right Doctrine.[156] *Bennett* is a careful blend of language rejecting natural right as a guiding principle, without going so far as to fully embrace best interests.[157] Instead, both doctrines become dissolved in the extraordinary-circumstances test, which allows for a less doctrinaire approach in subsequent decisions. The citation of *Bennett* in a later Iowa case coupled with the absence of the rhetoric characteristic of the pre-1970 decisions[158] may signal a desire by the Iowa courts to be less stridently united to the Best Interests Doctrine.

## California: A New Life for Natural Rights

An analysis of California law over a period from approximately 1950–1980 will demonstrate that the law of the jurisdiction has gone full circle from natural right to best interests and back again to natural right.

In 1953, at approximately the same time in which the leading Natural Right Decisions were written by the New York Court of Appeals,[159] the California Supreme Court was lining up on the same side of the issue. The decision in *Guardianship of Smith,* decided in 1953, concerned a brother and sister, 8 and 6 years old respectively, born out of wedlock and residing with an adult sister, subsequent to their mother's death.[160] The adult sister's petition for guardianship was opposed by the natural father of the minor children, who sought to take them into his current household and legitimate them, all with his wife's consent.[161]

In holding for the father, in a short majority opinion, the court expressed itself in the familiar rhetoric of the Natural Right Doctrine.

> It is settled in this state that in either guardianship proceedings or custody proceedings in a divorce action, the parents of a legitimate child have preference over a non-parent and the custody shall not be given to a non-parent unless the parent is found unfit. "Where a parent applying for custody is in a position to take the child and is not shown to be unfit, the court may not award custody to strangers merely because it feels that they may be more fit or that they may be more able to provide financial, educational, social or other benefits [citations omitted].[162]

In a trenchant concurring opinion prophetic in its delineation of such controversial issues, Justice Traynor suggested that the seemingly disruptive return of a child to its natural parents may not be the unmitigated disservice to the infant that some would believe.[163]

> [E]ven if the child is required to make some sacrifice to be with his natural parent or adjust to a new environment, it does not necessarily follow that his welfare will be correspondingly impaired. It may not be to the best interest of the child to have every advantage. He may derive benefits by subordinating his immediate interests to the development of a new family relationship with his own parents by giving as well as receiving. Thus, although a change in custody from an outsider to a parent may involve the disruption of a satisfactory status quo, it may lead to a more desirable relationship in the long run.[165]

The dissenting opinion of Justice Schauer is an expression of the Best Interests Doctrine and illustrative of its ascendent, and ultimately prevalent, influence.

> This case appears to me to again illustrate the poignant undesirability, which I pointed out in my [previous] dissents. . . . [citations omitted], of requiring the trial court to find a parent to be "unfit" before it can confide the custody of a child to another person, even when the child's best interests are found to be with others.[166]

Ten years after *Smith,* the Natural Right Doctrine, with all the typical rhetoric, remained undiluted in the intermediate appellate decision in *Stauffacher* v. *Stauffacher.*[167] Therein, the appellate court reversed the trial court's award of custody to foster parents, based on an absence of proof of parental unfitness. "[T]he natural right of a parent to the care of a minor child, if a fit and proper person shall prevail as against an entire stranger, the law presuming, in the absence of either evidence or findings showing the contrary, that either parent is a proper person to whom the minor's care should be awarded. . . . [citations omitted]."[168]

In *In Re Barassi,* another intermediate appellate decision, decided in 1968,[169] the court again dealt with three infants of a stormy marriage who were shuttled from foster home to maternal grandparents and back again following their mother's death. The children finally arrived on the doorstep of their maternal great-uncle.[170] The court found nothing in the record that disqualified the natural father from custody by reason of his unfitness or abandonment.[171] The trial court award to the great-uncle was reversed, and custody was granted to the natural father. The opinion rings with the litany of the same familiar rhetoric of the early natural-right decisions in both New York and California. A parent must be found to be "affirmatively unfit" before custody will be awarded to a third party.[172]

> One of the natural rights incident to parenthood, a right supported by law and sound public policy, is the right to the care and custody of a minor child, and can only be forfeited by a parent upon proof that the parent is unfit to have care and custody [citations omitted].[173]

An early indication of change in California law can be found in the language, if not the holding, in the decision in *Eugene W.*[174] The natural mother in *Eugene W.* was found, on competent evidence, to be mentally ill, such as to be unfit to care for her minor children.[175] The judgment of the trial court, freeing the children from parental custody and control, on the petition of an appropriate public-welfare authority, was affirmed.[176] This result is certainly consistent with California case law up to this point, inasmuch as mental disability is clearly within the unfitness exception to the Natural Right Doctrine. Therefore it must be viewed with some significance that the court's opinion should go out of its way to include rhetoric from the Best Interests Doctrine and thus signal a change in attitude and sentiment.

In an intermediate appellate decision, *In re Guardianship of Marino,*[177] a California court adopted, in the most unequivocal language up to that time, the principles of the Best Interest Doctrine as exemplified by the leading Iowa cases.[178] Donald Marino was 2 weeks old when his mother died, and he was placed by his father in the care of his maternal aunt and her husband.[179] The father, faced with the responsibility of caring for seven older children without help, took this step in what he considered to be the best interests of all concerned.[180] When Donald was about 6, his father, now remarried and established in a respectable home with his older children, initiated steps to regain Donald's custody.[181] A transitional program was arranged whereby the child would spend certain periods in the home of the natural father, with the prospect of his eventual return to his father's care.[182] The child reacted very negatively to the transition; his behavior was characterized by emotional upset, manifested by physical symptoms.[183]

Evidence of the child's attitude and the physical symptoms demonstrated in his reaction would be a sufficient basis for maintaining the child in his aunt's custody under the extraordinary-circumstances test, which was adopted in New York under *Bennett* v. *Jeffreys.* [184] This is to say that the same result might have been reached in adopting more tempered language and more moderate doctrinal ground. But the court chose to reach its result by the best-interests route. The court bases its decision on its interpretation of a statute that first became operative on January 1, 1970, subsequent to the decisions in *Smith,* [185] *Stauffacher,* [186] and *Barassi.* [187]

The statute, Section 4600 of the California Civil Code, provides in relevant part, that custody may be awarded to a nonparent over the objection of a parent if a court shall "make a finding that an award of custody to a parent would be detrimental to the child and the award to a nonparent is required to serve the best interests of the child."[188]

The *Marino* court interpreted this clause as statutory authority for the elimination of the requirement that a determination of parental unfitness must be made prior to a custody award in favor of a nonparent.[189] This interpretation will prove to be incorrect, as demonstrated herein, *infra.* [190] But the *Marino* court's erroneous reading of the statute is illustrative of the bandwagon best-interests psychology that characterized the period in which the opinion was written.

In the decision in *In re B.G.,* [191] the fever found its most unabashed outlet, representing the peak of best-interests dominance in California case law. In that intermediate appellate decision, the court upheld a trial court disposition in favor of the foster parents, adopted the *Marino* view of Section 4600,[192] and threw in the characteristic rhetoric to leave no doubts as to its intentions.

> California, by enacting [Section 4600] has now joined those majority jurisdictions placing greater emphasis on the "best interests" of the child than on the rights of a biological parent. . . . The new law would seem to emphasize the propriety of a policy placing a child with third persons where such child has become established in a wholesome and stable environment, and where parental custody would be detrimental, even though the parent or parents were not unfit by [pre-4600] standards of fitness.[193]

The court, in affirming the trial court's award to the foster parents, refused to "upset a stable and satisfactory situation for one which is uncertain and could be severely damaging psychologically."[194] Thus best interests would appear to have gained ascendency in California in the wake of the decision in *B.G.* Many observers came to that conclusion soon after its publication. But the Best Interests Doctrine would not survive the stunning overruling of *B.G.* by the Supreme Court of California.[195]

The Supreme Court dealt with the erroneous interpretation of Section

4600 by the lower *B.G.* court and thus not only reversed the lower court's decision, but the entire trend that had been building in favor of the Best Interests Doctrine.[196] Placing the issues between the Best Interests Doctrine and the Natural Right Doctrine in sharper focus, the Supreme Court in *B.G.* went so far as to express the need to "avoid a *Painter* v. *Bannister* situation in California."[197]

Cases subsequent to *In re B.G.* even throw in some of the pre-*Marino* catch phrases: "Parenting is a fundamental right, and accordingly, is disturbed only in the extreme case of a person acting in a fashion incompatible with parenthood. . . . Thus the involuntary termination of that relationship . . . must be viewed as a drastic remedy."[198]

In *Carmelita B.,* the Supreme Court clearly reaffirmed its decision in *B.G.,* in making specific reference to it as emphasizing "the gravity of this [parental] right, [and] holding that the doctrine preferring parental custody was not affected by the enactment of Section 4600. . . ."[199]

The evolution of the law of child custody in California, with specific reference to those adversary situations involving parent and nonparent, has been nothing less than dramatic. It is inconceivable that the Court of Appeals in *B.G.* would have so forthrightly adopted the best-interests test if it had anticipated its clear and unceremonious reversal by the Supreme Court. The Court of Appeals Judge who wrote in *In re B.G.* that "California . . . has now joined those majority jurisdictions placing greater emphasis on . . . 'best interests' "[200] no doubt had much occasion for reflection on his capacity to discern judicial trends.

The California experience is a cogent warning to those who are overanxious to bury the Natural Right Doctrine, and it is a clear vindication of the carefully worded, delicately balanced language in the New York decision in *Bennett* v. *Jeffreys.*[201]

## Notes

1. *Portnoy* v. *Strasser,* 303 N.Y. 539, 104 N.E.2d 859 (1952).
2. *Id.,* at 542–543.
3. See note 1, *supra.*
4. *Portnoy* v. *Strasser,* 303 N.Y., at 540.
5. *Id.*
6. *Id.,* at 541.
7. *Id.,* at 543–544.
8. *Id.,* at 545.
9. *Id.,* at 541.
10. *Id.,* at 544.
11. See chapters 2, Custody Disputes between Natural Parents, *supra,*

and 3, Current Standards for Determination of Custody Disputes between Parents, *supra.*

12. *Portnoy* v. *Strasser,* 303 N.Y., at 542.

13. *Meyer* v. *Nebraska,* 262 U.S. 390, 399 (1923), as cited in *Portnoy* v. *Strasser,* 303 N.Y., at 542.

14. *Meyer* v. *Nebraska,* 262 U.S., at 399.

15. *Portnoy* v. *Strasser,* 303 N.Y., at 542.

16. See The Waning of the Natural-Right Doctrine, *supra.*

17. *Kropp* v. *Shepsky,* 305 N.Y. 465, 113 N.E.2d 801 (1953).

18. *Id.,* at 466–467.

19. *Id.*

20. *Id.,* at 467.

21. *Id.*

22. *Portnoy* v. *Strasser,* 303 N.Y. 539, 104 N.E.2d 859 (1952).

23. *Meyer* v. *Nebraska,* 262 U.S. 390, at 399.

24. *Kropp* v. *Shepsky,* 305 N.Y., at 468.

25. *Id.*

26. *Id.,* at 469, citing *Matter of Benning,* 303 N.Y. 775 (1952). *Matter of Gostow,* 220 N.Y. 373 (1917); *Matter of Bock,* 280 N.Y. 349 (1939); *Matter of Stuart* 280 N.Y. 245 (1939).

27. *Kropp* v. *Shepsky,* 305 N.Y., at 469.

28. *Id.*

29. *Id.,* at 471.

30. *Scarpetta* v. *Spence Chapin Adoption Serv.,* 28 N.Y.2d 185, 321 N.Y.S.2d 65 (1971).

31. This scenario could not have occurred in more recent times under the *Uniform Child Custody Jurisdiction Act.* See N.Y. Dom. Rel. Law §§ 75a–75z (McKinney).

32. *Scarpetta* v. *Spence Chapin Adoption Serv.,* 28 N.Y.2d, at 189.

33. *Id.*

34. *Id.,* at 186, 196.

35. *Id.,* at 192–193.

36. *Compare Scarpetta* v. *Spence Chapin Adoption Serv.,* 29 N.Y.2d, at 196, *with Anonymous* v. *N.Y. Foundling Hosp.,* 17 A.D.2d 122, 232 N.Y.S.2d 479 (1962).

37. *Spence Chapin Adoption Serv.* v. *Polk,* 29 N.Y.2d 196, 324 N.Y.S.2d 937 (1971).

38. *Id.*

39. *Id.*

40. *Id.*

41. *Id.,* at 198.

42. *Id.*

43. *Scarpetta* v. *Spence Chapin Adoption Serv.,* 28 N.Y.2d, at 185.

44. N.Y. Soc. Serv. Law § 383(5) (McKinney), *as amended* 1972.

45. *Scarpetta* v. *Spence Chapin Adoption Serv.,* 28 N.Y.2d, at 192–193.

46. *Matter of Catherine S. and Darlene S.,* 74 Misc. 2d 154, 347 N.Y.S.2d 470 (Fam. Ct. 1973).

47. *Id.,* at 155.

48. *Id.*

49. *Id.*

50. *Id.,* at 156.

51. *Id.,* at 157.

52. See notes 1, 24, 30, and 37, *supra.*

53. *Matter of Catherine S. and Darlene S.,* 74 Misc. 2d, at 157–158.

54. *Id.,* at 158.

55. *Id.,* at 162.

56. *Id.,* at 159.

57. *Id.*

58. See notes 1, 24, 30, and 37, *supra.*

59. *Matter of Patricia A.W.,* 89 Misc. 2d 368, 392 N.Y.S.2d 180 (Fam. Ct. 1977).

60. *Matter of Confessora B.,* 75 Misc. 2d 576, 348 N.Y.S.2d 21. (Fam. Ct. 1973).

61. *Id.,* at 577.

62. *Id.*

63. *Id.,* at 580.

64. *Id.,* at 579.

65. *Benitez* v. *Llano,* 47 A.D.2d 566, 356 N.Y.S.2d 1016 (2d Dept. 1975).

66. *See Kropp* v. *Shepsky,* 305 N.Y. 465, 113 N.E.2d 801 (1953), *and Scarpetta* v. *Spence Chapin Adoption Serv.,* 28 N.Y.2d 185, 321 N.Y.S.2d 65 (1971).

67. *Benitez* v. *Llano* 47 A.D.2d, at 566.

68. *Bennett* v. *Jeffreys,* 40 N.Y.2d 543, 387 N.Y.S.2d 821 (1976).

69. *Id.,* at 544.

70. *Id.,* at 545.

71. *Id.*

72. *Id.,* at 544–545.

73. *Id.,* at 544.

74. *Id.,* at 544, 552–553.

75. *Id.,* at 545.

76. *Id.,* at 546.

77. See Parental Right Doctrine, *supra,* and The Natural Right Doctrine under Attack, *supra.*

78. *Bennett* v. *Jeffreys,* 40 N.Y.2d, at 543.

79. *Spence Chapin Adoption Serv.* v. *Polk,* 29 N.Y.2d, at 198.
80. *Bennett* v. *Jeffreys,* 40 N.Y.2d, at 548.
81. *Id.*
82. *Id.*
83. *Id.,* at 549.
84. *Id.*
85. See Iowa, Bastion of Best Interests, *supra.*
86. *Bennett* v. *Jeffreys,* 40 N.Y.2d, at 546.
87. *Id.*
88. *Gomez* v. *Lozado,* 40 N.Y.2d 839, 387 N.Y.S.2d 834 (1976).
89. *Id.,* at 840.
90. *Raysor* v. *Gabbey,* 57 A.D.2d 437, 395 N.Y.S.2d 290 (4th Dept. 1977).
91. *Tyrell* v. *Tyrell,* 67 A.D.2d 247, 415 N.Y.S.2d 723 (4th Dept. 1979), *aff'd,* 47 N.Y.2d 937, 393 N.E.2d 1041 (1979).
92. *Id.,* 67 A.D.2d, at 250.
93. *Matter of Patricia A.W.,* 89 Misc. 2d, at 375.
94. *See Bennett* v. *Jeffreys,* 40 N.Y.2d 543, 387 N.Y.S.2d 821 (1976); *Gomez* v. *Lozado,* 40 N.Y.2d 839, 387 N.Y.S.2d 834 (1976).
95. *Matter of Patricia A.W.,* 89 Misc. 2d, at 375.
96. *Matter of Catherine S. and Darlene S.,* 74 Misc. 2d, at 154.
97. *Matter of Patricia A.W.,* 89 Misc. 2d, at 375.
98. *Matter of Sanjavini K.,* 47 N.Y.2d 374, 391 N.E.2d 1316 (1979).
99. *Bennett* v. *Jeffreys,* 40 N.Y.2d 543, 387 N.Y.S.2d 821 (1976).
100. *Matter of Sanjavini K.,* 47 N.Y.2d, at 382.
101. *Tyrell* v. *Tyrell,* 47 N.Y.2d 937.
102. *Id.*
103. *Matter of Catherine S. and Darlene S.,* 74 Misc. 2d, at 154.
104. *Matter of Confessora B.,* 75 Misc. 2d, at 576.
105. *Le Roy* v. *Odgers,* 18 Ariz. App. 499, 503 P.2d 975 (Ct. App. 1972).
106. *Id.,* at 977.
107. *Id.*
108. *Id.*
109. *Id.,* at 976.
110. *Id.*
111. *Id.*
112. *Id.,* at 977.
113. *Gowland* v. *Martin,* 21 Ariz. App. 495, 520 P.2d 1172 (1974).
114. *Id.,* at 1173.
115. *Id.*
116. *Id.*
117. *Id.*

118. *Id.*

119. *Id.,* at 1175.

120. *Id.,* at 1174.

121. *Id.,* at 1175.

122. *Id.,* at 1174.

123. *Id.*

124. *In re Arias,* 21 Ariz. App. 568, 521 P.2d 1146 (Ct. App. 1974).

125. *Id.,* at 1146–1147.

126. *Id. See Gowland* v. *Martin,* 21 Ariz. App. 495, 520 P.2d 1172 (1974).

127. *In re Arias,* 521, P.2d. at 1147.

128. *Id.*

129. *Id.*

130. *Painter* v. *Bannister,* 258 Iowa 390, 140 N.W.2d 152, *cert. denied,* 384 U.S. 949 (1966).

131. *Id.,* 140 N.W.2d, at 154.

132. *Id.*

133. *Id.*

134. *Id.*

135. *Halstead* v. *Halstead,* 259 Iowa 526, 144 N.W.2d 861 (1966).

136. *Id.,* at 865.

137. *Id.*

138. *Id.*

139. *Id.,* at 867.

140. *Matter of Catherine S. and Darlene S.,* 74 Misc. 2d 154, 347 N.Y.S.2d 470 (Fam. Ct. 1973).

141. *Halstead* v. *Halstead,* 144 N.W.2d, at 868.

142. *Garvin* v. *Garvin,* 260 Iowa 1082, 152 N.W.2d 206 (1967).

143. *Id.,* at 211.

144. *Id.*

145. *Hulbert* v. *Hines,* 178 N.W.2d 354 (Iowa 1970).

146. *Id.,* at 361. *Doan Thi Hoang Anh* v. *Nelson,* 245 N.W.2d 511 (Iowa 1976).

147. *Hulbert* v. *Hines,* 178 N.W.2d, at 361.

148. *Doan Thi Hoang Anh* v. *Nelson,* 245 N.W.2d, at 517.

149. *Halstead* v. *Halstead,* 259 Iowa, at 256.

150. *Doan Thi Hoang Anh* v. *Nelson,* 245 N.W.2d, at 517–518.

151. *Id.,* at 518.

152. *Matter of Burney,* 259 N.W.2d 322 (Iowa 1977).

153. *Id.,* at 324.

154. *Id.*

155. *Id.; Bennett* v. *Jeffreys,* 40 N.Y.2d, at 543.

156. See The Waning of the National Right Doctrine, *supra.*

157. *Bennett* v. *Jeffreys,* 40 N.Y.2d, at 548.

158. *See Matter of Sams,* 256 N.W.2d 520 (Iowa 1977).

159. See General Considerations, *supra,* and Continued Prevalence of the Natural Right Doctrine in New York, *supra.*

160. *In re Guardianship of Smith,* 42 Cal. 2d 91, 265 P.2d 888, 889 (1954).

161. *Id.,* at 889–890.

162. *Id.,* at 889.

163. *Id.,* at 889–890.

164. *Compare Matter of Catherine S. and Darlene S.,* 74 Misc. 2d 154, 347 N.Y.S.2d 47. (Fam. Ct. 1973); *Painter* v. *Bannister,* 258 Iowa 390, 140 N.W.2d 152, *cert. denied,* 384 U.S. 949 (1966).

165. *In re Guardianship of Smith,* 265 P.2d, at 891–892.

166. *Id.,* at 895.

167. *Stauffacher* v. *Stauffacher,* 227 Cal. 2d 735, 39 Cal. Rptr. 31 (1964).

168. *Id.*

169. *In re Barassi,* 265 Cal. 2d 282, 71 Cal. Rptr. 249 (1968).

170. *Id.,* at 250.

171. *Id.,* at 253–254.

172. *Id.,* at 253.

173. *Id.*

174. *In re Eugene W.,* 29 Cal. 3d 623, 105 Cal. Rptr. 736 (1972).

175. *Id.,* at 738.

176. *Id.,* at 742.

177. *In re Guardianship of Marino,* 30 Cal. 3d 952, 106 Cal. Rptr. 655 (1973).

178. See Iowa, Bastion of Best Interests, *supra.*

179. *In re Guardianship of Marino,* 106 Cal. Rptr., at 656.

180. *Id.*

181. *Id.,* at 657.

182. *Id.*

183. *Id.*

184. See The Waning of the Natural Right Doctrine, *supra. Bennett* v. *Jeffreys,* 40 N.Y.2d, at 543.

185. *In re Guardianship of Smith,* 42 Cal. 2d, at 91.

186. *Stauffacher* v. *Stauffacher,* 39 Cal. Rptr., at 31.

187. *In re Barassi,* 71 Cal. Rptr., at 249.

188. Cal. Civ. Code § 4600(c) (renumbered § 4600(3)(c) (West).

189. *In re Guardianship of Marino,* 106 Cal. Rptr., at 659.

190. See notes 196 and 197, *infra.*

191. *In re B.G.,* 32 C.A.3d 365, 108 Cal. Rptr. 121 (1973).

192. *Id.,* at 132.

193. *Id.*, at 133.

194. *Id.*, at 136.

195. *In re B.G.*, 11 Cal. 3d 619, 114 Cal. Rptr. 444, 523 P.2d 244 (1974).

196. *Id.*, at 257.

197. *Id.; Painter* v. *Bannister,* 258 Iowa, at 290.

198. *In re Carmelita B.*, 579 P.2d 514, 518, 146 Cal. Rptr. 623 (1978).

199. *Id.*

200. *In re B.G.*, 108 Cal. Rptr., at 132.

201. *Bennett* v. *Jeffreys,* 40 N.Y.2d 543, 387 N.Y.S.2d 821 (1976).

# 6 Visitation

## Theoretical Development of the Law

Visitation of noncustodial natural parents with children has generally been viewed as a form of temporary custody. This is a view that has been distilled by the courts whenever a litigant has sought, for one purpose or another, to drive a wedge of distinction between the terms *custody* and *visitation* and the concepts they represent. Prior to the specific statutory grant of visitation rights to grandparents in Section 72 of the Domestic Relations Law,[1] it was held "[v]isitation is a form of custody and custody is a legal right which properly belongs to the parent only."[2] There are many references in New York decisions indicating the adoption of the view that custody is the whole of which visitation is a part thereof; that is, that visitation is a "species" of custody[3] or partial custody.[4]

The importance of this conceptual distinction is that a great deal of what can be applied in law to custody in judicial decisions may also be applied to visitation and vice versa. Moreover, the implicit inclusion of the lesser concept of custody has been carried by the courts into statutory interpretation wherein the term *visitation* may be wholly absent in the governing statute.

In one family court decision subsequently sanctioned by appellate review, the court denied a motion to dismiss a petition for visitation on the grounds that the said court lacked jurisdiction. Without raising any questions as to the merits, the respondent took the position that Section 651(b) of the Family Court Act, the enabling statute, conferred jurisdiction for determination of custody, but that any mention of the term *visitation* was wholly lacking. The court ". . . [did] not subscribe to the proposition that the term 'custody' as employed in [the statute] excludes visitation."[5]

## Other Jurisdictions: General Considerations

Other jurisdictions generally follow the conclusions reached by the New York Courts in defining visitation as a lesser included concept of the term *custody*. Georgia law, for instance, parallels New York's in that court decisions have found a statutory grant of jurisdiction over custody to implicitly include jurisdiction over visitation.[6]

Similarly, a Michigan appellate court, addressing itself to a statute that outlined court jurisdiction over child custody held, "While that act focuses on custody disputes, there can be little doubt that the act was intended to control visitation privileges as well."[7]

It is difficult to see, as a practical matter, how any other result could have been achieved. The mechanics of trying a custody case are almost identical to litigating a visitation dispute; that is, they include testimony and/or reports of expert witnesses, anecdotal testimony by the parties themselves and members of their families, in-camera interviews with the children, and so forth. Moreover, the overriding criteria that go into the decision of either a custody or a visitation dispute are generally identical as well.[8] Thus if the New York courts and those of other jurisdictions had failed to find the implicit grant of visitation jurisdiction, legislative initiative in effecting a change would not have been long in coming.

## Criteria on Which an Order of Visitation Is Made in Disputes between Natural Parents

It is generally held that the same standards that apply to adjudication of a custody proceeding will apply to a determination of an issue of visitation. When the standard of adjudication is the best-interests-of-the-child test, as it clearly is in New York,[9] then of necessity, that same standard must be applied in a visitation dispute.[10] The Best Interests Rule in custody disputes is not necessarily applicable to litigation between parent and nonparent, as discussed in chapter 5, Custody Disputes between Natural Parents and Third Parties, *supra,* and therefore may not apply when a visitation issue between a parent and a nonparent is presented.

## Modification of Visitation

It is clear under New York law that once visitation is agreed on or ordered by a court the custodial parent "bears a heavy burden of proof to establish convincingly that the agreed visitation provisions" are clearly detrimental to the children.[11] If visitation provisions are of the "customary and reasonable type," they will be presumed valid in the face of all but a "pressing concern" and substantial proof that visitation is clearly harmful to the welfare of the children.[12]

The court's attitude is not only meant to be protective of the rights of the noncustodial parent, but protective also of the valued right of a child to the companionship and attention of a loved one who contributes constructively to his development.[13]

The burden of proof required of a custodial parent seeking to curtail visitation is demanding to the extent that even expert psychiatric testimony as to the negative attitude of the children, coupled with clearly expressed negative feelings of the children themselves, will not be sufficient, in the absence of demonstrable harm.[14] Such hostility toward the noncustodial parent on the part of the children, even if verified by expert opinion, may be treated skeptically by the courts as the product of the custodial parent's influence and manipulation, subtle though it may be.[15]

The children's own objection to visitation, when no harm is demonstrated, may be discounted even to the extent of enforcing overnight visitation with the noncustodial parent when it has previously been agreed to between the parties. "[R]ound-the-clock living together is vital in preserving a child's bond to a father as a true parent—trustworthy and caretaking—rather than a casual host."[16]

Emotional trauma experienced by a child on the occasion of her father's visits because of an acromonious verbal exchange between the father and the mother's male friend was not considered sufficient to curtail visitation.[17] The court suggested that if this were the only detrimental aspect of the father's visitation, it could easily be remedied by the voluntary absence of the mother's friend at the time of the father's scheduled arrivals and departures. "Where there is animosity between parents, claims by the custodial parent that visitation is disturbing to the child should be received with the most cautious scrutiny. . . ."[18]

Even when a noncustodial parent seeks to use visitation as a means of harrassing the custodian, the courts are still reluctant to curtail visitation. The solution will be sought in the imposition of strictly regulated hours of visitation, the exercise of such visitation on adequate notice to the custodian, and specific prohibition against the visiting parent entering the custodian's premises.[19]

When the noncustodial parent is demonstrated to be clearly deranged by expert testimony, heavily corroborated anecdotal testimony, and even public records, visitation will be curtailed as the only remedy for the acute emotional distress suffered by the child as a result of the visits.[20]

In the absence of clear derangement, courts may still limit the time spent with the visiting parent when otherwise innocuous behavior leaves a severe, demonstrable detrimental effect on the child. When a noncustodial father had his paramour present during the entire period of overnight visitation with his children, the court found the severe stress placed on the children by the parent's recent separation was intensified. The father's havior showed, in the court's opinion, an insensitivity on his part to the children's needs.[21]

The presence of a paramour during visitation in itself, however, is not a sufficient basis for limiting or withholding visitation without the concrete demonstration of some harm to the child.[22]

As a general rule, concrete, substantive, corroborated evidence on a significant issue will tip the balance against the noncustodial parent in any litigation to curtail or eliminate visitation rights. The gravity and importance that courts attach to a parent's visitation rights, however, make judges reluctant to diminish them. Hence, the weight of the burden of proof that a petitioner carries in such a proceeding cannot be overemphasized.

It would probably be useful in discouraging needless, and ill-advised litigation if attorneys who handle such matters took the trouble to point out to clients and potential clients that visitation and custodial matters are not decided on narrow moral issues alone. There must be something more— some demonstrated adverse effect on the child resulting from the parent's "immoral" behavior.[23] Too often, in the bitter and emotionally charged atmosphere of divorce, disappointment and love turned to hate, one party or the other will pounce with relish on the social, sexual, and romantic irregularities of the former partner's present life-style. No matter how unsuited the outraged party may be (by reason of his or her own past behavior) to pass judgement, the common scenario finds the accusing party before a court of law, recounting the former partners' sins and expecting the court to respond with thunderbolts of opprobrium. The accusers, in turn, respond with amazement when their tales of sin and abomination fail not only to excite the prurient interest of the judge but to secure them the relief requested without a more definite showing of harm to the child. In our opinion, no responsible attorney should recommend the initiation of custody or visitation litigation without first consulting a qualified behaviorist.

The practitioner must be particularly cautious when dealing with potential litigants who have achieved a relatively high level of education and professionalism in a field that may bear some relationship to the behavioral sciences (for example, educators, psychologists, social workers, and physicians). A custodial parent with such a background may observe defects in the relationship between the child and the visiting parent that he or she considers significant. However valid such an observation may actually be and however valuable a basis it may provide for improving the interaction between child and visiting parent, the observed defect may very well fall short of the heavy burden of proof required by the courts to limit or end visitation. An emotionally involved custodial parent—no matter how intelligent or professionally qualified and no matter how credible he or she may sound in recounting incidents and drawing conclusions therefrom—is not a reliable source in determining the merits of a potential visitation action. An objective, expert opinion should be a prerequisite before any court papers are filed or served.

### Noncustodial Parent's Demand for Increased Visitation

Generally, the same criteria as apply to a diminution or deprivation of visitation affects an increase in visitation (that is, the best interests of the child). As in custody disputes, generally some change of circumstances must be satisfactorily shown to warrant a change in the status quo. Absent a showing by the petitioning parent that it is in the best interests of the child to have *increased* visitation, a court is not justified in expanding existing visitation provisions simply because there is no reason *not* to do so.[24]

### Other Jurisdictions' Modification

The same basic principle of law appears to apply in most other jurisdictions; that is, the dependency of the amount and frequency of visitation on the child's best interests.[25] The use of visitation as a means of "punishing either parent" is rejected.[26] As in New York, the burden of proving that any modification of existing provisions would be in the child's best interests is placed firmly on the shoulders of the party seeking modification.[27]

### Procedures

A proceeding to modify visitation may be started in the same fashion as a proceeding to modify custody; that is, in the form of a petition or order to show cause or a writ of *habeas corpus* brought in family court,[28] or as a petition or order to show cause in Supreme Court,[29] or as a writ of *habeas corpus* in Supreme Court,[30] or incident to a support proceeding in family court.[31]

A proceeding in Supreme Court may be referred by the Supreme Court to the family court.[32] Indeed, the expertise and ancillary services provided by the family court make this a favored practice.[33] The family court, however, may not modify a custody or visitation disposition contained in a judgment or order of the Supreme Court unless the order makes specific referral to the family court.[34] Silence in a Supreme Court order with respect to referral, while sufficient to authorize family court modification for money matters,[35] is not sufficient to authorize referral in custody and, implicitly, visitation proceedings.[36]

The issue of visitation must be decided after a full hearing and "may not be determined on the basis of recriminatory and controverted affidavits."[37] It has been held that the specific fixing of visitation rights for a parent may *not* be delegated by the court to a probation officer but must be decided by the court.[38]

The trial court may admit reports of psychiatrists and other professional investigators and behaviorists without the personal appearances of such professionals, if stipulated to by the parties.[39]

The court may, in its discretion, conduct an in-camera interview with the child or children, with or without the consent of the parties. An abuse of this discretion may be reviewed by an appellate court.[40]

Thus the basic elements of a visitation action, which are identical to any custody litigation, are as follows:

1.  Commencement of the action in an appropriate forum.
2.  Possible referral to another forum.
3.  Examination by the behavioral scientists retained by the parties.
4.  Examination and/or investigation by a court-appointed professional or the probation department or Mental Health Services Department or equivalent of the family court.
5.  Hearing encompassing the following: (a) anecdotal testimony by the parties (the children when appropriate, family members, friends, teachers, and so forth); (b) expert testimony by professional behaviorists retained by the parties; (c) submission of reports by court-appointed professionals and possible appearances by them for testimony.
6.  Possible in-camera interview with the children.

*New York Surrogate's Court*

In New York, the surrogate's court of each county has jurisdiction to appoint a "guardian of the person and property of an infant."[41] This power has its origins in the powers of the chancellor under English common law, the same source from which the Supreme Court derives its powers as *parens patriea*. Analogously, the surrogate's court also has jurisdiction over visitation.[42]

It is clear that the surrogate's court has concurrent jurisdiction with the Supreme Court in New York over custody,[43] and that, implicit in custody dispositions is jurisdiction over visitation.[44] It is the rare case, however, wherein a visitation order is made in surrogate's court unless there is some related issue (for example, an adoption or a neglect proceeding).[45] When visitation is incidental to matrimonial litigation, the Supreme Court and family court are better equipped to deal with the issue because of their similar jurisdictions, which are absent in surrogate's court, over such issues as support, enforcement, interpretation of separation agreements, and family offenses. Surrogate's court will tend *not* to assume jurisdiction in a custody or visitation dispute when the Supreme Court has already assumed jurisdiction of a related matrimonial action.[46]

### Effect of Illegitimacy on Visitation Rights

The traditional rule in New York, going back to English common law, is that the father of an illegitimate child has a right to custody of the child superior to the rest of the world but inferior to the right of the natural mother.[47] This is distinct from the right of a natural father who was married to the mother, in which case (at least theoretically) his right to custody is equal to the mother's.[48]

Illegitimacy, however, does not appear to put a natural father at any particular disadvantage with respect to visitation. It has been held that when a mother sought to terminate the father's visitation rights solely on the ground of the child's illegitimacy, "the best interests of the infant is the guiding principle in the determination of custody and the right of visitation. . . . The father of an illegitimate child may be awarded custody and *a fortiori,* the right of visitation. . . ."[49]

The minority view looked on an award of visitation to an unwed father as something justified only by some unfitness, misconduct, or disability in the mother when such an award is made over the mother's objections.[50] Further, the minority view looked on the visitation of out-of-wedlock fathers as an impediment to the establishment of an accepted place in the community for mother and child because of the stigma of their irregular relationship. "[T]here is the enforced continuance of a relationship between the unwilling mother and the father, stemming from a situation socially condemned and likely to be intolerable to explain or sustain."[51]

This minority view has now been completely discredited by more recent cases, and there is now no question "but that the father of an out-of-wedlock child has standing to be heard on the issue of visitation rights," and, in a proper case, be awarded such visitation.[52]

In at least one case, the court was sufficiently concerned with preserving the visitation rights of an out-of-wedlock father that after the mother's marriage to another man, the court denied the stepfather's application for adoption.[53] The court recognized the threat to the natural father's continued visitation with the child after adoption,[54] although it has by no means been established that an out-of-wedlock father may not continue visitation after adoption by a stepfather in a appropriate case.[55]

*Other Jurisdictions—Visitation by*
*Out-of-Wedlock Fathers*

The general rule in New York is overwhelmingly recognized in the majority of U.S. jurisdictions; that is, that the putative father of an illegitimate child should be awarded the right of visitation if such an award would be consistent with the child's best interests.[56]

The one exception of note to the general rule is the state of Illinois, which had, in effect, a statute—the Illinois Paternity Act—[57]providing that the father of an out-of-wedlock child has no right to custody and control of the child. This statute was also interpreted under case law as denying the father any right to visitation.[58] The particular statute, however, was declared unconstitutional and in violation of the Fourteenth Amendment to the U.S. Constitution by the U.S. Supreme Court.[59]

As a result of the U.S. Supreme Court decision, the Illinois legislature was induced to amend the statute, and the state courts were persuaded to change their views to conform to the statutory mandate. "Since the father of an illegitimate child is no longer barred from obtaining custody, courts now must consider the familiar 'best interests of the child' standard in each case. . . ." This rule was applied to visitation as well.[60]

Apparently at the time the *Stanley* v. *Illinois* case was decided, "Illinois was the only State, which, as a matter of law, refused to consider a putative father's request for visitation rights."[61]

Pennsylvania at one time also denied visitation rights to out-of-wedlock fathers as a matter of law.[62] This view was, however, specifically overruled by a later Pennsylvania case.[63] There remains one exception to the new general rule in Pennsylvania wherein the court denied visitation to the father on the theory that the mother's remarriage and new life-style made the father's visits a disruptive influence.[64] This view was specifically rejected in New York decisions.[65]

**Rights of Grandparents**

The rights of grandparents and other blood relatives to custody of a child are no greater than or more preferred than those of any other nonparents.[66] "Non-parent relatives stand in the same position as any other contestant for a child's custody and the sole criterion for determination is the 'best interests of the child.' "[67]

With regard to visitation, however, as distinct from custody, grandparents *do* enjoy a special status granted them by statute. In 1966, the New York legislature gave the first specific statutory standing to grandparents to seek such visitation.[68] This legislative mandate was probably inspired by a line of decisions that held judicial interference on behalf of grandparental visitation to be unwarranted.[69]

In its original form, Domestic Relations Law Section 72 enabled grandparents to apply for visitation rights by writ of *habeas corpus* if the parent of the infant who was, in turn, the offspring of the applicant was deceased.[70] The courts construed this provision strictly. This is to say that the statute set forth two basic requirements: (1) the parent of the infant who was the child of the applicant must be deceased, and (2) the visitation must be in the best interests of the child.[71]

The prerequisite of the death of the parent, it may be assumed, was based on the idealistic view of family interrelationships, which presumed that a living parent would see that his or her *own* parents established grandparental interaction with the infant concerned.

The unpleasant reality of our society, however, is that many noncustodial natural fathers and mothers abandon all interest in their offspring in pursuit of new lives, new loves, and the desire to be free of the obligations, distractions, and remembrances of their failed marriages. The grandparents, on the other hand, are typically seeking gratification from different sources and find themselves hurt and helpless at the loss of contact with the infant. This set of circumstances and the strict construction of the law in its original form by the courts ultimately brought about the amendment to the statute.[72] The amended version allows grandparents to bring a writ of *habeas corpus* not only when the parent of the minor child "is or are deceased," but also "where conditions exist which equity would see fit to intervene."[73]

The best interest of the child is still, however, the controlling factor in sustaining such a writ.[74] Expert medical testimony indicating that grandparental visitation will have a detrimental emotional impact on a child is sufficient to deny such a writ,[75] but animosity between the grandparents and the custodial parent would not be sufficient.[76]

The expressed wishes of the children themselves (even those who are in their teens) not to participate in grandparental visitation, will not by itself dissuade a court from ordering such visitation in the absence of some proven detriment.[77] Where visiting grandparents themselves create animosity by demonstrating a hostile attitude toward the custodial parent and her new spouse, the subjection of the infants to the resulting emotional stress and loyalty conflicts will justify abrogation of grandparental visitation rights.[78]

Adoption of the children by a stepparent will not automatically eliminate grandparental visitation rights under Domestic Relations Law Section 72.[79]

Generally speaking, the courts do not consider visitation applications by grandparents lightly. Great weight is given, apparently, to the fact that the legislature took the trouble to pass a specific statute for the benefit of encouraging grandparental visitation.[80]

Visitation rights have been ordered for grandparents, in some cases, not on direct application, but as a by-product to custody disputes. In one case, wherein the mother voluntarily relinquished custody to the paternal grandparents and then attempted to regain custody, the courts upheld maintenance of custody in the paternal grandparents. However, as a by-product, visitation was specifically ordered for the mother, the father, and the *maternal* grandparents as well.[81] In another case, the maternal great-aunt sought to obtain custody of the infant from the out-of-wedlock father after the mother's death. Custody in the father was upheld, but visitation for the maternal relatives was ordered in "consideration of [their] continuing interest . . . and . . . the child's desire to maintain a relationship with them."[82]

Of course, other blood relatives or even nonrelatives, may apply for visitation under ordinary writ of *habeas corpus* or order to show cause. Application can be made either under the inherent power of the Supreme Court[83] or under Family Court Act Section 651. But the special focus of grandparents provided by Domestic Relations Law Section 72 gives them a procedural advantage that is often interpreted by the courts as a substantive advantage.

**Other Blood Relatives**

There are instances in which natural fathers have been granted visitation after adoption, although this has not been held to have the same weight as statute-mandated grandparental visitation.[84] There is one case on record wherein the court sustained custody of two minor girls in the *unrelated* foster parents against the natural mother. At the same time, the court ordered visitation between the girls in the foster home and an older, natural brother, who remained in the custody of his natural paternal grandmother.[85]

**Grandparental Visitation in Other Jurisdictions**

The evolution of grandparental visitation in other jurisdictions is, in many cases, nearly identical to the development in New York case law. In New Jersey, as in New York, the courts did not originally recognize the existence of any visitation rights in the grandparents until statutory authority was enacted in 1972.[86] The New Jersey statute, as originally written, was strikingly similar to Section 72 of the New York Domestic Relations Law, providing for *habeas corpus* relief in a superior court for grandparents who desired visitation, when either or both of the parents of a minor were deceased.[87] In much the same way as the appurtenant New York statute was amended to expand its application, so as to eliminate the prerequisite death of one or both parents, the New Jersey statute was similarly amended, effective May 1973.[88]

New Jersey law also recognizes the right of grandparental visitation in an appropriate case even after the adoption of the child by a stepparent.[89] It has been held in New Jersey that a paternal grandmother's right to visitation under the statute cannot be denied because her absent son, the father of the infant, is in arrears in court-ordered support payments.[90]

Ohio also has a statute similar to New York Domestic Relations Law Section 72.[91] But the Ohio statute is a little broader in that it refers to "relatives," rather than grandparents in defining the group that is eligible to apply for visitation privileges. Ohio decisions also recognize the right of grandparents to continued visitation after adoption by a stepparent.[92]

In the absence of a statute similar to those in effect in New York, New Jersey, and Ohio, a Rhode Island appellate court found a trial court to be lacking in jurisdiction to order visitation for a paternal aunt and uncle of a child, subsequent to the father's death and stepfather's adoption.[93]

Washington has a broad statute allowing the court to order visitation for any person when visitation may "serve the best interests of the child."[94] It has been held, however, that this statute could not be used by a maternal grandmother to seek visitation with her grandchild when the mother was both alive and in custody of the infant.[95] In other words, if the infant's mother, the custodial parent, has such a poor relationship with her *own* mother that she refused her visitation, the courts are not going to intervene. Here is an indication as to the *real* purpose behind the statutes that we have considered like New York's Domestic Relations Law Section 72 and others: that is, to offer protection to grandparents against the in-law or former in-law custodian, now free from the influence or compulsion to voluntarily allow grandparents to visit, due to the death, divorce, or absence of a spouse.

### Enforcement of Visitation Privileges

*Security for Return of Child from Visitation and*
*Enforcement of Visitation Privileges*

Custodial parents are often faced with the fear of a spouse taking advantage of the opportunity afforded by visitation to flee the jurisdiction with the child. This is a problem that, for the most part, will be remedied by the new Uniform Child Custody Jurisdiction Act, effective September 1 1978.[96]

In the past, there has been decisional precedent for requiring security

from visiting parents in various forms. In a case wherein the father was a
foreign national, and there was reason to believe that he might take the
opportunity of his visitation to remove the child from U.S. soil, he was
required to leave his passport with the custodian-mother on each occasion
that he exercised his visitation rights.[97] So long as he observed this precondi-
tion, the court would not deny him visitation as the custodian mother had
requested.[98]

A monetary bond has been required by some courts to assure
visitation.[99]

### Threat of Custodial Deprivation as Sanction to Enforce Visitation

The continuance of custody with one parent or the other may be condi-
tioned on maintaining the child's residence within access of the visiting
parent.[100] This is particularly so when a court perceives no useful purpose
other than vengeance in the impending move of the custodial parent.[101] If,
on the other hand, the move can be justified by reasons of health for either
custodial parent or child, by reasons of livelihood, or even by reason of the
custodial parent's family ties in the vicinity of the proposed new residence,
then the courts will not penalize the custodial parent.[102]

See chapter 3, Current Standards for Determination of Custody Disputes between Parents, *supra,* on transfer of custody as a sanction for contempt generally.

### Suspension of Support and Alimony Provisions as Sanction for Denial of Visitation

A court may refuse to enforce a husband's or ex-husband's obligation to
pay alimony to a wife or ex-wife, if, as the custodial parent, she withholds
visitation with a child or children unless it can be demonstrated that such
visitation is detrimental to the child or children.[103] In all such cases, the
parent seeking to curtail or withhold visitation, without suffering a penalty,
"bears a heavy burden of proof" to establish detriment to the infant.[104]
Moreover, when the original visitation provisions are part of a separation
agreement or stipulation they will be "presumptively valid" and subject to
modification only under a "pressing concern" for the welfare of the children.[105] To avoid loss of alimony, it is not enough that the custodial parent
acted in good faith at the time she adjudged visitation to be harmful. In
other words, if a court subsequently finds insufficient support for the custodian's position, it will not help her in recouping lost alimony that her
motives were pure and not vindictive.[106]

Generally speaking, it is only the withholding of alimony payments that will be upheld by a court as a sanction to enforce visitation. Withholding of child support is generally not favored "apparently on that theory that payments should be withheld only from the person responsible for the breach or that a father's common law duty of child support continues independent of contract or decree."[107]

There is at least one case in New York contrary to this point of view, wherein the court held that the noncustodial father's right to suspend support payments "applies to child support as well as to support for a mother. Thus, it seems clear that the right of the children to housing, clothing, etc., claimed by [the mother's] attorney does not have priority over the father's right of visitation. . . ."[108] This particular case may be distinguishable in that there was no alimony due to the wife to withhold as a sanction. In addition, the wife herself was apparently self-sufficient, and the father continued, voluntarily, to pay a portion of the child support.[109]

Obviously, cases are not decided in a vacuum, and it may have been easy for a judge to decide that the father's visitation rights were *not* subordinate to the children's need for "housing, clothing, etc." when they were getting it anyway. One can only speculate if the court's brave words might have been somewhat tempered when a real deprivation of necessaries could be demonstrated on the record.[110]

On a contractual basis, support and visitation provisions are deemed interdependent so that recovery of arrears in support under a separation agreement may be denied when visitation is also provided but not honored.[111] There appears to be some conflict as to whether the separation agreement must survive independently and not be merged in a judgment in order for the rule to apply after divorce.[112] When the support and visitation provisions are specifically made independent covenants in a separation agreement, support will be enforced though visitation is denied.[113] Of course, when there is a demonstrated need on the part of either the wife or child, provisions of a separation agreement may be implicitly or explicitly modified or ignored altogether.[114]

## Enforcement by Contempt Proceedings

The obvious remedy available for failure of a custodial parent to allow visitation as provided by a court order or decree incorporating a separation agreement or stipulation is to apply to an appropriate court to hold the offending party in contempt. This power is available in the New York Supreme Court under Judiciary Law Sections 750 and 753, which include the traditional powers of punishment by fine and imprisonment or both. With regard to custody provisions, these same powers are incorporated by reference into the Family Court Act in Section 156.[115] The judiciary law contempt provisions are also incorporated by reference into the Surrogate's Court Procedure Act in Sections 606 and 607.

There is at least one reported case in New York of a mother being held in contempt and fined for failing to allow visitation to the father of her children.[116] There are no reported cases in New York that have come to our attention wherein the contempt powers of the courts have been used to commit a custodial parent to jail. It is, we suspect, an unlikely situation. The prospect of a mother who is otherwise fit being confined to prison, away from her children, is rather more drastic than most judges would be able to sanction. And of course, if the custodial parent were unfit, the court would have the option of transferring custody of the children to the other parent or some other party.

The aggrieved noncustodial party will more likely be forced to rely on the implied threat of custodial change and the economic sanctions of withheld alimony and/or child support when seeking to enforce court ordered or contractual visitation. The new Uniform Child Custody Act will no doubt go far toward simplifying enforcement across state lines and making some present case law obsolete.

Generally, a court's attitude toward enforcement of visitation in a particular case will depend on (1) the best interests of the child with regard to the visitation, (2) the motivation behind the custodial parent's violation of the visitation provisions, and (3) the interdependence of the visitation and support provisions, as either agreed on by the parties or a decreed by the court.

It is, of course, an interesting question, as to how grandparents and other beneficiaries of court-ordered visitation would enforce their rights without the sanction of contempt of court. In most such cases, the visiting party is neither a likely alternative custodian not responsible for any support.

## Other Jurisdictions

There is a wide range of court reactions and imposed sanctions against a custodial parent who withholds visitation. An appellate court in Vermont has held that it was in error *not* to hold a custodial mother in contempt for denying visitation to the father in a case wherein the father *was* held in contempt for failing to pay support.[117] In Idaho, an appellate court sustained a refusal of the trial court to enforce arrears in child support due to the custodian mother's denial of jury-ordered visitation.[118] In Massachusetts, however, child-support payments were ordered continued although the mother had removed the children to the Virgin Islands, well beyond reasonable access of the father.[119]

## Visitation Provisions in Separation Agreements and Stipulations

It is our experience that in attempting to resolve visitation disputes in conferences prior to trial, the court and the parties are most aided by visitation provisions that are specific and detailed. Most people consider themselves to be and want to be considered law-abiding. Specific provisions that do not leave room for argument, interpretation, and petty disputes lend powerful moral force to the trial judge's attempts to settle disputes before the storm of acrimonious litigation engulfs both the parties and the court. Agreements and stipulations that provide for "liberal" visitation or for details to be worked out between the parties inevitably lead, sooner or later, to disagreement, misunderstanding, and surrender to the temptation (always present between divorced spouses) to make the issue of custody a battleground. Provisions that spell out dates, times, places, and conditions are strongly recommended.

## Notes

1. See Rights of Grandparents, *supra.*
2. *People ex rel. Hacker* v. *Strongson,* 141 N.Y.S.2d 859 (Sup.Ct. 1955).
3. *People ex rel. "Jean Francois"* v. *"Olga Ivanova,"* 14 A.D.2d 317, 221 N.Y.S.2d 75 (1st Dept. 1961).
4. *Ex parte People ex rel. Cox,* 124 N.Y.S.2d 511 (Sup. Ct. 1953).
5. *In re Juan R.* v. *Necta V.,* 55 A.D.2d 33, 389 N.Y.S.2d 126 (2d Dept. 1976).
6. *Hopkins* v. *Hopkins,* 237 Ga. 845, 229 S.E.2d 751 (1976).
7. *Stevenson* v. *Stevenson,* 74 Mich. App. 656, 254 N.W.2d 337 (1977).
8. *In re Juan R.* v. *Necta V.,* 55 A.D.2d, at 35.
9. See chapter 2, Custody Disputes between Natural Parents, *supra.*
10. *In re Juan R.* v. *Necta V.,* 55 A.D.2d 33, 389 N.Y.S.2d 126 (2d Dept. 1976).
11. *In re Doe* v. *Doe,* 86 Misc. 2d 194, 197, 378 N.Y.S.2d 269 (Fam. Ct. 1975), cited with approval in *Marciano* v. *Marciano,* 56 A.D.2d 735, 392 N.Y.S.2d 747 (4th Dept. 1977); *accord, Petraglia* v. *Petraglia,* 56 A.D.2d 923, 392 N.Y.S.2d 697 (2d Dept. 1977), *appeal dismissed,* 42 N.Y.2d 805. *See Kresnicka* v. *Kresnicka,* 48 A.D.2d 929, 369 N.Y.S.2d 522 (2d Dept. 1975).
12. *In re Doe* v. *Doe,* 86 Misc. 2d, at 197.
13. *Id.*

14. *Id.*

15. *Id.*

16. *Id.*

17. *Marciano* v. *Marciano,* 56 A.D.2d 735, 392 N.Y.S.2d 747 (4th Dept. 1977).

18. *Id.*

19. *Petraglia* v. *Petraglia,* 56 A.D.2d 923, 392 N.Y.S.2d 697 (2d Dept. 1977). *Compare with Molier* v. *Molier,* 53 A.D.2d 996, 386 N.Y.S.2d 226 (3d Dept. 1976).

20. *Hotze* v. *Hotze,* 57 A.D.2d 85, 394 N.Y.S.2d 753 (4th Dept. 1977).

21. *Dodd* v. *Dodd,* 93 Misc. 2d 641, 403 N.Y.S.2d 401 (Sup. Ct. 1978).

22. *Compare Dodd* v. *Dodd, id., with Repetti* v. *Repetti,* 50 A.D.2d 913, 914, 376 N.Y.S.2d 1019 (2d Dept. 1975).

23. *Feldman* v. *Feldman,* 45 A.D.2d 320, 358 N.Y.S.2d 507 (2d Dept. 1974).

24. *Carter* v. *Carter,* 58 A.D.2d 890, 397 N.Y.S.2d 96 (2d Dept. 1977).

25. *Hock* v. *Hock,* 50 Ill. App. 3d 583, 365 N.E.2d 1025 (1977).

26. *Id. See also Keefer* v. *Keefer,* 107 Ill. App. 2d 74, 245 N.E.2d 784 (1969); *Nye* v. *Nye,* 411 Ill. 408, 105 N.E.2d 300 (1952); *Malone* v. *Malone,* 5 Ill. App. 2d 525, 126 N.E.2d 505 (1955).

27. *Valencia* v. *Valencia,* 46 Ill. App. 3d 741, 360 N.E.2d 1384 (1977). *See Pate* v. *Pate,* 348 So. 2d (La. Ct. App. 1977), a Louisiana decision for comparison with a jurisdiction with a civil-law background. See chapter 1, Jurisdiction, *supra,* and chapter 1, note 41, *supra.*

28. N.Y. Fam. Ct. Act § 651(b) (McKinney 29A).

29. N.Y. Dom. Rel. Law § 240 (McKinney).

30. N.Y. Dom. Rel. Law §§ 70, 240 (McKinney).

31. N.Y. Fam. Ct. Act § 447 (McKinney 29A).

32. N.Y. Fam. Ct. Act §§ 651(a), 652, 467 (McKinney 29A).

33. *See In re Juan R.* v. *Necta V.,* 55 A.D.2d, at 37.

34. N.Y. Fam. Ct. Act §§ 467, 652 (McKinney 29A); *Harrington* v. *Harrington,* 60 A.D.2d 982, 401 N.Y.S.2d 342 (4th Dept. 1978).

35. N.Y. Fam. Ct. Act §§ 461(b), 466 (McKinney 29A).

36. *Harrington* v. *Harrington,* 60 A.D.2d 982, 401 N.Y.S.2d 342 (4th Dept. 1978).

37. *Kresnicka* v. *Kresnicka,* 48 A.D.2d 929, 369 N.Y.S.2d 522 (2d Dept. 1975); *Fischbein* v. *Fischbein,* 55 A.D.2d 885, 391 N.Y.S.2d 6 (1st Dept. 1972).

38. *Brown* v. *Brown,* 71 Misc. 2d 818, 887 N.Y.S.2d 465, *aff'd,* 39 A.D.2d 897, 334 N.Y.S.2d 1005 (1st Dept. 1972).

39. *Falkides* v. *Falkides,* 40 A.D.2d 1074, 339 N.Y.S.2d 445, 108 N.E.2d 402 (1962); *Isaacs* v. *Murcin,* 38 A.D.2d 673, 327 N.Y.S.2d 126 (4th Dept. 1971); *Lincoln* v. *Lincoln,* 24 N.Y.2d 270, 273, 247 N.E.2d 659 (1969).

40. *Falkides* v. *Falkides,* 40 A.D.2d 1074, 339 N.Y.S.2d 445, 108 N.E.2d 402 (1962); *Lincoln* v. *Lincoln,* 24 N.Y.2d, at 273; *but compare with Ehrlich* v. *Ressner,* 55 A.D.2d 953, 391 N.Y.S.2d 152 (2d Dept. 1977).

41. See chapter 1, Jurisdiction, *supra,* and Theoretical Development of the Law, *supra. In re Camp,* 126 N.Y. 377, 389 (1891); *In re Throne's Estate,* 126 Misc. 96, 213 N.Y.S. 419, 421 (Sur. Ct. 1925); *In re Lamb's Estate,* 139 N.Y.S. 685 (Sur. Ct. 1912); *In re Stuart,* 280 N.Y. 245, 20 N.E.2d 741 (1939); *In re Bock,* 280 N.Y. 349, 21 N.E.2d 186 (1939); *In re Leslie Marie L.,* 75 Misc. 2d 305, 348 N.Y.S.2d 46 (Sur. Ct. 1973).

42. *See* chapter 1, Jurisdiction.

43. *In re Yardum,* 228 A.D.2d 854 (2d Dept. 1930).

44. *In re Juan R.* v. *Necta V.,* 55 A.D.2d 33, 389 N.Y.S.2d 126 (2d Dept. 1976).

45. See chapter 1, Jurisdiction, *supra.*

46. *In re Stillman,* 117 Misc. 61, 190 N.Y.S. 495 (Sur. Ct. 1921). *Compare In re Lee,* 220 N.Y. 532, 116 N.E. 352 (1917), *with In re Rosenberg's Estate,* 130 N.Y.S.2d 316 (Sur. Ct. 1954).

47. See chapter 4, Effect of Illegitimacy, *supra.*

48. See chapter 2, Custody Disputes between Natural Parents, *supra.* N.Y. Dom. Rel. Law § 70 (McKinney).

49. *People ex rel. "Jean Francois"* v. *"Olga Ivanova,"* 14 A.D.2d 317, 221 N.Y.S.2d 75 (1st Dept. 1961). *See also People ex rel. Meredith* v. *Meredith,* 272 A.D. 79, 69 N.Y.S.2d 462, *aff'd,* 297 N.Y. 692, 77 N.E.2d 8 (1947).

50. *People ex rel. "Jean Francois"* v. *"Olga Ivanova,"* 14 A.D.2d, at 318. *Compare with In re Cronell* v. *Hartley,* 54 Misc. 2d 732, 69 N.Y.S.2d 462 (Fam. Ct. 1967).

51. *People ex rel. "Jean Francois"* v. *"Olga Ivanova,"* 14 A.D.2d, at 318.

52. *In re Pierce* v. *Yerkovich,* 80 Misc. 2d 613, 363 N.Y.S.2d 403 (Fam. Ct. 1974). *See also Stanley* v. *Illinois,* 405 U.S. 645 (1972); N.Y. Fam. Ct. Act § 549 (McKinney 29A).

53. *In re Gerald G.G.,* 61 A.D.2d 521, 526, 403 N.Y.S.2d 57 (2d Dept. 1978).

54. *Id.*

55. See Other Blood Relatives, *supra. Scranton* v. *Hutter,* 40 A.D.2d 296, 339 N.Y.S.2d 708 (4th Dept. 1973); *People ex rel. Simmons* v. *Sheridan,* 98 Misc. 2d 331, 414 N.Y.S.2d 83 (1979); *In re Geri* v. *Fanto,* 79 Misc. 2d 947, 361 N.Y.S.2d 984 (Fam. Ct. 1974).

56. *See* 15 A.L.R.3d 887 (1967); *Gardiner* v. *Rothman,* 345 N.E.2d 370, 372 (Mass. 1976).

57. Ill. Rev. Stat. ch. 106 3/4, § 62 (1971).

58. *DePhillips* v. *DePhillips,* 35 Ill. 2d 154, 219 N.E.2d 465 (1966); *Wallace* v. *Wallace,* 60 Ill. App. 2d 300, 210 N.E.2d 4 (1965).

59. *Stanley* v. *Illinois,* 405 U.S. 645 (1972).

60. *People ex rel. Vallera* v. *Rivera,* 29 Ill. App. 3d 775, 351 N.E.2d 391, 393 (1976); *see also In re Jones,* 34 Ill. App. 3d 603, 340 N.E.2d 269, 272 (1975).

61. *People ex rel. Vallera* v. *Rivera,* 351 N.E.2d, at 393 n.1.

62. *Commonwealth ex rel. Golembewski* v. *Stanley,* 205 Pa. Super. Ct. 101, 208 A.2d 49 (1965).

63. *Commonwealth* v. *Rozanski,* 206 Pa. Super. Ct., 397, 213 A.2d 155 (1965).

64. *Commonwealth* v. *Spano,* 68 Pa. D. & C. 248 (1949).

65. Compare *People ex rel. "Jean Francois"* v. *"Olga Ivanova,"* 14 A.D.2d 317, 221 N.Y.S.2d 75 (1st Dept. 1961).

66. *Matter of Grace V.,* 78 Misc. 2d 77, 80, 355 N.Y.S.2d 540 (Fam. Ct. 1974).

67. *Id.* at 80.

68. N.Y. Dom. Rel. Law § 72 (McKinney).

69. *Noll* v. *Noll,* 277 A.D. 286, 98 N.Y.S.2d 938 (4th Dept. 1950); *People ex rel. Hacker* v. *Strongson,* 141 N.Y.S.2d 859 (1955); *Ex parte People ex rel. Cox,* 124 N.Y.S.2d 511 (1953).

70. N.Y. Dom. Rel. Law § 72 (McKinney).

71. *People ex rel. Feliciano* v. *Alexander,* 34 A.D.2d 526, 308 N.Y.S.2d 446 (1st Dept. 1970).

72. *Id.,* at 526.

73. N.Y. Dom. Rel. Law § 72 (McKinney), *as amended* 1975.

74. *Lo Presti* v. *Lo Presti,* 40 N.Y.2d 522, 526–527, 355 N.E.2d 372 (1976).

75. *Id.,* at 525.

76. *Id. See also Lachnow* v. *Barasch,* 57 A.D.2d 896, 394 N.Y.S.2d 284 (2d Dept. 1977); *Sagumeri* v. *Fortunato,* 55 A.D.2d 936, 391 N.Y.S.2d 377 (2d Dept. 1977); *Vacula* v. *Blume,* 53 A.D.2d 633, 384 N.Y.S.2d 208 (2d Dept. 1976).

77. *Ehrlich* v. *Ressner,* 55 A.D.2d 953, 391 N.Y.S. 248 (4th Dept. 1977).

78. *In re Geri* v. *Fanto,* 79 Misc. 2d 947, 361 N.Y.S.2d 984 (Fam. Ct. 1974).

79. *Id.; Scranton* v. *Hutter,* 40 A.D.2d 296, 339 N.Y.S.2d 708 (4th Dept. 1973); *People ex rel. Simmons* v. *Sheridan,* 98 Misc. 2d 331, 414 N.Y.S.2d 83 (1979).

80. *See Ehrlich* v. *Ressner,* 55 A.D.2d 953, 391 N.Y.S.2d 152 (2d Dept. 1977).

81. *Gallinger* v. *Gallinger,* 55 A.D.2d 1036, 391 N.Y.S.2d 248 (4th Dept. 1977).

82. *People ex rel. Blake* v. *Charger,* 76 Misc. 2d 577, 351 N.Y.S.2d 322 (1974).

83. See chapter 1, Jurisdiction, *supra.*

84. *In re Raana Beth N.,* 78 Misc. 2d 105, 355 N.Y.S.2d 956 (Sur. Ct. 1974); *In re Abraham L.,* 53 A.D.2d 669, 385 N.Y.S.2d 103 (2d Dept. 1976).

85. *In re Patricia A. W.,* 89 Misc. 2d 368, 392 N.Y.S.2d 180 (Fam. Ct. 1977).

86. *Mimkon* v. *Ford,* 66 N.J. 426, 332 A.2d 199 (1975).

87. N.J. Stat. Ann. § 9:2–7.1 (West).

88. *Mimkon* v. *Ford,* 332 A.2d, at 201 n.1.

89. *Id. Compare with Scranton* v. *Hutter,* 40 A.D.2d 296, 339 N.Y.S.2d 708 (4th Dept. 1973); *In re Geri* v. *Fanto,* 79 Misc. 2d 947, 361 N.Y.S.2d 984 (Fam. Ct. 1974).

90. *Bennett* v. Bennett, 150 N.J. Super. 509, 376 A.2d 191 (1977).

91. Ohio Rev. Code Ann. § 3109.11 (Page).

92. *Grazino* v. *Davis,* 50 Ohio App. 2d 83, 361 N.E.2d 525 (1976).

93. *Ryan* v. *De Mello,* 116 R.I. 264, 354 A.2d 734 (1976).

94. Wash. Rev. Code § 26.09.240.

95. *Carlson* v. *Carlson,* 16 Wash. App. 595, 558 P.2d 836 (1976).

96. See N.Y. Dom. Rel. Law §§ 75a–z (McKinney).

97. *Kresnicka* v. *Kresnicka,* 42 A.D.2d 607, 354 N.Y.S.2d 118 (2d Dept. 1973).

98. *Id.*

99. *People ex rel. Halvey* v. *Halvey,* 185 Misc. 52, 55 N.Y.S.2d 761 (Sup. Ct. 1945), *aff'd,* 269 A.D. 1019, 59 N.Y.S.2d 396 (1st Dept. 1945), *Sweet* v. *Rose,* 25 A.D.2d 805, 269 N.Y.S.2d 530 (3d Dept. 1966); *In re Reinhart* v. *Reinhart,* 33 Misc. 2d 80, 227 N.Y.S.2d 39 (Sup. Ct. 1961).

100. *In re Denberg* v. *Denberg,* 34 Misc. 2d 980, 987, 229 N.Y.S.2d 831 (Sup. Ct. 1962).

101. *Id.*

102. *Id.,* at 986; *Whittemore* v. *Whittemore,* 202 Misc. 175, 178, 109 N.Y.S.2d 216 (Sup. Ct. 1951).

103. *In re Doe* v. *Doe,* 86 Misc. 2d, at 196 and at 202. *See also Sawyer* v. *Larkin,* 37 A.D.2d 929, 326 N.Y.S.2d 270 (1st Dept. 1971).

104. In re Doe v. *Doe,* 86 Misc. 2d, at 196.

105. *Id.,* at 197; *Callender* v. *Callender,* 37 A.D.2d 360, 325 N.Y.S.2d 420 (1st Dept. 1971).

106. *In re Doe* v. *Doe,* 86 Misc. 2d 194, 378 N.Y.S.2d 269 (Fam. Ct. 1975).

107. *Id.,* at 202; Smith v. *Smith,* 255 A.D. 652, 9 N.Y.S.2d 188 (2d Dept. 1939); *Harris* v. *Harris,* 197 A.D. 646, 189 N.Y.S.2d 215 (1st Dept. 1921).

108. *In re Sandra B.* v. *Charles B.,* 85 Misc. 2d 663, 380 N.Y.S.2d 861 (Fam. Ct. 1976).

109. *Id.*

110. *Id.*

111. *Callender* v. *Callender,* 37 A.D.2d 360, 325 N.Y.S.2d 420 (1st Dept. 1971).

112. *Compare Callender* v. *Callender, id., with Abraham* v. *Abraham,* 44 A.D.2d 675, 353 N.Y.S.2d 794 (2d Dept. 1974).

113. *Geller* v. *Schulman,* 45 Misc. 2d 824, 257 N.Y.S.2d 632 (Civ. Ct. 1965).

114. *McMains* v. *McMains,* 15 N.Y.2d 283, 206 N.E.2d 185 (1965).

115. See Practice Commentaries by Douglas J. Besharove; N.Y. Fam. Ct. Act § 156 (McKinney 29A).

116. *Lefkowitz* v. *Lefkowitz,* 17 Misc. 2d 958, 186 N.Y.S.2d 925 (Sup. Ct. 1959).

117. *Boone* v. *Boone,* 133 Vt. 322, 340 A.2d 53 (1975).

118. *Heidemann* v. *Heidemann,* 96 Idaho 602, 533 P.2d 96 (1974).

119. *Ruquist* v. *Ruquist,* 367 Mass. 662, 327 N.E.2d 742 (1975).

# 7 Counsel Fees

## General Considerations

The topic of counsel-fee awards in matrimonial and related causes of action is in itself substantial enough for a book-length treatise. We consider it advisable to avoid excessive tangential discussion herein and maintain the focus on counsel fees as applied to custody matters. Nevertheless, some background discussion is necessary for perspective.

## Counsel-Fee Origins

The origins of the authority of the courts of New York to grant awards of counsel fees in matrimonial actions are referable to the powers inherited by the Supreme Court as successor to the English Court of Chancery.[1] Prior to 1787, there was no jurisdiction conferred on *any* tribunal in New York to grant a divorce or any incidental relief whatever.[2] The only recourse, up until that time, for the domestically discontented was an application for a personal bill of divorce from the New York legislature.[3] When jurisdiction was conferred on the courts by the legislature, it was specifically granted to the Court of Chancery, to which the Supreme Court succeeded.[4] In the earliest cases, it has been held that the power to grant counsel fees is implicit in the power to grant a divorce in every case wherein the English Courts had that power, even when specific authoritization was lacking in the statute.[5]

> [I]t must be assumed that when they vested the Court of Chancery with the power to exercise that jurisdiction, they considered that it would be vested by implication with those equitable powers to guard the rights of wives, which had always been regarded as incidents of such jurisdiction, and were customarily exercised by the courts engaged in its administration. . . . It must be remembered that the jurisdiction was conferred not upon a common-law court, but upon the Court of Chancery, and in view of its general powers to adjust remedies and annex conditions to the exercise of rights and redress of injuries.[6]

Thus from the earliest devolution of authority to grant counsel fees to the Supreme Court, there was an explicit distinction between the equitable power to grant an award and the common-law right to obtain a reimbursement for counsel fees by a suit for necessaries.[7]

The case-law origins of present-day counsel fees focused on the English chancellor's *incidental* authority to grant counsel fees in conjunction with his authority to grant divorces. The first instance of *judicial* authority to grant a divorce in New York State, however, was the legislative enactment of 1787, whereby the Court of Chancery received its power to grant divorce by statute. Thus the origin of the court's powers in New York stems from a legislative enactment with a prior nonstatutory common-law tradition. Therefore later cases make reference to the pertinent statute as the authority and to English precedent as the source of amplification and elaboration on the statutory authority.[8]

Later discussions pertain to the statutory authority as essentially the last word and tend to deny awards when specific statutory authority is found to be lacking.[9] Based on precedents dating from the early part of this century, the appellate division has explicitly held that "[t]he authority of any court to grant counsel fees is purely statutory" and can only be sustained if authority for it can be found in a pertinent statutory provision.[10] The discussion of counsel fees as applied to custody matters is, therefore, a discussion of the pertinent statutes and their application to specific circumstances.

### Counsel Fees as Distinguished from Necessaries

While the right to a counsel-fee award originates in the powers of the English chancellor,[11] the right to bring a plenary action for counsel fees as necessaries has a common-law provenance and no basis in statutory authority. The common-law liability of a husband to supply his wife and children with necessaries in general was considered "well-settled" when *Keller* v. *Phillips*[12] was decided by the Court of Appeals in 1868.

> The rule of law relating to the powers of the wife to bind her husband to payment for goods purchased by her for the use of herself and the family are well settled. The husband is bound to provide for her and them whatever is necessary for their suitable clothing and maintenance according to his and their situation and condition in life.[13]

It is beyond question that this same principle applies to the necessaries of children who are entitled to look to their father for support.

> "A parent is under a natural obligation to furnish necessaries for his infant children; and if the parent neglect that duty, any other person who supplies such necessaries is deemed to have conferred a benefit on the delinquent

parent, for which the law raises an implied promise to pay on the part of the parent" [citation omitted]. This rule has long been recognized as the law both in England and this country.[14]

It is also well settled that the obligation to pay attorney's fees is included within the definition of necessaries.

> Where a wife, living with her husband whom he is obliged to support, is arrested on a criminal charge, or prosecuted in a civil action, which may result in her incarceration, the necessity for a lawyer may be as urgent and as important as the necessity for a doctor when she is sick. Her health is a very important matter in the maintenance of the home and the happiness or even existence of the marital state. Of like importance is her presence in the home which may be interrupted and the home broken up by taking her therefrom on a criminal charge. The mental suffering and anguish which may result from an unwarranted suit for alleged libel may be as disastrous in its effects as any other mental sickness or disorder. Such actions may, therefore . . . require the husband to pay a reasonable lawyer's bill for services in protecting his wife.[15]

The more recent cases continue to hold that "legal services rendered to a wife in a matrimonial action are necessaries and her lawyer has a common law right to bring a plenary action against the husband for having supplied such services."[16]

The provision of various statutory remedies for the award of counsel fees does not deprive a wife from electing the common-law plenary alternative.[17] In a plenary action, the attorney "may not claim for himself any greater right than the wife's or a different standard of determining his right to compensation."[18] Moreover, "in such a plenary suit the amount of the counsel fees is fixed with reference to the results actually achieved in the matrimonial litigation."[19]

A parent may still elect between the statutory right to a counsel-fee award or a plenary action under the common law. Generally, the existence of the statutory remedy is not deemed to preclude the alternative common-law remedy for necessaries.[20] In disposing of an application for a counsel fee under an authorizing statute, however, the courts will generally decline to award a counsel fee for services long since past and uncompensated.[21] To secure favorable disposition of an application for a counsel fee, the application must be made during the pendency of the cause of action for which the award is sought, or the right to do so at a later date must be reserved.[22]

> If the wife has made application for attorney's fees during the pendency of the matrimonial action, the court's fixation of such fees is the measure of the husband's obligation with respect to the action, and the wife will be deemed to have made an election barring further plenary suit against the husband for such fees.[23]

When, however, "an application for counsel fees has been made and considered in an underlying proceeding and conclusively disposed of a common-law plenary action is barred."[24] When the record is inconclusive as to a disposition by the court on an application for counsel fees, or when moving papers are so inadequate such that no application can be deemed to have been properly presented to the court, then a common-law plenary action will survive.[25]

Legal services rendered to either parent in a custody proceeding clearly come within the definition of necessaries rendered on behalf of a minor child.[26] Thus there is a right to proceed in common-law plenary action for counsel fees incurred in connection with a custody proceeding, so long as the defendant is properly chargeable with liability for the necessaries of the child on whose behalf the custody proceeding was brought. This is so even when authority may be lacking for a counsel-fee award under one or more of the applicable statutes.[27]

In *Errico* v. *Manville,* a 1969 Westchester County Court decision,[28] a remarried mother sought to obtain custody of her child from her former husband.[29] The mother initiated the litigation and possessed monetary means far superior to those of the father.[30] In a decision that might possibly *not* have been made today,[31] the court denied the father's application for a counsel fee, on a narrow reading of the pertinent statutes. The court found that the statutory language clearly provided only for payment of a counsel fee by the husband and father to the wife, or ex-wife, and mother.[32] Therefore, no counsel fee could be awarded in favor of the father as against the mother, although the court did find that the father had recourse to a common-law plenary suit against the mother for the necessary fees.[33] Possibly, the father in *Errico* was able to take some comfort in the alternative offered to him by the county court by way of its expressed dictum. It is certainly far more economical, however, in terms of an attorney's time and effort, to obtain a statutory counsel-fee award as incidental relief to an underlying custody or other matrimonial action. Attempting to collect the same, or possibly a lesser amount of money, in an additional lawsuit with all of its potential discovery and motion practice, trial effort, and subsequent collection practice is unproductive. To be relegated to a common-law plenary action places an attorney at a distinct disadvantage; the client is also at a disadvantage by reason of the chilling effect this circumstance will have on a lawyer's willingness to take a case.

## Pertinent Statutory Authority

### The Domestic Relations Law

The most significant of the pertinent statutory sections in New York is Domestic Relations Law Section 237,[34] which provides in Section 237(a) that a counsel fee may be awarded to either spouse in divorce, annulment, separation, or related actions. By inference, therefore, the court may award a counsel fee in any general matrimonial action in which a prayer for a custody award is brought as requested incidental relief.[35] Such an award may be made "by one or more orders from time to time before final judgment, or by both such order or orders and the final judgment."[36]

Under Section 237(b), the court may award a counsel fee in any action to amend or modify any outstanding order or judgment for custody or visitation, among other things.[37] Further, the court may make such an award pursuant to a writ of *habeas corpus* or petition and order to show cause concerning custody or visitation. The power to make the award under the statute was, until recently, directed against the father or husband and for the benefit of the wife or mother, but the most recent amendment to the statute has made it gender-neutral in conformity with current case law.[38] The award may be made only in the order or judgment by which the particular application or proceeding is finally determined.[39] Careful study of the last sentence of Section 237(b) and the second sentence of Section 237(a) will reveal the importance of recording an application for counsel fees prior to the final order or judgment or a reservation of the right to do so thereafter.

## The Family Court Act

Under Article 4 of the Family Court Act, the family court may make an order of custody or visitation pursuant to a petition for support when it otherwise has original or referred jurisdiction.[40] The family court's jurisdiction to award custody or visitation also extends to all matters referred from the Supreme Court during the pendency of a divorce, separation, or annulment action.[41] There is further jurisdiction under Article 4 of the Family Court Act to award custody or visitation pursuant to an order of protection incidental to an application for support.[42]

When relief is sought under any pertinent provision of Article 4 of the Family Court Act, a counsel-fee application will be entertained by the court pursuant to Section 438.[43] The Section provides that counsel fees may be awarded "at any stage of the proceeding,"[44] again putting the attorney on notice that the right to the fee may be lost if not timely made.[45]

The statutory jurisdiction of the family court to award custody or visitation also extends to applications that come before it pursuant to paternity proceedings.[46] As a consequence, a custody issue litigated pursuant to a paternity petition may result in a counsel fee being awarded to the mother, but only after an order of filiation has been entered.[47] This particular provision is unique in that a successful disposition on the action in chief is an absolute prerequisite to a counsel-fee award. But the rationale behind the requirement is readily apparent inasmuch as if there is no paternity established, there is no *prima facie* standing to challenge custody or demand visitation.[48]

An additional source of family court jurisdiction in custody and visitation awards is Section 842(e), which provides for such an award incidental to an order of protection obtained in the course of a family-offense proceeding.[49] Article 8 of the Family Court Act makes no provision for the award of a counsel fee pursuant to any order or incidental relief obtained under the article. It thus appears that no counsel-fee award is available if a custody award is made incidental to an order of protection under Article 8. Section 817 of the Family Court Act provides that the court, however, on its own motion and at any time may convert a petition under Article 8 to a petition, among other things, under Article 4 for support or Article 5 for paternity.[50] This raises the inference that the counsel-fee remedies available under Sections 438 and 536 would become available on such conversion.[51]

Under Sections 651(a) and 651(b), the family court has, by inference, inherited all of the powers of the Supreme Court concerning custody and visitation issues, wherein relief is sought following referral from the Supreme Court or pursuant to the family court's original jurisdiction.[52] Further, under Section 652 of the Family Court Act, a custody issue may be referred to the family court by the Supreme Court during the pendency of a matrimonial action for divorce, annulment, separation, and so forth.[53] Although there is no specific statutory provision for an award of counsel fees under Article 6 of the Family Court Act, as compared to Articles 4 and 5,[54] there is ample decisional authority for the view that the family court's authority to award a counsel fee is implicit in its statutory exercise of Supreme Court powers granted to it under Section 651.[55] There is precedent supporting the family court's power to award a counsel fee pursuant to both a referral under Section 651(a) and an action on the court's original jurisdiction under Section 651(b).[56]

The family court's jurisdiction over custody and visitation is further augmented by Section 34-a of the Uniform Support of Dependent's Law.[57] Under Section 34-a, an award may be made in respondent's favor, pursuant to a Uniform Support of Dependents Law (U.S.D.L.) petition for support, so long as the petitioner and the child who is the subject of the requested relief both reside in another county of New York.[58] To the extent that counsel fees are available under the U.S.D.L., it would appear that they may be awarded incidental to an order granting custody or visitation under Section 34-a.

Earlier case law held that no counsel-fee awards were available under the U.S.D.L. for want of specific statutory authorization.[59] Later cases, however, have favored a broader interpretation by inferring from Section 438 of the Family Court Act[60] the authority to award a counsel fee under a Uniform Support of Dependents Law proceeding.[61]

*The Surrogate's Court Act*

Except in relation to abandoned, neglected, and involuntarily surrendered children, or with respect to adoption matters,[62] the surrogate's court rarely uses its authority to adjudicate custody and visitation matters.[63] To the extent that the court has such powers, it appears to have incidental authority to award counsel fees inferred from its succession to the *parens patriae* equity powers of the chancellor.[64]

In a 1932 surrogate's court decision, the maternal aunt and uncle of infant children (de facto custodians of the children, following the death of their mother) sought reimbursement from the estate of the children for legal expenses incurred in defending a *habeas corpus* proceeding against the natural father of the infants.[65] The court held that "[a]n infant's estate is liable for moneys advanced for the necessaries of life" and allowed the charge against the estate based on that principle and the court's inherent powers.[66]

> If the court has the inherent power to indemnify out of trust property for proper expenses in connection with the property of infants, then it must be held that a court of equity has the inherent power to pay reasonable expenses to secure a ruling as to the proper and fit control of the persons of infants, where such payments are beneficial and necessary to the persons of the infants.[67]

There is also statutory authority for the Surrogate's court to award a counsel fee from estate funds to an attorney for services rendered to "a fiduciary or to a deviser, legatee, distributee, or any person interested."[68] Such an award may be made "at any time during the administration of an estate and irrespective of the pendency of a particular proceeding."[69] The petitioner may be a "fiduciary of the estate or a person interested or an attorney who has rendered services."[70]

The trend in case law has been such that there is little opportunity in recent years for the surrogate's court to exercise its authority in custody litigation in general.[71] A necessary consequence of this cycle is a sparsity of cases applying either general equity powers or the compensation statute with regard to counsel-fee awards in such matters.[72]

## Timely Application in Family Court

Section 438 of the Family Court Act[73] provides for a counsel-fee award "in any proceeding" under Article 4 before a family court judge.[74] *Cassieri* v. *Cassieri,* decided by the appellate division in 1969, ignited a notable judicial controversy as to the timeliness of counsel-fee applications in the family court.[75] The court in *Cassieri* interpreted the phrase "in any proceeding" to mean "at any stage of the proceeding."[76] Thus because the counsel-fee application was not formally made until after the family court judge had entered an order of support, the appellate division reversed the family court's subsequent award of a counsel fee.[77]

> In our opinion the instant application for counsel fees was not made "at any stage of the proceeding [citing case]." The entry of the order terminating the proceeding deprived the Family Court of jurisdiction to entertain the application for counsel fees and to make the order appealed from awarding counsel fees.[78]

*Reed* v. *Reed,* a 1970 New York County Family Court decision, took extreme exception to the appellate division's ruling in *Cassieri* and justified its position on the lack of a controlling opinion in the first department.[79] "Unlike the Supreme Court's final judgments in matrimonial litigation, the Family Court's orders . . . do not 'terminate' a Family Court proceeding . . . 'continuing jurisdiction of Family Court is expressly provided by Section 451'."[80]

The court in *Reed* held that the construction by the appellate division in *Cassieri* of "in any proceeding" as synonymous with "any stage of the proceeding" was far too narrow.[81] Further, to follow the rule in *Cassieri* "would be to establish a mined trap to cut off discretion in Family Court to award counsel fees by an obscure application of a doctrine of instantaneous laches which would detonate at the instant of termination of any hearing leading to a final order."[82] The application for a counsel fee, in the opinion of the court in *Reed,* should be permitted within a "reasonable time after trial or disposition."[83]

It has been held that, when an attorney made an oral application for a counsel fee to a family court judge, and the judge directed him to submit a supplemental written application, the court had itself extended the proceeding for the continuation of the counsel-fee request.[84] It appears that the whole problem of the opinion in *Cassieri* versus the opinion in *Reed* is best resolved by the simple expedient of reserving, at the time of trial in family court, the right to submit a posttrial written application for counsel fees.

It has been further held that even if the rule in *Reed* were to be applied, the application for a counsel fee must be made within a "reasonable time."[85] In following the reasonable-time rule, the court denied a counsel-fee application submitted 18 months from the date of entry of the original order.[86] Whatever defect was present in the application for a counsel fee for services that resulted in the original order, however, none would be imputed to a timely application for counsel fees for services rendered on subsequent petitions for modifications.[87]

## Eligibility for Counsel Fees in Custody Proceedings

*Nonparents*

It is plain from published decisions that, although one need not be a natural parent to achieve standing to contest custody or visitation, there is no statutory authority for a counsel-fee award to nonparent third parties. It was held as follows in *Koch* v. *Koch,* a 1979 decision:[88]

> Domestic Relations Law Section 237(b), the applicable statute, provides that only a husband or father can be directed to pay counsel fees in a custody proceeding. This section was amended in 1978 and the legislature saw fit not to alter the above stated provision despite the fact that existing Domestic Relations Law Section 72 gave a grandparent the right to petition for visitation of grandchildren under certain circumstances. Thus, we hold that the special financial interdependence that exists between spouses and parents that gives rise to the obligation to pay counsel fees in a custody proceeding does not exist between a mother-in-law as in the case at bar.[89]

It should be noted that Section 237 was further amended in 1980 to make the language therein gender-neutral and eliminate any confusion as to whether the courts had the authority to award a counsel fee to a father as against a mother. There was still no intent indicated by the legislature, however, to bring third parties within the ambit of the statute.

In a decision similar to that in *Koch* v. *Koch, supra,* the Duchess County Family Court denied an application for a counsel fee in a custody dispute that pitted the natural mother against her own parents.[90]

> A petitioner who is emancipated from her parents is a stranger to them insofar as her ability to obtain any form of support is concerned. As is the case with any litigants, who, from a legal point of view, are strangers, absent statutory or case law to the contrary, one may not exact counsel fees from the other. . . . [T]his court may not attempt to legislate in an effort to right an apparent wrong.[91]

*Father's Standing to Collect Counsel Fees as against the Mother*

It is now the "law of the land," not to mention the law of New York, that all statutes granting courts authority to award counsel fees in matrimonial actions must be interpreted as gender-neutral. This is to say that when a statute provides for an award to a wife, the constitutional requirement of equal protection of the laws mandates that either spouse may benefit from the enabling authority of the statute "on a gender-neutral, needs only basis."[92] This conclusion was reached by the appellate division in the second department on direct remand of the Supreme Court of the United States[93] for reconsideration in light of *Orr* v. *Orr,* the historic alimony-equalizer case.[94]

The effect of the gender-neutral inference, however, was made retroactive only to March 5, 1969, the date of the United Supreme Court's decision in *Orr* v. *Orr*.[95]

> All other awards of counsel fees which had been conclusively adjudicated as of that date shall not be affected by our holding today. There exists no constitutional impediment to applying changes in law only in cases pending as of the date of such decision (citations omitted).[96]

*Childs* v. *Childs* was cited as the direct authority for the second department's declaration that an inference of gender neutrality must also be applied to Section 438 of the Family Court Act.[97] It appears to be a fair inference that the gender neutral rule is now applicable to all counsel-fee statutes presently in effect in New York as to any application made on or before March 5, 1979.

Additionally (see Counsel Fees as Distinguished from Necessaries, *supra,* and Eligibility for Counsel Fees in Custody Proceedings, Non-parents, *supra*) Section 237 has been amended in its most recent addition to make its language gender-neutral.

The gender-neutral rule in counsel-fee awards was a long time in coming. The principles promulgated in *Childs*[98] were anticipated in certain far-sighted trial-court decisions as long ago as 1976.[99] But the instances wherein courts failed to recognize the discriminatory aspects of the enabling statutes or even address the issue were more numerous. The U.S. Supreme Court has held that "discrimination by a state between different classes of its citizens must . . . have some relevance to the purpose for which the classification is made."[100] This constitutional quality-control criterion, as applied to sex-discrimination statutes, was once deemed satisfied relative to counsel-fee statutes on the following grounds:

> The purpose of the statute is to allow a wife [or former wife on behalf of her children] to present and prosecute her action properly. Without the power to award a needy wife counsel fees, the rights of the woman, in many cases, could not be adequately protected.[101]

Moreover, there was considerable avoidance by the appellate courts of direct address to the sex-discrimination issue wherever and whenever such avoidance could be adroitly accomplished.[102]

In *Errico* v. *Manville,* a 1969 county-court decision,[103] the mother of the minor child involved divorced the child's father and married one Mr. Manville, one of the more notorious and romantic heirs to great wealth of twentieth-century America.[104] As part of a separation agreement, the mother conceded custody of her daughter to the father and even agreed to pay the father $150 per week toward the child's support.[105]

Some 9 years after the divorce and soon after the death of Mr. Manville (in 1967), Mrs. Manville commenced a *habeas corpus* proceeding in Supreme Court to obtain custody of her child.[106] The mother's application was denied, and therefore the father, whose means were far inferior to those of the mother, assumed the status of the victorious party in a custody proceeding.[107] Nevertheless, the court cited with approval the rule of another judge of coordinate jurisdiction who had denied the father's application for a counsel fee under the enabling statute.[108] " '[T]he legislative intent seems to be to confine the obligations to pay the other party's counsel fees to the husband or father. Without express statutory authorization, the court is without power to grant this form of relief.' "[109]

The court ruled, however, that the mother was liable for the fair value of the services of the father's attorney in a plenary action by the attorney for necessaries.[110] In a difficult case, of course, a sensitive court will find a way to accomplish an objective that it might otherwise find to be proscribed. The decision in *Childs* v. *Childs,*[111] by its gender-neutral, judge-made modification of all outstanding counsel-fee statutes, has made exotic and creative solutions unnecessary. Gradually, all pertinent statutes will no doubt be amended to bring their language into line with the principle as expressed in *Childs.*

## Standards for Awards

Section 237 of the Domestic Relations Law[112] provides that the criterion for an award is that "in the court's discretion, justice requires, having regard to the circumstances of the case and of the respective parties."[113] The important word appears to be "discretion" as opposed to "justice" or "circumstances," at least in the pragmatic analysis. Discretion leaves a great deal of room in which a judge may maneuver, effectively limited only by what an appellate court will consider to be an abuse of discretion.

It was held in *Ansorge* v. *Armour,* a *habeas corpus* proceeding brought to obtain the custody of a child, that the initiators of the proceeding "had the burden of proving facts showing such necessity for the proceedings as well as a necessity for a change in the custody of the child."[114] Therefore, ". . . in the absence of any evidence in this record showing that the welfare of the child demands a modification or change in the custody as awarded by the divorce decree, we cannot find that justification for a habeas corpus proceeding which makes it necessary for the father to pay the lawyer hired by the mother to conduct it."[115] Thus in denying a mother's request to modify the provisions of a separation agreement incorporated into a divorce decree, this court also denied the mother a counsel fee.[116]

But the *Ansorge* decision was made in a plenary action brought by the mother's attorney against the father. It is questionable as to whether the heavy burden to demonstrate necessity for the proceeding could be established by anything less than success. Hence it is doubtful, based on the rule as cited hereinabove, whether the prerequisite of success is meant to apply to applications brought under statutory authority, which refers to an award based on justice and circumstances of the respective parties. There is no inference that can be drawn from the statute to indicate that success on the merits is a basis for an award. Thus the language placing the burden of proving necessity on the initiator of a custody proceeding can be severely misinterpreted when taken out of context. Moreover, the court in *Ansorge* appeared to be significantly influenced by its view of the custody proceeding as an opportunistic means of leverage by the mother to gain an upward modification of her support.[117] The sincerity of her interest in the welfare of the children was treated by the court with skepticism.[118]

The language of *Ansorge,* misleading when taken out of context, was used in the worst possible fashion in *People ex rel. Fousier* v. *Uzielli.* [119]

> As to the counsel fee, petitioner [mother] has the burden of proving facts showing such necessity for the proceeding as well as a necessity for a change in custody of [the children] [citations omitted]. On the record before us petitioner did not meet that burden.[120]

*Fousier,* unlike *Ansorge,* was not a plenary action. With that distinction in mind, what is the significance of the language in *Fousier* regarding the burden of proving necessity? Conceivably, the petitioner might show necessity for a change of custody and receive an award in her favor on the case in chief yet fail to receive a favorable disposition of a counsel-fee application because, even though victorious, the custody proceeding was not deemed necessary at the inception. On the other hand, the petitioner might have shown the proceeding to be necessary at the inception but fail to receive a favorable disposition on the case in chief and thus forfeit a counsel fee on that basis alone, in spite of the statutory admonition that an award be made according to justice and the relative circumstances of the parties.

The case examples in this section will generally demonstrate that an award of a counsel fee in a custody or visitation matter will depend on the court's perception of the relative merits of the positions of each party, including the degree of sincerity of each party as perceived by the court. As a practical matter, these factors will take vigorous precedence over such other elements as the relative financial circumstances of the adversaries or the ultimate success of either of them.

In a 1955 Westchester County decision, the Supreme Court addressed the petition of a custodial mother seeking to modify the visitation provisions of a separation decree. (A divorce was a rare and cherished commodity in the New York courts under the law current in 1955.)[121] The court considered copious testimony, including that of behavioral experts, to the effect that the father's visitation was injurious to the children by reason of the following: (1) the presence of a young woman friend, (2) verbal altercations with the mother's relatives occurring at times when the father called for the children, and (3) derogatory remarks of the mother made by the father and his relatives in the presence of the children.[122] The court concluded that the children had developed emotional problems arising from "the breach of relationship[s] between the father and mother and are such as are frequently found among children of broken or disturbed homes and are a traumatic incident of separation or divorce."[123]

Although the court, throughout the remainder of its decision, wrote of the need for both parents to behave responsibly under the distressing circumstances of matrimonial strife, its award of relief left little doubt that it placed the blame for the dissension on the father.[124] In modifying the visitation provisions, all of the new restrictions were placed on the father, and most of the admonitions were addressed in his direction.[125] Additionally, on the collateral issue of child support, the court found that the father had enjoyed a considerable increment in his standard of living since the time when the separation decree was entered.[126] It must then come as no surprise that the court also found that "[i]t was necessary and beneficial to the children that their mother's counsel render her services in connection with this motion."[127] There was no mention in the decision of the mother's relative means—her indigency or lack of it—relating to her ability to pay her own counsel. It was enough for the court that the father was at fault and could afford to pay the price.

In a 1971 first department case, the custodial mother had removed the infant to Florida for a period of 6 months immediately after the grant of a decree of divorce wherein the father was awarded "reasonable visitation."[128] Having effectively deprived the father of his visitation for 6 months, the custodial mother returned to New York, where the father initiated a proceeding, by order to show cause, to secure his rights under an outstanding divorce decree.[129] The father succeeded in his application, which was in turn upheld by the appellate division. Additionally, the appellate court affirmed the trial court's denial of a counsel fee to the mother for the postjudgment proceeding.[130]

We should not disturb the [trial court's] determination when there are no special circumstances. The wife argues that the father has not seen the child since she went to Florida. To use that as a basis for reducing visitation would be to permit that deprivation by distance to be used to assist the party responsible. As to counsel fees, those already awarded were more than ample. . . . There is no need to continue with additional counsel fees.[131]

If there is a conclusion to be drawn, it appears to be that, regardless of the means, sex, or circumstances of either party, the standard according to which a counsel fee is deemed merited will be the relative display of wilfulness, defiance, arrogance, or stubbornness of the adversary party who most offends the court. The breadth of discretion allowed to the court by the statute is understandably too tempting not to be taken advantage of in this fashion, despite the seeming limitations of the "justice" and "circumstances" language.

Even an attorney's behavior, over and above the issue of the mother's indigency, can prejudice her application for counsel fees, when subjected to a judicial scrutiny empowered with such broad discretion. In *People ex rel. Schack* v. *Schack,* the appellate division substantially reduced a trial court counsel fee award in a *habeas corpus* proceeding, on concluding that "a substantial amount of time expended by counsel for both parties was in the nature of tactics rather than substance."[132]

In a 1977 memorandum decision by the first department, the appellate division reversed a $500 counsel-fee award to the noncustodial mother, which had been granted on her motion concerning visitation provisions of an outstanding divorce judgment.[133] The appellate division concluded that the mother's original application had been wholly frivolous and that the mother had "failed to meet the burden of proving facts showing a necessity for the motion, a vital factor in determining whether a counsel fee award was warranted."[134]

In addition to some showing of merit on the application that underlies a counsel-fee request, the party seeking the award needs to make some showing of a financial inability to carry on a custody proceeding without counsel-fee relief.[135] The courts, needless to say, exercise broad discretion in determining an applicant's necessary indigency with respect to counsel awards in all domestic relations cases, whether or not a child-custody controversy is presented. Nevertheless, indigency sufficient to inhibit pursuit of adequate legal relief is an abiding principle of counsel-fee awards, no matter how vague its application.

In a novel 1975 Nassau County case, a mother of six children, seeking to put the cares of housework and parenthood behind her and find personal gratification in a broader sphere, petitioned the Supreme Court to award custody not to herself but to her husband.[136] Her purpose was to be free of the responsibilities of childcare in order to join the U.S. Army.[137] The father, although continuing to maintain physical custody of the children, opposed the mother's application.[138] The proceeding was occasioned by the U.S. Army's requirement that, before accepting the enlistment of a woman with children, the military candidate must submit a court order to the effect that her children are not in her custody.[139]

The court denied the mother's application as contrary to the best interests of the children and, further, denied her a counsel fee in that "her application is not predicated on the well-being of the children, or for her necessaries, but in furtherance of her own personal desire to join the United States Army."[140]

In a similar mode, a 1978 family court decision found that the proceeding before it was occasioned solely by the custodial mother's intransigent and unjustifiable denial of visitation to the father.[141] In denying a counsel-fee award, the court held as follows:

> The touchstone upon which an award should be predicated is that the wife's or mother's claim or defense be rooted in reason and have some merit [citing cases]. Success is of no importance. For if success were the *sine qua non* for the award of counsel fees, women understandably would be reluctant to chance the vagaries and uncertainties of litigation. . . . [However] without the condition that the wife or mother have some merit to her claim or defense the beneficent design of [the statute] would be corrupted and the husbands and fathers victimized by unscrupulous wives and mothers.[142]

A capsule rule may be stated thus, by way of conclusion: The failure of a female applicant, be she wife, ex-wife, and/or mother, to present some meritorious grounds for a counsel-fee award and her failure to avoid offending the sensibilities of the court by reason of essentially unfair behavior on her part will result in the denial of the award. It appears that the rule is more accurately stated in the negative than in the positive sense.

## Other Jurisdictions

### Illinois

Illinois, like New York, has a specific statute addressed to the award of counsel fees that applies to matrimonial actions in general and, implicitly, to custody disputes in particular.[143] As with the currently applicable New York statute,[144] the Illinois code provisions tell part, but not all, of the story. The power to construe is great, and the scope of discretion is wide when an enabling statute provides that a court "may" enter such an award.[145] Bearing in mind the distinction between "may" and "must," an attorney needs no greater reason to ask for a retainer in advance.

Yet the drafters of the Illinois code exhibited the most tender sensitivity to the needs of the hardworking practitioner. They provided that a court may set a fee and order payment by a party to his or her *own* attorney, in addition to or as an alternative to an award to the adversary attorney.[146] Further, the court may appoint an attorney to represent a child's interest in a custody or visitation matter and order that payment be made by either or both parents "or against the child's separate estate."[147] In New York, the provisions for payment of a "law guardian" to represent the child's interests place the burden of the fee on the court.[148]

The breadth of the court's authority to award a counsel fee extends to the "maintenance or defense of any proceeding" and the "enforcement or modification of any order or judgment" under the Illinois Marriage and Dissolution Act.[149] Implicitly, then, an award may be made in a custody or visitation proceeding that is defined in chapter 40, paragraph 610 of the same act.[150] Certainly, the same general rules that pertain to the application of the statute to matrimonial actions in general will apply to awards in custody disputes in particular. The commentaries to the counsel-fee section, paragraph 508, provide guidance in this regard.

> Subsection(a) provides that the court "may" order either spouse to pay costs and attorney's fees. In so doing, this section retains Illinois' adherence to the general rule that the allowance of such fees and costs in divorce proceedings is not a matter of right [citing cases] but rests within the sound discretion of the trial court [citing case]. In exercising its discretion, the court may consider, in addition to the abilities of the parties to pay, the questions at issue, the significance or importance of the subject matter, the degree of responsibility involved, the standing or skill of the person employed and the time and labor involved. . . . In exercising its discretion, under prior law, the court also considered the circumstances which prompted judicial proceedings. Fees could not be assessed against a party who had "done nothing which necessitated or required judicial action. . . ." Such rules continue to apply under this section.[151]

At the outset, then, assuming the accuracy of the commentaries, the general rule for standards of awards encompasses the same elements as those promulgated in New York.[152] The more significant distinction is the effective elimination in Illinois of the need for a plenary action or a suit for necessaries as the means to collect legal fees in custody cases[153] because of the court's statutory power to award a fee to a disputant's *own* attorney and to award a fee directly to a law guardian appointed for a child.[154] The commentaries reflect on the 1970 amendment to the Illinois Constitution[155] that "abolished differences between law and equity and conferred upon the circuit courts original jurisdiction in all judiciable matters."[156] In furtherance of that general principle, the legislature empowered the court to order counsel-fee awards in favor of, and adverse to, any party or combination of parties in a custody dispute, including the subject children.[157] It is interesting that this greater exposure on the part of one parent party for payment of attorney's fees can work to the disadvantage of the other party, while the person who benefits is the court-appointed law guardian.

In *In re Scott*, a 1979 intermediate appellate case, the father and former husband petitioned the court for a modification of the custody provisions of a prior divorce decree.[158] Based on lengthy testimony from various behavioral scientists, the trial court concluded that the child's best interests were best served by a transfer of custody to the father and his second wife "because of the possibility of the recurrence of the mother's schizophrenia."[159]

The appellate court upheld the trial court decision as contrary to the weight of the evidence and well within the proper exercise of the trial court's discretion.[160] The denial of a counsel-fee award to the mother by the trial court was also upheld on appeal as properly within the court's discretion.[161]

> The party seeking to recover attorney's fees must show financial inability to pay and the ability of the other spouse to do so. . . . In the instant case, the facts indicate that each party had approximately $100.00 left after the payment of their monthly expenses. Although the [father's] income is larger than [the mother's] his obligations are also comparably greater and include, in addition to his own attorney's fees, payment of the child's attorney's fees. He is still making payment on debts incurred during his marriage to respondent, and he has the obligation to support his child.[162]

Interestingly, though, the appellate court reversed the trial court's order that both parties bear the cost of the psychiatric testimony of an impartial expert appointed by the court.[163] The appellate court analyzed the statutory mandate authorizing the court to require the services of the expert and concluded that its intent was for the court to bear the expense.[164] The applicable provision "is patterned after the New York impartial medical testimony plan which requires the expert's compensation be paid by the court."[165] It is remarkable that, unlike in New York, whenever the services of a lawyer are required, it is the intention of the Illinois courts and legislature to place the burden of his fee on some resource other than the public purse. Yet a distinction is made when the expert services of other professionals are required.

A review of the language of some of the more pertinent Illinois appellate cases will disclose a somewhat greater disposition to rely on the outcome of the custody case in chief as a criterion for a counsel-fee award, in addition to the respective merits of the positions of the adversary parties.

**Relevant Cases.** In a 1979 opinion, *In re Borowczyk,*[166] the divorced mother of two daughters, 7 and 8 years old, respectively, at the time of the original proceeding, moved to terminate her former husband's visitation rights on the grounds that the welfare of her children would otherwise be jeopardized.[167] Her petition was precipitated by a postvisitation physical examination of her younger daughter wherein a diagnosis of gonorrhea was made.[168] A trial followed in which voluminous medical and psychological expert testimony was presented to the court. At the conclusion of the hearing, the court held that, although the children had been sexually active during their visitation with their father, the circumstances were such that neither neglect nor abuse could be attributed to him or his second wife. Therefore, on balance, the court decided that the best interests of the children would *not* be served by a termination of the father's visitation rights.[169]

The mother did not appeal the denial of her modification petition. She did appeal an award of attorney's fees in favor of the father against *her* and a denial of her own application for reimbursement of her own attorney's fees.[170] The appellate court reversed the award of the counsel fee against the mother, citing two primary grounds.[171] The first was her seemingly complete inability to pay.

> In the present case, the pleadings disclose certain undisputed facts. Petitioner [the mother] is unemployed and owns no property other than her clothing, household furnishings, and an old automobile. Petitioner's mother permits her to live in a rent-free apartment, and petitioner's only income is the weekly child-support award she received from respondent [the father]. Respondent [the father] at no time made any showing to the trial court of his inability to pay attorney's fees. He never submitted any pleadings or affidavits setting forth his income or expenses, nor did he deny any of petitioner's statements regarding his earnings. There was no basis in fact for the trial court's holding that petitioner pay fees to respondent's attorney. Conversely, the only facts elicited revealed that petitioner was unable to pay her attorney's fees and that respondent was in a superior position financially.[172]

The appellate court reversed the award of a counsel fee against the mother and in favor of the father, reversed the denial of an award to the mother, and remanded the issue of the mother's counsel-fee award to the trial court.[173] Further, the review court specifically rejected the contention of the father that the trial court's decision on the counsel-fee issue was proper as a punitive measure against the mother's bad-faith motivations.[174]

> [The mother] was informed of her child's symptoms by [the father's] present wife. Two doctors diagnosed the child as being infected with gonorrhea. There was evidence that both children had sexual contact with a male known to them. Petitioner was informed of the younger child's condition while the children were on vacation in respondent's household. *If [the mother] had not sought the assistance of the court under such circum-*

*stances, her fitness to have custody of the children would be open to question. The trial court did not find that the proceedings were brought in bad faith or as harrassment; it merely held that the evidence was insufficient to terminate [the father's] visitation rights* [emphasis added].[175]

The appellate court leaves no doubt as to what the primary considerations are in determining a counsel-fee award: The person against whom the award is made must be capable of paying it, and the opposing party must be unable to do so.[176] Thereafter, factors such as good faith, harrassment, and a sufficient factual basis may come into play. Although the appellate court awarded a counsel fee to the mother and against the father in spite of the father's prevalence on the merits of the cases, the court leaves the distinct impression that, had there been a less convincing record of the sound factual basis for the mother's petition, they may well have agreed with the trial court's conclusions adverse to the mother. Thus, although the bottom-line result may not be the ultimate determination of a counsel-fee application, the final view of the evidence in the broad picture appears to be most significant.

A most succinct statement of all of the applicable general rules was made in *Kuhns* v. *Kuhns,* a 1972 First District opinion.[177]

The allowance of fees in divorce proceedings rests in the sound discretion of the trial court and will be disturbed on review only when the exercise of discretion is clearly abused [citing case]. The allowance of attorney's fees depends upon the unique characteristic of each case [citing case]. In determining whether an allowance of fees is proper, it is necessary to examine the circumstances which initiate the invocation of judicial proceedings for relief [citing case]. And where the party upon whom the fees are sought to be imposed has done nothing which necessitated or required judicial action the allowance of fees is error [citing case].[178]

The father in *Kuhns* petitioned the court for a modification of the divorce decree in which the mother had been awarded custody.[179] At the time of the hearing, the father had de facto custody with the mother's consent, following the apprehension, on a fugitive warrant, of the mother's paramour. The father charged, among other things, that the mother had led a nomadic life-style accompanied by the children until her lover was arrested. Further, the mother was accused of habitual intoxication, use of dangerous drugs, child abuse, and various other character traits suggesting the most flagrant instability.[180] The appellate court did not pass on the sufficiency of proof of each of the allegations. It was enough for the court that the mother "by her own misconduct, precipitated these post-decree proceedings" and that the father was "compelled" by her behavior to "seek the assistance of the court in order to protect the welfare of the children."[181]

Moreover, the mother was surely not destitute (she had already paid her lawyers some $6,500.)[182] "Although the record reveals that [the father] is possessed of more income and assets than [the mother] we believe that it would be inequitable and unfair to further punish [the father] by requiring him to pay fees to [the mother's] attorney."[183] The trial court's award was reversed in what was clearly labeled "an abuse of discretion."[184]

It is interesting to note that in determining the ability of a disputant to afford the services of counsel, the courts may take into consideration the means of a *present* spouse, even though he is not the father of the children for whose benefit the services are retained. There is no precedent for the consideration of this factor in any New York case that has come to our attention. (See Standards for Awards, *supra.*) In *Kjellesvik* v. *Shannon,* the appellate court upheld the trial court's denial of a counsel fee to the mother at the conclusion of a hearing in which custody was modified adverse to her and in favor of the father.[185] The court concluded that a substantial medical malpractice settlement obtained by the stepfather during the pendency of the custody litigation provided a sufficient basis for the trial court's conclusion that sufficient means were available to the mother.[186]

One of the more remarkable developments in Illinois law with respect to counsel fees in custody cases is a specific statutory mandate to impose counsel fees punitively on a party seeking a custody modification "if the court finds that the modification action is vexatious and constitutes harrassment."[187] Although the basis for such a punitive award may be difficult to prove, and courts may severely limit the application of the statute for fear of a chilling effect on legitimate grievances (for example, *In re Borowczyk, supra*), its very existence provides a powerful reserve weapon with which to discourage the more splenetic abuses of the court's process.

Illinois provides an alternative remedy for relief in child-custody disputes by means of a writ of *habeas corpus* for nonparent parties.[188] We have not found a case on point, as we did in New York, specifically denying counsel-fee relief to third party nonparents in custody litigation.[189] It would appear, however, that the same lack of specific statutory authority for such an award would bar that relief, except as permitted under the Marriage and Dissolution Act.[190]

## California

In California, the Family Law Act is denoted as part 5 of the Civil Code, and it covers the entire scope of matrimonial, dissolution, support, custody, and property distribution matters. Section 4370 of the act provides that the court may order "the husband or wife, father or mother, as the case may be, to pay such amount as may be reasonably necessary for the cost of maintaining or defending the proceeding, and for attorney's fees.''[191] The section continues with the expected language extending the mandate to supplementary proceedings and appeals.[192] What is notable is that attorney's fees are lumped together throughout with "costs.''[193] In fact, the black letterheading of the section reads "costs and attorney fees pendentelite.''[194]

The New York Statute refers to counsel fees and expenses.[195] The distinction in terms appears to signal an identification of attorney's fees less with the attorney's expenses and time than with the traditional concept of court costs. The award of costs is a subject over which courts traditionally exercise broad, often sparsely explained, and even arbitrary discretion. The leading California appellate cases on standards for counsel-fee awards are not very instructive with respect to identification of grounds. Rather, they monotonously give generalized, stylized support for the principle that judicial discretion is paramount so long as the applicant can show sufficient need. In *Straub* v. *Straub,* the court held as follows:[196]

> A court may allow counsel fees on an application for modification of a custody award [citations omitted]. A motion for such fee is addressed to the sound discretion of the court, and in the absence of a clear showing of abuse, its determination will not be disturbed on appeal [citations omitted]. . . . Requisite to the granting of such relief, however, is a finding that the award is necessary. The burden of establishing such necessity is upon the applicant [citations omitted]. . . . It has also been a long-established rule in this state that in the allowance of attorney's fees, or the determination of the value of legal services rendered by an attorney, the experience of the trial judge furnishes every element necessary to fix the value of services rendered by an attorney in handling a legal problem [citations omitted]. The judge's experience and knowledge offer sufficient basis for fixing the amount of an attorney's fee, even in the absence of specific evidence on the subject [citations omitted]. This last-mentioned rule is predicated upon the basis that evidence as to the reasonable value of the services is necessarily before the trial court when it hears the case, and that the trial court judge, being a lawyer, can readily ascertain from the case the value of the services performed in his presence and the approximate time spent in preparation [citations omitted]. *Because the matter of awarding compensation for services rendered by an attorney is left, to so great a degree, in the judicial discretion of the trial court, its determination will not be disturbed unless the sum allowed is plainly and palpably exorbitant and such as shocks the conscience of an appellate court.*[197]

Surely this tribute to judicial rectitude and percipience is a heartwarming experience for any member of the bench to read. Why is it that the attorneys who appear before one so often fail to convey the same faith and confidence as expressed by the honorable tribunal that wrote the words above? The principle of broad, nearly unrestricted judicial discretion appears to apply to the issue of the award itself as well as the amount. It is so unequivocally announced in *Straub* as to make that case the source of authority for the principles of counsel-fee awards even in nonmatrimonial cases.[198]

The inclination to place such limitless discretion in judicial hands may be an outgrowth of the identification of attorney's fees with court costs generally. More likely, it is explained by California's long-standing community-property law background, whereby a trial court may view a counsel-fee award as just one more component in the equitable distribution of assets and benefits in the course of a marital dissolution. Hence the counsel-fee award is not perceived as a sufficiently distinct issue to be analyzed, explained, justified, or supported in its disposition.

As observed herein, the current statute provides for the payment of counsel fees for the benefit of "husband or wife, father or mother, as the case may be."[199] No provision is made for nonparent parties to custody litigation to qualify for an award of such fees. Again, as in Illinois (Other Jurisdictions, Illinois, *supra*) and New York (Pertinent Statutory Authority, *supra*), this omission appears to have been intentional. Section 4370, the applicable California statute,[200] allows that an award may be made for any proceeding under the same part 5 of the code.[201] Section 4600 delineates who may contend for the custody of a child and the order of preference in making such an award.[202] The participation of nonparent parties is clearly contemplated.[203] Yet it is just as plain that no intention is manifested to include nonparent parties in a counsel-fee award. As in Illinois, however (Other Jurisdictions, Illinois, *supra*), California does provide for the appointment of a law guardian to represent the child's independent interests in any custody proceeding with an award to be made against one or both parents in the court's discretion, but *not* against the child's separate estate.[204]

## Texas

Texas law has much in common with that of California, probably to a large degree because the two states share the same community-property heritage from the Spanish legal tradition. Texas's applicable statute goes even further in its language than does California's in identifying attorney's fees with costs generally and, thus, suggesting that the broadest judicial discretion will be tolerated.[205]

> In any proceeding under this subtitle, the court may award costs as in other civil cases. Reasonable attorney's fees may be taxed as costs, and may be ordered paid directly to the attorney, who may enforce the order for fees in his own name.[206]

The subtitle referred to in the quotation above is "Subtitle A, The Parent Child Relationship and the Suit Affecting the Parent Child Relationship."[207]

Texas, however, clearly goes further than any other jurisdiction that has been examined heretofore in that it specifically provides for the inclusion of third-party nonparent litigants as eligible applicants for counsel fees. The mandate is found by implication in the definition of the parent-child relationship under the subtitle[208] and the supplementary definition of parties with standing before the court in parent-child litigation.[209] Those who have standing to contest and thus qualify as a counsel-fee recipient are defined as follows:

> A suit affecting the parent-child relationship may be brought by any person with an interest in the child, including the child [through a representative authorized by the court], any agency of the state or of a political subdivision of the state, and any authorized agency.[210]

The suggestion of wide judicial discretion as implicit in the statutory language identifies attorney's fees with costs "as in other civil cases."[211] Further suggestion for this policy is linked to the community-property tradition, and access is given by the code mandate to nonparent parties.[212] This suggestion is generally borne out by the appellate cases. Decisions as to grounds for the award are generally limited to the recitation of statutory authority and deference to the judicial discretion of the court below.[213]

## Notes

1. N.Y. Const. arts. VI, VII(a); N.Y. Jud. Law § 140(b) (McKinney). See chapter 1, Jurisdiction, *supra*.

2. *Griffin* v. *Griffin*, 47 N.Y. 134, 138 (1872).

3. *Id.*

4. *Id.*, at 139; see note 1, *supra*.

5. *Id.*, at 140–141.

6. *Id.*, at 141.

7. *Id.*, see Counsel Fees as Distinguished from Necessaries, *supra*.

8. *Higgins* v. *Sharp*, 164 N.Y. 4, 58 N.E. 9 (1900).

9. *Johnson* v. *Johnson*, 206 N.Y. 561, 100 N.E. 408 (1912); *Ramsden* v. *Ramsden*, 91 N.Y. 281 (1883).

10. *Hockenbrought* v. *Hockenbrought*, 44 A.D.2d 767, 354 N.Y.S.2d 257 (4th Dept. 1974); *Lambert* v. *Lambert*, 45 A.D.2d 715, 356 N.Y.S.2d 95 (2d Dept. 1975); *Blaine* v. *Blaine*, 20 A.D.2d 903, 248 N.Y.S.2d 960 (2d Dept. 1964).

11. See Counsel-Fee Origins, *supra*.

12. *Keller* v. *Phillips*, 39 N.Y. 351 (1868).

13. *Id.*, at 354.

14. *DeBrauwere* v. *DeBrauwere,* 203 N.Y. 460, 462, 96 N.E. 722, 723 (1911).

15. *Elder* v. *Rosenwasser,* 238 N.Y. 427, 429–430, 144 N.E. 669, 670 (1924); *see also Dravecka* v. *Richard,* 267 N.Y. 180, 196 N.E. 17 (1935).

16. *Tompkins & Lauren* v. *Glass,* 44 Misc. 2d 239, 240, 253 N.Y.S.2d 465, 467 (Sup. Ct. 1964). *See also Schwartz* v. *Aberbach,* 66 Misc. 2d 246, 247, 319 N.Y.S.2d 1021, 1022 (Civ. Ct. 1971); *Levine* v. *Levine,* 48 Misc. 2d 15, 263 N.Y.S.2d 997 (Civ. Ct. 1965), *aff'd,* 50 Misc. 2d 39, 269 N.Y.S.2d 243 (Sup. Ct. 1966).

17. *Schwartz* v. *Aberbach,* 319 N.Y.S.2d, at 1022–1023; *Levine* v. *Levine,* 263 N.Y.S.2d, at 1002.

18. *Schwartz* v. *Aberbach,* 319 N.Y.S.2d, at 1022.

19. *Tompkins & Lauren* v. *Glass,* 253 N.Y.S.2d, at 467. *See also Weidlich* v. *Richards,* 276 A.D. 386, 94 N.Y.S.2d 546, 548 (1st Dept. 1950).

20. *Levine* v. *Levine,* 263 N.Y.S.2d, at 1002; *Schwartz* v. *Aberbach,* 319 N.Y.S.2d, at 1022.

21. *Tompkins & Lauren* v. *Glass,* 253 N.Y.S.2d, at 467. *See also Sussman* v. *Sussman,* 13 A.D.2d 464, 212 N.Y.S.2d 95 (1st Dept. 1961); *Fisher* v. *Fisher,* 223 A.D. 19, 227 N.Y.S. 345 (1st Dept. 1928), *aff'd,* 250 N.Y. 313, 165 N.E. 460 (1929).

22. *Tompkins & Lauren* v. *Glass,* 253 N.Y.S.2d, at 467.

23. *Id. See also Turner* v. *Woolworth,* 221 N.Y. 425, 117 N.E. 814 (1917); *Dravecka* v. *Richard,* 267 N.Y., at 180.

24. *Schwartz* v. *Aberbach,* 319 N.Y.S.2d, at 1023.

25. *Id.*

26. *Errico* v. *Manville,* 59 Misc. 2d 549, 552, 299 N.Y.S.2d 914, 918–919 (Westchester County Ct. 1969). *See also Friou* v. *Gentes,* 11 A.D.2d 124, 204 N.Y.S.2d 836 (2d Dept. 1960); *Siegel & Hodges* v. *Hodges,* 20 Misc. 2d 243, 191 N.Y.S.2d 984 (Sup. Ct. 1959), *aff'd,* 10 A.D.2d 646, 197 N.Y.S.2d 246 (2d Dept. 1960), *aff'd,* 9 N.Y.2d 747, 174 N.E.2d 533 (1961).

27. *Errico* v. *Manville,* 299 N.Y.S.2d, at 920.

28. *Id.*, at 914.

29. *Id.*

30. *Id.*, at 921.

31. See Father's Standing to Collect Counsel Fees as Against the Mother *supra.*

32. *Errico* v. *Manville,* 299 N.Y.S.2d, at 920.

33. *Id.*

34. N.Y. Dom. Rel. Law § 237 (McKinney 1977).

35. *Id.*, at § 237(a). See Counsel-Fee Origins, *supra.*

36. *Id.*

37. *Id.* at § 237(b). See chapter 1, Jurisdiction, *supra.*

38. *Id.* See Eligibility for Counsel Fees in Custody Proceedings, Father's Standing to Collect Counsel Fees as Against the Mother, *supra.*

39. *Id.*

40. N.Y. Fam. Ct. Act § 447 (McKinney 29A 1975). See chapter 1, Jurisdiction, *supra.*

41. *Id.,* at § 467. See chapter 1, Jurisdiction, *supra.*

42. *Id.,* at § 446. See chapter 1, Jurisdiction, *supra.*

43. *Id.,* at § 438.

44. *Id.*

45. See Pertinent Statutory Authority, *supra,* and Timely Application in Family Court, *supra.*

46. N.Y. Fam. Ct. Act. §§ 549, 551 (McKinney 29A 1975). See chapter 1, Jurisdiction, *supra.*

47. *Id.,* at § 536.

48. See chapter 4, Effect of Illegitimacy, *supra.*

49. N.Y. Fam. Ct. Act § 842(e) (McKinney 29A 1975).

50. *Id., at* § 817.

51. *Id.,* at §§ 438, 536.

52. *Id.,* at §§ 651(a), (b). See chapter 1, Jurisdiction, *supra.*

53. *Id.,* at § 652.

54. *Id.,* at §§ 438, 536.

55. *Id.,* at §§ 651(a), (b); *Kapzynski* v. *Kapzynski,* 30 A.D.2d 962, 294 N.Y.S.2d 345 (2d Dept. 1968), *motion for leave to appeal denied,* 23 N.Y.2d 643 (1969); *Hockenbrought* v. *Hockenbrought,* 44 A.D.2d 767, 354 N.Y.S.2d 257 (4th Dept. 1974).

56. *Dagaev* v. *Dagaev,* 90 Misc. 2d 962, 397 N.Y.S.2d 317 (Fam. Ct. 1977).

57. N.Y. Dom. Rel. Law § 34-a (McKinney 1980).

58. *Id.* See chapter 1, Jurisdiction, *supra.*

59. *Dannheim* v. *Babbitt,* 48 Misc. 2d 310, 264 N.Y.S.2d 639 (Fam. Ct. 1965).

60. N.Y. Fam. Ct. Act § 438 (McKinney 29A 1975).

61. *Murdock* v. *Settembrini,* 21 N.Y.2d 759, 288 N.Y.S.2d 234, 235 N.E.2d 222 (1968); *In re Schneider,* 72 Misc. 2d 423, 425, 339 N.Y.S.2d 52, 55 (Fam. Ct. 1972); *Sorbello* v. *Cook,* 93 Misc. 2d 998, 1001, 403 N.Y.S.2d 434, 436 (Fam. Ct. 1978).

62. See chapter 1, Jurisdiction, *supra;* see chapter 1, Jurisdiction, note 28, *supra.*

63. See chapter 1, Jurisdiction, *supra;* see chapter 1, Jurisdiction, notes 24, 25, and 26, *supra.*

64. See chapter 1, Jurisdiction, *supra.*

65. *In re Boulware's Will,* 144 Misc. 235, 258 N.Y. 522 (Sur. Ct. 1932).

66. *Id.,* at 532.

67. *Id.*, at 533.

68. N.Y. Surr. Ct. Proc. Act § 2110 (McKinney 58A 1967).

69. *Id.*, at § 2110(1).

70. *Id.*, at § 2110(2).

71. See chapter 1, Jurisdiction, *supra.*

72. N.Y. Surr. Ct. Proc. Act § 2110 (McKinney 58A 1967).

73. N.Y. Fam. Ct. Act § 438 (McKinney 29A 1975).

74. *Id.*

75. *Cassieri* v. *Cassieri,* 31 A.D.2d 927, 298 N.Y.S.2d 844 (2d Dept. 1969).

76. *Id.*, at 845.

77. *Id.*

78. *Id.*

79. *Reed* v. *Reed,* 63 Misc. 2d 459, 461, 311 N.Y.S.2d 657, 659 (Fam. Ct. 1970).

80. *Id.*, at 659.

81. *Id.*, at 658.

82. *Id.*, at 661.

83. *Id.*, at 662.

84. *Hoover* v. *Hoover,* 74 Misc. 2d 13, 344 N.Y.S.2d 61 (Fam. Ct. 1973).

85. *Brown* v. *Brown,* 82 Misc. 2d 759, 761, 370 N.Y.S.2d 421, 422 (Fam. Ct. 1975).

86. *Id.*, at 423.

87. *Id.*

88. *Koch* v. *Koch,* 99 Misc. 2d 124, 415 N.Y.S.2d 369 (Fam. Ct. 1979).

89. *Id.*

90. *Carnese* v. *Carnese,* 93 Misc. 2d 558, 403 N.Y.S.2d 174 (Fam. Ct. 1978).

91. *Id.*, at 175.

92. *Childs* v. *Childs,* 69 A.D.2d 406, 419 N.Y.S.2d 533 (2d Dept. 1979).

93. *Id.*, at 536. *See also Childs* v. *Childs,* 60 A.D.2d 639, 400 N.Y.S.2d 356 (2d Dept. 1977), appeal dismissed, 43 N.Y.2d 946, 403 N.Y.S.2d 896, 374 N.E.2d 1247 (1978), *vacated,* 440 U.S. 952 (1979).

94. *Orr* v. *Orr,* 440 U.S. 268 (1979).

95. *Childs* v. *Childs,* 419 N.Y.S.2d, at 542.

96. *Id.*

97. N.Y. Fam. Ct. Act § 438 (McKinney 29A 1975); *Seward* v. *Seward,* 75 A.D.2d 583, 426 N.Y.S.2d 798 (2d Dept. 1980).

98. *Childs* v. *Childs,* 419 N.Y.S.2d, at 533.

99. *Marcia D.* v. *Donald D.,* 85 Misc. 2d 637, 380 N.Y.2d 904 (Fam.

Ct. 1976); *Thaler* v. *Thaler,* 89 Misc. 2d 315, 319–325, 391 N.Y.S.2d 331, 334–340 (Sup. Ct. 1977), *rev'd on other grounds,* 58 A.D.2d 890, 396 N.Y.S.2d 815 (2d Dept. 1977).

100. *Baxstrom* v. *Herold,* 383 U.S. 107, 111 (1966).

101. *Reisch* v. *Reisch,* 85 Misc. 2d 107, 109, 379 N.Y.S.2d 275, 277 (Fam. Ct. 1975).

102. *See Childs* v. *Childs,* 419 N.Y.S.2d, at 533; *Carter* v. *Carter,* 65 A.D.2d 765, 410 N.Y.S.2d 119 (2d Dept. 1978).

103. *Errico* v. *Manville,* 59 Misc. 2d 549, 299 N.Y.S.2d 914 (Westchester County Ct. 1969).

104. *Id.,* at 917.

105. *Id.*

106. *Id.*

107. *Id.*

108. *Id.,* at 918.

109. *Id.*

110. *Id.*

111. *Childs* v. *Childs,* 69 A.D.2d 406, 419 N.Y.S.2d 533 (2d Dept. 1979).

112. N.Y. Dom. Rel. Law § 237 (McKinney).

113. *Id.; Mester* v. *Mester,* 58 Misc. 2d 790, 797, 296 N.Y.S.2d 193, 201 (Sup. Ct. 1969).

114. *Ansorge* v. *Armour,* 267 N.Y. 492, 501, 196 N.E. 546 (1935).

115. *Id.,* at 502.

116. *Id.*

117. *Id.*

118. *Id.*

119. *People ex rel. Foussier* v. *Uzielli,* 23 A.D.2d 260, 260 N.Y.S.2d 329 (1st Dept. 1965), *aff'd,* 16 N.Y.2d 1057, 266 N.Y.S.2d 131, 213 N.E.2d 460 (1965).

120. *Id.,* at 265.

121. *Ross* v. *Ross,* 143 N.Y.S.2d 234, 235 (Sup. Ct. 1955).

122. *Id.*

123. *Id.,* at 236.

124. *Id.,* at 236–238.

125. *Id.,* at 238.

126. *Id.,* at 239.

127. *Id.*

128. *Weltz* v. *Weltz,* 38 A.D.2d 520, 326 N.Y.S.2d 568 (1st Dept. 1971).

129. *Id.,* at 569.

130. *Id.*

131. *Id.*

132. *State ex rel. Schack* v. *Schack,* 48 A.D.2d 791, 792, 369 N.Y.S.2d 159, 160 (1st Dept. 1975).

133. *Salk* v. *Salk,* 57 A.D.2d 519, 393 N.Y.S.2d 566 (1st Dept. 1977).

134. *Id.*

135. *Noel* v. *Derrick,* 71 A.D.2d 704, 705, 418 N.Y.S.2d 481, 483 (3d Dept. 1979). *See also Sharp* v. *Kieserman,* 102 Misc. 2d 667, 424 N.Y.S.2d 103 (Fam. Ct. 1980).

136. *La Rosa* v. *La Rosa,* 83 Misc. 2d 1059, 1060, 373 N.Y.S.2d 985, 987 (Sup. Ct. 1975).

137. *Id.*

138. *Id.*

139. *Id.,* at 988.

140. *Id.,* at 988–989.

141. *P.* v. *P.,* 98 Misc. 2d 52, 413 N.Y.S.2d 81 (Fam. Ct. 1978).

142. *Id.,* at 83.

143. Ill. Ann. Stat. ch. 40, § 508 (Smith-Hurd 1980).

144. N.Y. Dom. Rel. Law § 237 (McKinney 1972); see Pertinent Statutory Authority, *supra.*

145. Ill. Ann. Stat. ch. 40, § 508(a) (Smith-Hurd 1980). *Compare with* N.Y. Dom. Rel. Law §§ 237(a), (b) (McKinney 1972).

146. Ill. Ann. Stat. ch. 40, § 508 (Smith-Hurd 1980).

147. *Id.,* at § 506.

148. N.Y. County Law Art. 18–B (McKinney 1972); N.Y. County Law §§ 722(4), 722-c (McKinney 1972); N.Y. Fam. Ct. Act §§ 249, 262(a)(iv), (v), (vii) (McKinney 1975); N.Y. Surr. Ct. Proc. Act § 407 (McKinney 58A 1980).

149. Ill. Ann. Stat. ch. 40, § 508(a)(1), (2) (Smith-Hurd 1980).

150. *Id.,* at §§ 601 *et seq.*

151. *Id.,* at § 508 Commentaries.

152. See Standards for Awards, *supra.*

153. See Counsel Fees as Distinguished from Necessaries, *supra.*

154. Ill. Ann. Stat. ch. 40, §§ 506, 508 (Smith-Hurd 1980).

155. Ill. Const. art. VI, 9.

156. Ill. Ann. Stat. ch. 40, §508 Commentaries (Smith-Hurd 1980).

157. *Id.*

158. *In re Scott,* 75 Ill. App. 3d 710, 712, 394 N.E.2d 779, 781 (1979).

159. *Id.,* at 781.

160. *Id.,* at 782.

161. *Id.*

162. *Id.*

163. *Id.,* at 783.

164. *Id.*

165. *Id.;* See note 148, *supra.*

166. In re Borowczyk, 31 Ill. App. 3d 425, 397 N.E.2d 71 (1979).

167. *Id.*, at 72.

168. *Id.*

169. *Id.*, at 73.

170. *Id.*

171. *Id.*

172. *Id.*, at 74.

173. *Id.*, at 75.

174. *Id.*, at 74.

175. *Id.*

176. *Id.*

177. *Kuhns* v. *Kuhns,* 7 Ill. App. 3d 884, 288 N.E.2d 884 (1972).

178. *Id.*, at 886.

179. *Id.*, at 885.

180. *Id.*

181. *Id.*, at 886.

182. *Id.*

183. *Id.*

184. *Id.*

185. *Kjellesvik* v. *Shannon,* 41 Ill. App. 3d 674, 355 N.E.2d 120 (1976).

186. *Id.*, at 125.

187. Ill. Ann. Stat. ch. 40, § 610(c) (Smith-Hurd 1980).

188. *Id.*, at ch. 65, §§ 1 *et seq.; People ex. rel. Elmore* v. *Elmore,* 46 Ill. App. 3d 504, 361 N.E.2d 615 (1977).

189. See Eligibility for Counsel Fees in Custody Proceedings, Non-parents, *supra,* and note 88, *supra.*

190. Ill. Stat. ch. 41, §§ 506, 610(c) (Smith-Hurd 1980); *see also People ex rel. Elmore* v. *Elmore,* 46 Ill. App. 3d 504, 361 N.E. 2d 615 (1977).

191. Cal. Civ. Code § 4370(a) (West 1981).

192. *Id.*

193. *Id.*

194. *Id.*

195. *See Pertinent Statutory Authority, The Domestic Relations Law, supra;* N.Y. Dom. Rel. Law § 237 (McKinney 1977).

196. *Straub* v. *Straub,* 213 Cal. App. 2d 792, 29 Cal. Rptr. 183 (1963).

197. *Id.*, at 187–188; see also Hicks v. *Hicks,* 249 Cal. App. 2d 964, 969, 58 Cal. Rptr. 63, 66 (1967); *Cope* v. *Cope,* 230 Cal. App. 2d 218, 235–236, 40 Cal. Rptr. 917, 928 (1964).

198. *Fed-Mart Corp.* v. *Price,* 111 Cal. App. 3d 215, 168 Cal. Rptr. 525, 531 (1980).

199. Cal. Civ. Code § 4370(a) (West 1981).

200. *Id.*

201. Cal. Civ. Code § 4600 (West 1970).

202. *Id.*

203. *Id.*

204. Cal. Civ. Code § 4606 (West 1981); *compare with* Ill. Stat. Ann. ch. 40, § 506 *supra.* (Smith-Hurd 1980).

205. Tex. Fam. Code Ann. tit. 2, § 11.18(a) (Vernon 1975).

206. *Id.*

207. *Id.*

208. *Id.,* at tit. 2, §§ 11.01, 11.01(1), (5), 12.04.

209. *Id.,* at tit. 2, § 11.03.

210. *Id.*

211. *Id.,* at tit. 2, § 11.18(a).

212. *Id.,* at tit. 2, § 11.03.

213. *Reyna* v. *Reyna,* 584 S.W.2d 926 (Tex. Civ. App. 1979); *Bradford* v. *Campdera,* 581 S.W.2d 501, 509 (Tex. Civ. App. 1977); *Derbonne* v. *Derbonne,* 555 S.W.2d 507, 509 (Tex. Civ. App. 1977); *Labowitz* v. *Labowitz,* 542 S.W.2d 922, 926 (Tex. Civ. App. 1976); *Forney* v. *Jorrie,* 511 S.W.2d 379, 387 (Tex. Civ. App. 1974).

# Index

173

# About the Authors

**Shirley Wohl Kram** was appointed family court judge by Mayor John Lindsay in May 1971 and reappointed for a second ten-year term by Mayor Ed Koch in May 1981. She has served in every county in New York State and is a member of the statewide Rules Committee for Family Court. Judge Kram also serves as chairperson of the Advisory Committee to the Appellate Division in the First Department.

Before her appointment to family court, Judge Kram served with the Mental Health and Narcotics Division of the Legal Aid Society as a staff lawyer and later as attorney-in-charge. She has also served in private practice in general litigation, specializing in matrimonial law. She has published extensively in law journals and other legal periodicals on the subjects of family and matrimonial law.

**Neil A. Frank** is a member of the bar of the State of New York, of the federal courts for the Eastern and Southern Districts of New York, and of the U.S. Supreme Court. He received the B.A. from Hunter College in 1967 and the J.D. from Fordham University Law School in 1972. Mr. Frank's career has been marked by a broad range of pursuits relating to children and the family and their interaction with society's institutions. His past occupations have included instructor in the New York City Public School system, caseworker for the New York City Department of Social Services, law assistant to the judges of the Family Court of the State of New York for New York City, and assistant corporation counsel for the City of New York, Family Court Division. He currently serves as principal law clerk to the Honorable Joseph Cohen, judge of the Court of Claims of the State of New York.

Mr. Frank has also served as law assistant to the justices of the Supreme Court of the State of New York, Bronx County, and has been associated with various law firms engaged in general practice. A member of the faculty of the American Institute for Paralegal Studies, Mr. Frank has also published several articles on domestic relations, many of them with Judge Shirley W. Kram, his coauthor.